Pro Active Record

Databases with Ruby and Rails

Kevin Marshall, Chad Pytel, Jon Yurek

Apress®

Pro Active Record for Ruby: Databases with Ruby and Rails

Copyright © 2007 by Kevin Marshall, Chad Pytel, Jon Yurek

ISBN-13 (pbk): 978-1-59059-847-4

ISBN-10 (pbk): 1-59059-847-4

Printed and bound in the United States of America 9 8 7 6 5 4 3 2 1

Lead Editor: Jonathan Gennick
Technical Reviewer: Adam Stein
Editorial Board: Steve Anglin, Ewan Buckingham, Gary Cornell, Jonathan Gennick, Jason Gilmore, Jonathan Hassell, Chris Mills, Matthew Moodie, Jeffrey Pepper, Ben Renow-Clarke, Dominic Shakeshaft, Matt Wade, Tom Welsh
Production Director and Project Manager: Grace Wong
Copy Editor: Heather Lang
Associate Production Director: Kari Brooks-Copony
Production Editor: Katie Stence
Compositor and Artist: Kinetic Publishing Services, LLC
Proofreader: Nancy Sixsmith
Indexer: Broccoli Information Management
Cover Designer: Kurt Krames
Manufacturing Director: Tom Debolski

Distributed to the book trade worldwide by Springer-Verlag New York, Inc., 233 Spring Street, 6th Floor, New York, NY 10013. Phone 1-800-SPRINGER, fax 201-348-4505, e-mail orders-ny@springer-sbm.com, or visit http://www.springeronline.com.

For information on translations, please contact Apress directly at 2855 Telegraph Avenue, Suite 600, Berkeley, CA 94705. Phone 510-549-5930, fax 510-549-5939, e-mail info@apress.com, or visit http://www.apress.com.

The source code for this book is available to readers at http://www.apress.com in the Source Code/Download section. You will need to answer questions pertaining to this book in order to successfully download the code.

To my wife, Catherine, I love you . . . more.
—KM
To my wife, Rachel, I love you all the way to the moon, and back.
—CP
To my fiancée, Karen, for making everything fun and for making me happy.
—JY

Contents at a Glance

Contents vii

About the Authors xv

About the Technical Reviewer xvii

Acknowledgments xix

Introduction xxi

■**CHAPTER 1**   Introducing Active Record 1

■**CHAPTER 2**   Active Record and SQL 25

■**CHAPTER 3**   Setting Up Your Database 43

■**CHAPTER 4**   Core Features of Active Record 59

■**CHAPTER 5**   Bonus Features 91

■**CHAPTER 6**   Active Record Testing and Debugging 125

■**CHAPTER 7**   Working with Legacy Schema 161

■**CHAPTER 8**   Active Record and the Real World 187

■**APPENDIX**   Active Record Methods in Detail 215

■**INDEX** 267

Contents

About the Authors. xv

About the Technical Reviewer. xvii

Acknowledgments. xix

Introduction. xxi

■**CHAPTER 1**   **Introducing Active Record**. 1

The Story Behind Active Record 2

Active Record Mostly Adheres to the ORM Pattern 2

Active Record Is a Different Kind of ORM 3

Active Record Is One Part of the MVC Concept 4

Active Record Is Primarily Used for CRUD Database Transactions 4

The Active Record Library Is Ruby Code 5

From Active Record Objects to Database Records and Back Again 5

Creating an Active Record Object 6

Manipulating or Accessing the Attributes of the Object 6

Saving the Attributes as a Record in the Database 6

Why Active Record Is a Smart Choice 7

Installing and Configuring Active Record. 8

Installing the Active Record Gem 8

Installing Any Additional Required Libraries or Gems 9

Supplying the Adapter-Specific Information 10

Learning More 16

Building Your First Active Record Program 18

Your First Example. 18

Active Record Assumptions and Conventions. 19

Overriding the Assumptions. 20

Retrieving Objects from the Database 21

Exploring Active Record Relationships. 22

Them's the Basics! 24

■CHAPTER 2   **Active Record and SQL** 25

Creating a Record 25
Reading a Record 27
    :conditions 28
    :include 29
    :order 31
    :select 31
    Dynamic Finders 33
Updating a Record 34
Deleting a Record 35
Completely Nondynamic Finders 37
Transactions 38
Locking 40
    Optimistic Locking 41
    Pessimistic Locking 42
CRUD Isn't Cruddy 42

■CHAPTER 3   **Setting Up Your Database** 43

Designing Active Record–Friendly Tables 43
Traditional Database Management 44
Common Problems with the Traditional Approach 45
Managing Your Database with Migrations 46
    How the DSL Works 46
    Using Migrations 47
    Executing Migration Scripts 48
    The Anatomy of a Migration File 50
    Migrations in Action 50
Migrations Are Easier Than They Sound 57

■CHAPTER 4   **Core Features of Active Record** 59

Callbacks 59
    Implementing Callbacks 60
    Callback Macros 61
    Specific Types of Callbacks 63
    One Down, Two to Go 69

Associations 69
    Farmers, Cows, Milk, and How They Relate 69
    Association Types 70
    Association Modifiers 76
    Two Core Features Down, One to Go 80
Validations 80
    Why Bother with Validations? 80
    Implementing Validations 81
    Convenience Functions 83
Your Core Is Strong 89

■CHAPTER 5   **Bonus Features** 91

Active Record Observers 91
Canned Functionality 92
    Acting as a List 93
    Acting as a Tree 97
    Acting as Nested Sets 101
Aggregations 105
    Step 1: Calling the composed_of Method 106
    Step 2: Defining Your Value Object 107
    Putting It All Together: Using Aggregations 108
Extending Active Record 109
    Extending Active Record the Easy Way 109
    Writing Code That Writes Code 110
    Meet method_missing 112
    What Column Did You Want, Again? 116
    But What About the Farmer? 117
    Adding Class Methods 120
Don't Shoot Yourself in the Foot 123

■CHAPTER 6   **Active Record Testing and Debugging** 125

Unit Testing 125
    Why Write Unit Tests? 126
    How to Write Good Unit Tests 127
    Assertions 129
    Fixtures 139
    Fixture Formats 142
    Wrapping It All Up 144

Active Record Errors and Exceptions 144
    Active Record Error Methods 144
    Preparing for Problems 153
Debugging Tips and Tricks 153
    Active Record and Logging 153
    Active Record Benchmarking 159
    Testing Is Fun! 160

▪CHAPTER 7   **Working with Legacy Schema** 161

Give and Take 162
    How Much Do You Want to Do in Active Record? 162
    Who's Responsible? 163
    How Do Things Get Done? 163
    Is There an Easier or More Efficient Way? 163
Configuration Options for Active Record 164
    primary_key_prefix_type 164
    table_name_prefix 165
    table_name_suffix 166
    pluralize_table_names 166
    colorize_logging 167
    default_timezone 167
    allow_concurrency 168
    generate_read_methods 169
    schema_format 169
    set_table_name 170
    set_primary_key 171
    set_Inheritance_column 171
    set_sequence_name 172
Making the Complex Easier 173
    CRUD Operations and Complex SQL Statements 175
    Improving Performance and Cutting Out the Middle Man 177
    Stored Procedures, Custom Functions, and Sequences 179
    Data Types 181

Importing and Exporting 181
    Exporting XML 182
    Importing XML 183
    Exporting YAML 184
    Importing YAML 184
    Exporting CSV 185
    Importing CSV 185
You're on Your Way to Becoming a Legend 186

CHAPTER 8   Active Record and the Real World 187

Exploring Active Record Source Code 187
    Finding the Code 188
    Following the Code Trail 188
    Putting It All Back Together 191
The Future of Active Record 192
    The Keys to the Enterprise 192
    Little by Little, Big Things Will Happen 193
    Two Steps Forward, One Step Back 193
    A World of Resources 194
    Active Record on Its Own 195
    Adding Your Own Two Cents 195
Alternatives to Active Record 196
    DBI 196
    Og 197
    ActiveRelation 199
    Database-Specific Libraries 199
    Active Resource 200
    Even More Alternatives 201
Common Active Record Questions and Answers 201
    How Do I Use Multiple Databases with Active Record? 201
    How Do I Handle Internationalization and Localization? 204
    How Do I Use Composite Primary Keys? 205
    How Do I Use GUID/UUID Primary Keys? 205
    Can I Use Active Record in a Multithreaded Program? 206
    How Do I Ensure Proper Handling of Decimal Numbers? 206
    What Database Locking Mechanisms Does Active
        Record Support? 206

Does Active Record Support Prepared Statements? 207

How Do I Select a Random Record from the Database? 207

How Do I Model X with Active Record? 208

What Support Does Active Record Have for Database
Foreign Keys? 210

How Do I Properly Use find_by_sql? 210

How Do I Ensure that All My Records Are Valid? 211

Can I Use the Same Name for a Database Column
and an Active Record Model? 212

Does Active Record Support enum Column Types? 213

Does Active Record Support Adding Security to Individual
Models or Columns? 213

What Is the Difference Between has_one and belongs_to? 213

How Can You Paginate Active Record Results? 213

Where Can I Get More Active Record Help? 214

■APPENDIX **Active Record Methods in Detail** 215

ActiveRecord::Base 215

Public Class Methods 215

Protected Class Methods 224

Public Instance Methods 225

ActiveRecord::Calculations::ClassMethods 231

Public Instance Methods 231

ActiveRecord::Callbacks 233

Public Instance Methods 233

ActiveRecord::ConnectionAdapters::AbstractAdapter 235

Public Instance Methods 235

Protected Instance Methods 236

ActiveRecord::ConnectionAdapters::Column 236

Public Class Methods 236

Public Instance Methods 237

ActiveRecord::ConnectionAdapters::DatabaseStatement 238

Public Instance Methods 238

Protected Instance Methods 240

ActiveRecord::ConnectionAdapters::Quoting 240

Public Instance Methods 240

ActiveRecord::ConnectionAdapters::SchemaStatements 241

Public Instance Methods 241

Protected Instance Methods 245

ActiveRecord::ConnectionAdapters::TableDefinition 245
    Public Class Methods 245
    Public Instance Methods. 245
ActiveRecord::Errors 246
    Public Instance Methods. 246
ActiveRecord::Migration 249
    Public Class Methods 249
ActiveRecord::Observer 250
    Public Class Methods 250
    Protected Instance Methods 250
ActiveRecord::Observing::ClassMethods. 250
    Public Instance Methods. 250
    Protected Instance Methods 251
ActiveRecord::Reflection::ClassMethods. 251
    Public Instance Methods. 251
ActiveRecord::Reflection::MacroReflection 252
    Public Class Methods 252
ActiveRecord::Schema 252
    Public Class Methods 252
ActiveRecord::Transactions::ClassMethods 253
    Public Instance Methods. 253
ActiveRecord::Validations. 254
    Public Instance Methods. 254
    Protected Instance Methods 255
ActiveRecord::Validations::ClassMethods 255
    Public Instance Methods. 255

■INDEX 267

About the Authors

KEVIN MARSHALL is a software developer at heart. He is a consultant to a number of companies and currently runs a number of sites on his own—many of which are now happily taking advantage of Active Record with the Ruby on Rails framework, including the popular Draftwizard.com. As a technology writer, Kevin has published a short article, "Web Services with Rails," contributed a few recipes to the *Ruby Cookbook* (Lucas Carlson and Leonard Richardson. O'Reilly, 2006), and contributed a number of articles to the Association of Computing Machinery's periodical, Computing Reviews (available online at http://www.reviews.com).

Kevin is also a member of the Pro Football Writers Association, the Fantasy Sports Trade Association, and the Fantasy Sports Writers Association. When he's not deep into coding, building content, or talking football, he's generally off playing with his two sons or spending time with his amazing wife Catherine. To learn more about what he's up to right now, you can visit his company site, http://falicon.com, or just drop him a note at info@falicon.com.

CHAD PYTEL is president of thoughtbot, inc., a software development consulting firm located in Boston and New York that specializes in agile, test-driven web application development using the Ruby on Rails framework. With a history in Java and EJB development, thoughtbot switched to Ruby on Rails as its primary development platform in 2005. Chad is a firm believer in the model-view-controller design pattern and realistic software development, and those philosophies, combined with Ruby and Ruby on Rails, represent a new, exciting, and better way to develop software.

Chad lives with his wife in Ambler, PA. When not managing projects and writing code, Chad enjoys acting in and producing theater, film, and improv comedy. To follow along with Chad and the rest of the thoughtbot team's ideas on business, design, development, and technology, visit their blog at http://giantrobots.thoughtbot.com.

JON YUREK is the chief technical officer at thoughtbot, inc. Born a programmer, Jon has been developing software professionally since 1999. After seeing the elegant and expressive power of Ruby, Jon quickly moved all new development at thoughtbot away from Java and Perl to using Ruby and Rails.

Jon is a graduate of Worcester Polytechnic Institute and currently lives in Somerville, MA.

About the Technical Reviewer

ADAM STEIN is a software engineer and has been working in Java and ColdFusion for the past eight years. He has always been curious about Ruby, and toying with Active Record was his first venture into the Ruby world. Adam is most proud of his wonderful wife, Marcy, and their three great children: Thomas, Joseph, and Julia.

Acknowledgments

We would like to give special thanks to Yukihiro "Matz" Matsumoto for getting the ball rolling by creating the Ruby language. We would also like to thank David Heinemeier Hanson and the many other contributors to the Ruby on Rails framework, especially for their work on the Active Record library. Without their innovation and selfless dedication to creating something as special as Active Record, this book would not have been possible.

KM, CP, JY

I would like to thank my wife Catherine for sharing life's adventures with me; my coauthors Chad and Jon and the entire thoughtbot staff for making this book ten times better than I could have done on my own; Anthony Molinaro for being a good friend and inspiring me to do more than just code; Keith Nordberg for always listening (and encouraging) my crazy ideas and plans; Mike Cole for being the good person I can only strive to be; my half-brother Mike for sharing his wisdom, life experience, and wonderful family with me; my mother Barbra Taylor, my sister Kim, my aunt K.T., and my grandmother Nancy for raising me; Bruce Antelman and the Reviews.com staff as well as the various clients I've worked for over the years for giving me exciting challenges and a reason to always keep learning; and finally, thank you to both my sons Timothy and Brady for making every day a fun day.

KM

Thank you to everyone at thoughtbot for your hard work, determination, and commitment to excellence and to my awesome wife Rachel for her love and support. Additionally, thank you to all the friends, clients, colleagues, and teachers—good and bad—who have shaped the way that I think about life, programming, and business.

CP

Thanks to the guys at thoughtbot for challenging me every day and to anyone who ever had a kind word or a harsh one about anything I've done; the praise kept me going, and the criticism made me better.

JY

Introduction

When we first shared the idea for this book with some of our peers in the Ruby community, they all had the same initial question, "Is there really enough to talk about in Active Record to fill a whole book?"

Our answer, then and now, is, "Yes and no."

You see, at the time of this writing, Active Record has primarily been covered as a subsection, or maybe as a chapter or two, within a larger scoped book generally about the Ruby on Rails (RoR) framework. And almost all of those books actually do a great job of introducing you to the basics of Active Record; they go a long way toward getting you started with the library. However, because they are addressing a larger scope, all of the existing books also fall short in exposing the hidden features and benefits of using the Active Record library, and almost none even mention the fact that you can get many of the same advantages in your Ruby programs outside of the Rails framework.

If all we were going to do was get you enough knowledge to use the basics of Active Record as you build new Ruby on Rails projects, then no, there would not be enough to fill an entire book. Within this book however, we go much deeper into the library than any other source has to date. We explore the raw source code for the Active Record library. We help to explain the concepts, the rules, and the goals for the Active Record library—and we show you how to bend and break the library as you see fit for your own applications. We do this with lots and lots of examples, so you can try it all for yourself and learn by doing.

Our motivation for writing this book goes back to our beginnings using the Ruby on Rails framework. When first introduced to Ruby on Rails, we really liked what we were seeing. Clearly, Ruby on Rails was a powerful and intuitive framework that would make us more productive in our daily work. In our enthusiasm for the newfound tool, we began applying Ruby on Rails to many of our existing projects—and those words, "existing projects," are key here. They are at the root of our motivation to write this book.

Active Record can be deceptively simple to use in an environment that you develop around Ruby on Rails from the very beginning. But sooner or later, you'll run into a database that's been designed without Active Record in mind, or you'll need to design a database yourself that doesn't conform to all of Active Record's defaults. And that's where this book comes in. Many, if not all of the books about Ruby on Rails that we have read assume that you will only be building a stand-alone Rails application from scratch. But this isn't the case for us! It probably won't be the case for you either. We saw a clear need for a book to help developers take full advantage of the Ruby on Rails framework while continuing to use legacy databases that their other business applications depend on.

Among the three of us, we have a pretty fair bit of experience in applying Active Record to the problem of legacy databases. In our work with clients, we often find ourselves writing ad-hoc Ruby scripts using Active Record to manage various client databases or to perform various incidental tasks. Whether it's pulling data from an Oracle database for a Ferret indexing script for Reviews.com, pulling and pushing content from an MS SQL Server database for the SportsXchange, or doing simple data manipulation and calculations in a local MySQL instance, we can now do it all in Ruby with the Active Record library.

However, the steps it took us to get to this comfort level opened our eyes to the fact that there is no real, centralized source of Active Record information. We had to piece together what's in this book over time by collecting tips, playing with code, using trial and error, and digging through all the source code line by line. While we didn't mind the work (and we got lots of help from the Ruby community), we thought it would be selfish not to share our new-found experience and knowledge with everyone else and hopefully save a few of you some time. Maybe we'll even convert a few new people over to Ruby who've been using the "I can't work with my legacy schema" argument as a reason for not trying it.

So, long story short, if you are looking to know more about Active Record than the basics covered in other books, if you want to know how your Ruby on Rails applications really do all that magic communication with your database (and how to improve it for your specific situation), if you want to work with Active Record but have a legacy schema you need to deal with, or if you simply want an easy way to create ad-hoc database-driven Ruby scripts, then this book was written just for you. The combination of Ruby on Rails and Active Record can be just as powerful against legacy databases as against databases that you build with Active Record to begin with. The magic is there. We want to show it to you. We hope that we've succeeded.

CHAPTER 1

■■■

Introducing Active Record

One of the first jobs Kevin had as a teenager was as a dishwasher at a local diner. For those of you who aren't familiar with the job, dishwashers are generally at the bottom of the totem pole in most kitchens. If there's a job nobody wants to do, like digging through the trash for a retainer someone left on a plate, the dishwasher is the one who ends up having to do it. As you can imagine, he hated that job. Still, he did learn a lot of good life lessons, and he learned to be a jack-of-all-trades at an early age.

As a developer, you can probably relate to the jack-of-all-trades situation (though we hope you don't have to dig through the trash like Kevin did!). Developers are expected to know everything there is to know about our language of choice, our development and production platforms, our database software, and, of course, our business logic. In reality, that's a lot of stuff, and just completing a simple task often requires changing hats from a developer to a database administrator to a designer to an end-user. Active Record helps free our brains up a little bit by combining some of these roles into one simple skill set—that of Active Record developer.

Since this entire book covers the niche topic of Active Record for Ruby, it's probably safe to assume that you already know at least the very basics of what the Ruby Active Record library is. That is, you've heard that it's an object relational mapping (ORM) library that is the model part of the Rails model, view, controller (MVC) framework and primarily allows for create, read, update, and delete (CRUD) database operations. If nothing else, you got that much information from the back cover of this book!

But maybe you skipped the back cover and just flipped to this section to see if this book is worth buying (it is, and we recommend two copies; we hear it makes a great gift!), or maybe you're like us and hate acronyms, or your eyes just glaze over when you hear many technical terms in a row like that. Whatever the case, we don't feel like this explanation helps people to understand what Active Record really is or what can actually be done with it. So here's our layman's explanation, which we hope is a bit more direct and easier to digest:

Active Record is a Ruby library that allows your Ruby programs to transmit data and commands to and from various data stores, which are usually relational databases.

In even more basic terms, you might say:

Active Record allows Ruby to work with databases.

Admittedly, there's a lot more to Active Record than just this basic explanation, but hopefully, this gives you the core idea of what the Active Record library was designed to accomplish. Throughout the rest of this book, we'll dig into a lot of little tips, tricks, and features that will turn you into a master of Active Record for Ruby. But before we get too deep into the guts of it all, let's lay a little groundwork and cover some of the background of the Active Record library and the concepts it incorporates, just so we're all on the same page at the start.

The Story Behind Active Record

Active Record is actually a design pattern originally published by Martin Fowler in his book *Patterns of Enterprise Application Architecture* (Addison-Wesley Professional, 2002). The now-famous creator of Rails, David Heinemeier Hansson (commonly referred to online and throughout the rest of this book as simply DHH), took the concepts laid out by Mr. Fowler and implemented them as a Ruby library that he also called Active Record.

■**Note** Since both the design pattern and the Ruby library are called Active Record, it can quickly become confusing which we're referring to throughout this book. Since the majority of this book is specifically written for and about the Active Record library for Ruby, when we refer to something as simply "Active Record," we mean the Active Record library for Ruby. Therefore, when we refer to the Active Record design pattern, we will use the full label "Active Record design pattern."

When DHH released the Rails framework to the public, Active Record was part of the core bundle, and it's now also available as its own Ruby gem.

As is often the case with open source projects, once the initial library was out there, a number of Ruby and Rails contributors took it upon themselves to take the next step so that the library could be used with almost all of the popular database applications. They did this by developing various database-specific adapters for Active Record. Active Record adapters are basically custom implementations of various parts of the Active Record library that abstract the proprietary bits of each database system, such as connection details, so that the Active Record library pretty much works the same regardless of the backend database system you are using. The most popular and widely used of these adapters are now also directly included as part of the library (we'll mention many of the contributors and developers later in this chapter when we cover the specifics of each database adapter for Active Record).

Active Record Mostly Adheres to the ORM Pattern

The core concept of Active Record and other object relational mapping (ORM) libraries is that relational databases can be represented reasonably in object-based code if you simply think of database tables as classes, table rows as objects, and table fields as object attributes. Looking at a quick example will help to explain this concept best, so assume we had something like the following accounts table in some type of database:

```
Accounts table
    ID field (integer; auto-incremented; primary key)
    Username field (text type field)
    Password field (text type field)
```

Our Active Record Account class, or model as it's commonly referred to, would look something like this:

```
Class Account < ActiveRecord::Base
end
```

And finally, throughout our Ruby or Rails code, we would create instances of account objects like this:

```
# creates a new account object in memory and a new account record in our database
newacc = Account.new
newacc.Username = "Kevin"
newacc.Password = "Marshall"
newacc.save

# creates an Account object in memory from data in Account table with ID of 1
# (equivalent to the ANSI SQL statement of "select * from accounts where ID = 1")
findacc = Account.find(1)

# deletes records from database that have username of "Kevin"
Account.delete("username = 'Kevin'")
```

Don't worry if all this sort of seems like magic at this point—right now, we're simply trying to show you the ORM concept without any clutter. We'll dive into the details of all this stuff and explain all the ins and outs of Active Record syntax in later chapters.

Active Record Is a Different Kind of ORM

Active Record differs from other ORM libraries, such as Java's Hibernate, mostly in the way it's configured or, rather, in the general lack of initial configuration it requires. Out of the box, Active Record makes a number of configuration assumptions, without requiring any outside XML configuration files or mapping details, so nearly everything just works as DHH believed most would expect or want it to—in fact, our previous example showed this was the case and took full advantage of Active Record assumptions. We weren't required to do any additional configuration or set up any special files or instructions. We just opened a text program and typed a few short lines of code, and before you knew it, we had a fully functional Active Record program.

In fact, the lack of configuration and taking advantage of the default assumptions Active Record makes on our behalf is most likely why the previous example felt like magic. Later in the book, we'll go into more detail about configuration and the default assumptions Active Record makes, as well as how to override any of those assumptions whenever you need.

Active Record Is One Part of the MVC Concept

Active Record is probably most famous as being an important part of the Ruby on Rails framework. And if we had to pick one single thing about the Rails framework that we think makes it successful, it would be the fact that it adheres to the MVC design. The concept of MVC is to break code into logical groupings and programs into logical functional groupings. Traditionally, the model section is where the majority of your business logic code would be; the view is where your user interface code would be, and the controller code primarily deals with the communication between the model and view. Rails MVC implementation is a little bit different. With Rails, the model section is generally your Active Record classes and other data-descriptive or data-communication code. The view section remains primarily for the user interface, which tends to be a heavy dose of HTML in most Rails applications. The controller also handles the communication between the models and the views; however, it also tends to host a larger part of the business logic than traditional MVC systems might.

Since we are focusing on Active Record and not Rails throughout this book, we won't spend too much time on MVC concepts or details. From strictly an Active Record developer's point of view, it doesn't really matter where our code is located or how it's sectioned off. But the MVC design is worth knowing about when you plan to build programs of any serious size. And it's especially important to understand where Active Record fits into the picture of the MVC framework when you are building Rails applications.

Active Record Is Primarily Used for CRUD Database Transactions

There are four general tasks you perform when working with databases: creating (C), reading (R), updating (U), and deleting (D) rows of data. As a group, these actions are often referred to as CRUD. Almost all modern applications perform CRUD operations, and Active Record was specifically designed to make CRUD operations easy to write and understand. The following examples display the four basic CRUD operations as you would see them in most Active Record programs:

```
newacc = Account.new(:username => "Kevin")
newacc.save #=> creates the new record in the account table

temp = Account.find(1)
# => selects the record associated with id of 1 from the account table
temp.username = 'Kevin' # => assigns a value to the username attribute of the object
temp.save #=> does the actual update statement applying the changes we just stated.

Account.destroy_all(1) #=> deletes the record in the account table with id of 1
```

Of course, there are a lot more options and ways to do things than the preceding examples show, but these are the most generic, and probably most common, ones you'll see in Active Record applications. In the next chapter, we'll talk about the Active Record CRUD operations and their various options in detail.

The Active Record Library Is Ruby Code

Probably the most important thing to remember when working with Active Record is that in the end, it's all really just Ruby code. This means anything you can do with Ruby objects, such as inheritance, overriding of methods, metaprogramming, and more, also can be done with Active Record objects. True, the object attributes are generally populated with data pulled from a database through SQL statements, and in most cases, the object attribute values are eventually written out to a database through SQL statements. But outside of those two important processes, everything else you do with or to Active Record objects is really done just like you are working with any other Ruby object.

Though the whole idea is to represent database records as objects, it's important to remember that they really are two separate things: Ruby objects and database records. As such, you can (and will) sometimes have your database record in a different state or with a different value than its corresponding Active Record object and its attributes. This is probably most obvious when you are dealing with data validations. When a data validation fails during an attempt to save, your Active Record object attribute will still have the value assigned by your application (which fails validation), but your database record will not have been updated. We talk more about this issue, and data validation in detail, in Chapter 4.

From Active Record Objects to Database Records and Back Again

Even though Active Record objects are really just Ruby objects, when packaged as the Active Record library, they do go through a number of built-in steps or methods each time they are created, accessed, updated, or deleted. Whether you are saving new records, updating existing ones, or simply accessing data with Active Record, there are three general steps to follow:

1. Create an Active Record object.

2. Manipulate or access the attributes of the object.

3. Save the attributes as a record in the database.

As mentioned previously, updating data can be done using the previous steps or with a special update call shown in the following example:

```
Account.update(1, "Username = Kevin")
```

Deleting data from a database, on the other hand, is a little bit of a special situation, since you often want your database records to exist long after your Active Record objects have been destroyed or gone out of scope. If we tied the deletion of data from the database to the life cycle of our objects, every time our code was finished executing, our objects would be removed from memory and our data deleted from our database. That would be a very bad thing. Therefore, deleting data is done by special destroy or delete statements—not by simply removing the object from memory. The following example shows one way of deleting the record with a primary key of 1:

```
Account.delete(1)
```

If it seems like we are glossing over the details of all this, don't worry; we'll break down the specifics of each of these steps throughout different parts of this book. For now, let's just take a peek at the basics of these three steps, so you have a base understanding of how things work.

Creating an Active Record Object

Most often, you create your Active Record objects with a call to the create or new method. Both of these methods also allow you to set the values of your object's attributes directly, as shown in the following example:

```
example = Account.new(:Account_Name => "Kevin Marshall",
 :Account_Username => "Falicon")
```

The other common way to create an Active Record object is to use one of the various find methods. All of these methods populate the object's attributes from records in the database that matched the search criteria. The following example creates an object that is populated with the data of the record with a primary key of 1:

```
example = Account.find(1)
```

Again, we will cover all the various details and options of create, new, update, delete, and find methods throughout the following chapters.

Manipulating or Accessing the Attributes of the Object

Once you have an Active Record object, you have the ability to set or get all of its attributes. The attributes are usually directly mapped from the fields of your database table. So for example, if our Account table had an Account_Username field, then our Account Active Record objects would have a corresponding Account_Username attribute. The following example shows one way of directly setting an attribute's value as well as how to access the value of a given attribute:

```
example.Account_Username = "Falicon"
puts "Your username is now #{example.Account_Username}"
```

Saving the Attributes as a Record in the Database

It's important to remember that when you are working with an Active Record object you are really only setting and accessing the attributes of a Ruby object. Your changes are not reflected within your database until you make a call to the ActiveRecord::Base.save method.

The save method is where most of the real action and power of the Active Record library takes place:

```
Example.save
```

It's this method that has built-in support for things like callbacks, data validations, and many of the other features explained throughout the remainder of this book.

Why Active Record Is a Smart Choice

Active Record is easy to install, simple to write and read, and full-featured object-based code. Out of the box, it comes with support for most all modern database systems, is platform independent, and goes a long way in abstracting the messy details of dealing with various database implementations. All this means that you, as a developer, can focus on learning just one thing, Active Record, to deal with storing and retrieving data from your database. You don't have to worry about learning all the ins and outs of your specific database software, the unique version of SQL it supports, or the related tips and tricks for massaging data in and out of the database. That leaves you more time and energy for coding your real applications.

If you've been reading through this chapter in hopes of deciding if Active Record is worth learning more about, we hope that you are now anxious to dive into the details with us. However, if you aren't yet quite sold on working through the rest of the book, consider the following list of added benefits to the Active Record approach, each of which we will cover in detail throughout the remainder of this book:

- Simplified configuration and default assumptions

- Automated mapping between tables and classes and between columns and attributes

- Associations among objects

- Aggregation of value objects

- Data validations

- Ability to make data records act like lists or trees

- Callbacks

- Observers for the life cycle of Active Record objects

- Inheritance hierarchies

- Transaction support on both the object and database level

- Automatic reflection on columns, associations, and aggregations

- Direct manipulation of data as well as schema objects

- Database abstraction through adapters and a shared connector

- Logging support

- Migration support

- Active Record as an important part of the Ruby on Rails framework

- Active Record as it's integrated in other emerging frameworks like Merb and Camping

This is just a small list of the features of Active Record, but I hope it gives you an idea of just how powerful Active Record can be. Still, before you can take advantage of anything Active Record has to offer, you must first get it installed and configured, so let's get started with that step now.

Installing and Configuring Active Record

One of the primary design goals of Active Record (and Rails for that matter) was to favor, as DHH puts it, "convention over configuration." This means, from a developer's point of view, it should be very quick and simple to install and start to use. A developer should not have to spend hours setting up and learning about all the various configuration options and files before even starting to do some real coding. As you can imagine, this is a lofty goal for any library designer, but it's one that DHH was actually able to achieve! In fact, it's probably the single biggest reason that Active Record (and Rails) is being so quickly adapted by developers around the world. In this chapter, we'll walk you through the very simple three-step process to get Active Record installed for your specific situation.

Since Active Record is really just a collection of Ruby code, it stands to reason that you must first have Ruby correctly installed on your machine. And since Active Record is primarily distributed as a gem, it should be no surprise that you must also have the Ruby Gem system correctly installed on your machine. There are many good books and resources that cover the installation of these requirements, so we won't go into the details of these here and will instead assume that you already have them installed.

■Note If you are looking for more information on installing Ruby or the Ruby Gem system, two good web sites full of Ruby resources are `http://www.rubycentral.com` and `http://www.rubyforge.com`.

Assuming that you do, in fact, have Ruby and the Ruby Gem system installed correctly on your machine, installing Active Record requires just three simple steps:

1. Install the Active Record gem.

2. Depending on the database adapter you intend to use, install the required files or libraries.

3. Supply the adapter-specific connection information to make a connection to the database.

Let's look at each of these steps in a little more detail. When we're finished with this chapter, you'll have Active Record fully installed, and you'll be ready to dive into coding!

Installing the Active Record Gem

You are probably already familiar with the idea of Ruby Gems—a simple system for packaging, distributing, and installing various Ruby libraries. You're probably also already aware that `www.rubyforge.com` is the default remote gem distribution site. So it should be no surprise to learn that Active Record is, in fact, a gem available through the RubyForge.com system and that the most basic command to install the Active Record gem is to simply type **gem install activerecord** at a command line. The gem system should then walk you through any additional steps that are required for installing the library, including installing the Active Support library, which is a Ruby requirement for Active Record.

■**Note** If you prefer, you can download the Active Record library for local installation from www.rubyforge.com. However, it's generally easier and, therefore, recommended that you simply use the remote gem installation procedure described in this section.

Installing Any Additional Required Libraries or Gems

Active Record handles communication between your code and the database through the use of database-specific adapters. Because each of these adapters is unique and specific to the database that it communicates with, each adapter also has unique and varying underlying requirements in addition to those required by the general Active Record library.

Since Active Record is really just Ruby code, you can view the source code at any time. The source code for each Active Record adapter can be found in your Ruby installation directory under the lib/ruby/gems/1.8/gems/activerecord-1.15.1/lib/active_record/connection_ adapters directory. Looking directly at the source code is the best possible way to get familiar with the real ins and outs of what each adapter actually does and supports. If you're serious about becoming an Active Record expert, I highly recommend taking a peek at the inner workings of each. It's also a great way to see high-level Ruby programming and design in action.

Out of the box, Active Record comes with adapters for connecting to the most popular and commonly used databases currently on the market: DB2, Firebird, FrontBase, MySQL, Open-Base, Oracle, PostgreSQL, SQLite, SQL Server, and Sybase. Let's take a little more detailed look at the specific dependencies of each database adapter:

DB2: The DB2 adapter was written and is currently maintained by Maik Schmidt. The adapter requires the ruby-db2 driver or Ruby DBI with DB2 support to be installed on the machine as well. You can obtain the ruby-db2 library or the Ruby DBI files from www. rubyforge.org/projects/ruby-dbi.

Firebird: The Firebird adapter was written and is currently maintained by Ken Kunz. The adapter requires the FireRuby library to be installed on the machine as well. You can install the FireRuby library via the gem command gem install fireruby.

FrontBase: The FrontBase adapter does not currently have any author or maintenance information in its source code. The adapter requires the ruby-frontbase library to be installed on the machine as well. You can obtain the ruby-frontbase library via the gem command gem install ruby-frontbase.

MySQL: The MySQL adapter does not currently have any author or maintenance information in its source code. The adapter requires the MySQL library to be installed on the machine as well. You can obtain the MySQL library via the gem command gem install mysql.

OpenBase: The OpenBase adapter does not currently have any author or maintenance information it in its source code. The adapter requires the OpenBase library to also be installed on the machine. You can obtain the OpenBase library via the gem command gem install openbase.

Oracle: The Oracle adapter was originally written by Graham Jenkins and is currently maintained by Michael Schoen. The adapter requires the ruby-oci8 library, which itself requires that the OCI8 API be installed on your machine. The OCI8 API can be installed as part of the Oracle client available via www.oracle.com, and the ruby-oci8 library files can be obtained from www.rubyforge.org/projects/ruby-oci8.

PostgreSQL: The PostgreSQL adapter does not currently have any author or maintenance information in its source code. The adapter requires the ruby-postgres library to be installed on the machine as well. You can obtain the ruby-postgres library via the gem command gem install ruby-postgres.

SQLite: The SQLite adapter was originally written by Luke Holden and was updated for SQLite3 support by Jamis Buck. The adapter requires the sqlite-ruby library for SQLite2 support and the sqlite3-ruby library for SQLite3 support. You can obtain the sqlite-ruby library via the gem command gem install sqlite-ruby. You can obtain the sqlite3-ruby library via the gem command gem install sqlite3-ruby.

SQLServer: The SQLServer adapter was written by Joey Gibson with updates provided by DeLynn Berry, Mark Imbriaco, Tom Ward, and Ryan Tomayko. The adapter is currently maintained by Tom Ward. The adapter requires the Ruby DBI library and support for either ADO or ODBC drivers be installed on the machine. You can obtain the DBI library from www.rubyforge.org/projects/ruby-dbi. If you intend to use the ADO drivers, included in the DBI download should be the file bdi-0.1.0/lib/dbd/ADO.rb. Once the DBI library is installed, this ADO.rb file should be copied to your-ruby-install-directory/lib/ruby/ site_ruby/1.8/DBD/ADO/ directory. ODBC driver support varies for each operating system and is outside of the scope of this book. Please refer to your specific operating system's documentation for details on properly setting up ODBC driver support.

■**Note** You will probably need to manually create the ADO directory within the DBD directory before placing the ADO.rb file in it.

Sybase: The Sybase adapter was written and is maintained by John R. Sheets. The adapter requires the Sybase-ctlib library to be installed on the machine as well. You can obtain the Sybase library via http://raa.ruby-lang.org/project/sybase-ctlib/.

Supplying the Adapter-Specific Information

The final step before you can start to actually use Active Record is to establish a connection to your specific database. If you are connecting to Active Record through a Rails application, you generally provide these details in a database.yml file in your applications config directory. You supply these connection details in YAML format. However, the YAML approach is really just Rails syntactic shorthand for calling the ActiveRecord::Base.establish_connection method. Since this is a book about Active Record (and not Rails), throughout our examples, we will generally call the establish_connection method rather than use the YAML file option.

The establish_connection method expects parameters to be passed as hash values, and each adapter has its own set of acceptable parameters. Let's take a look at each situation in detail. We will also provide an example call of the `establish_connection` method for each adapter.

DB2 Parameters

The minimum DB2 requirements are the adapter and database parameters. Here is the complete list of parameters to consider:

adapter: Specifies that this is connection information for a DB2 database. The value can be either `db2` or `ibm-db2` for the IBM adapter.

database: The name of the database that you are attempting to connect to.

username: Optional parameter containing the username of the user as whom you wish to connect to the database. The default value is nothing.

password: Optional parameter containing the password of the user as whom you wish to connect to the database. This value is provided in plain text. The default value is nothing.

schema: Optional parameter containing the initial database schema to be set.

The following example shows how to open an Active Record database connection for DB2:

```
ActiveRecord::Base.establish_connection(:adapter => "db2",
 :database => "artest", :username => "kevin", :password => "test")
```

Firebird Parameters

The minimum Firebird requirements are the adapter and database parameters. Here is the complete list of parameters to consider:

adapter: Specifies that this is connection information for a Firebird database. The value should be `firebird`.

database: The name of the database that you are attempting to connect to. This value can be either an alias of the Firebird database, the full path of the database file, or a full Firebird connection string.

■Note If you provide a full Firebird connection string in the database parameter, you should not specify the host, service, or port parameters separately.

---

username: Optional parameter containing the username of the user as whom you wish to connect to the database. If this value is not provided, the underlying operating system user credentials are used (on supporting platforms).

password: Optional parameter containing the password of the user as whom you wish to connect to the database. This value is provided in plain text. This parameter is required if the username parameter is supplied but should be omitted if the username is not provided.

host: Optional parameter containing the domain name of the machine that hosts your database. You should not provide this parameter if you are providing the full connection information in the database parameter. Some platforms require that you set this to localhost when connecting to a local Firebird instance through a database alias.

port: Optional parameter containing the port on which the database is available for connections. This parameter is required only if the database is only available on a nonstandard port and the service parameter is not provided. If the service parameter is provided, this value will not be used.

service: Optional parameter containing the service name. This parameter is required only if the host parameter is set and you are connecting to a nonstandard service.

charset: Optional parameter containing the character set that should be used for this connection. You should refer to your Firebird documentation for the valid values that can be used with this parameter.

The following example shows how to open an Active Record database connection for Firebird:

```
ActiveRecord::Base.establish_connection(:adapter => "firebird",
 :database => "test", :host => "www.yourdbserver.com",
:username => "kevin", :password => "test")
```

FrontBase Parameters

The minimum FrontBase requirements are the adapter, database, and port parameters. Here is the complete list of parameters to consider:

adapter: Specifies that this is connection information for a FrontBase database. The value should be frontbase.

database: The name of the database that you are attempting to connect to.

username: Optional parameter containing the username of the user as whom you wish to connect to the database.

password: Optional parameter containing the password of the user as whom you wish to connect to the database. This value is provided in plain text.

host: Optional parameter containing the domain name of the machine that hosts your database.

The following example shows how to open an Active Record database connection for FrontBase:

```
ActiveRecord::Base.establish_connection(:adapter => "frontbase",
 :database => "test", :host => "www.yourdbserver.com")
```

MySQL Parameters

The minimum MySQL requirements are the adapter and database parameters. Here is the complete list of parameters to consider:

adapter: Specifies that this is connection information for a MySQL database. The value should be `mysql`.

database: The name of the database that you are attempting to connect to.

username: Optional parameter containing the username of the user as whom you wish to connect to the database.

password: Optional parameter containing the password of the user as whom you wish to connect to the database. This value is provided in plain text.

socket: Optional parameter that contains the socket that should be used to communicate with the MySQL database. If this parameter is omitted, the adapter assumes a value of `/tmp/mysql.sock`.

port: Optional parameter containing the port on which the database is available for connections.

sslkey: Required parameter if you are connecting to a MySQL database via SSL.

sslcert: Required parameter if you are connecting to a MySQL database via SSL.

sslca: Required parameter if you are connecting to a MySQL database via SSL.

sslcapath: Required parameter if you are connecting to a MySQL database via SSL.

sslcipher: Required parameter if you are connecting to a MySQL database via SSL.

The following example shows how to open an Active Record database connection for MySQL:

```
ActiveRecord::Base.establish_connection(:adapter => "mysql", :database => "test",
:username => "kevin", :password => "test")
```

OpenBase Parameters

The minimum OpenBase requirements are the adapter and database parameters. Here is the complete list of parameters to consider:

adapter: Specifies that this is connection information for an OpenBase database. The value should be `openbase`.

database: The name of the database that you are attempting to connect to.

username: Optional parameter containing the username of the user as whom you wish to connect to the database.

password: Optional parameter containing the password of the user as whom you wish to connect to the database. This value is provided in plain text.

host: Optional parameter containing the domain name of the machine that hosts your database.

The following example shows how to open an Active Record database connection for OpenBase:

```
ActiveRecord::Base.establish_connection(:adapter => "openbase",
:database => "test", :host => www.yourdbserver.com,
:username => "kevin", :password => "test")
```

Oracle Parameters

The minimum Oracle requirements are the adapter and database parameters. Here is the complete list of parameters to consider:

adapter: Specifies that this is connection information for an Oracle database. The value should be oracle.

database: The name of the database that you are attempting to connect to.

username: Optional parameter containing the username of the user as whom you wish to connect to the database.

password: Optional parameter containing the password of the user as whom you wish to connect to the database. This value is provided in plain text.

The following example shows how to open an Active Record database connection for Oracle:

```
ActiveRecord::Base.establish_connection(:adapter => "oracle",
 :database => "test", :username => "kevin", :password => "test")
```

PostgreSQL Parameters

The minimum PostgreSQL requirements are the adapter and database parameters. Here is the complete list of parameters to consider:

adapter: Specifies that this is connection information for a PostgreSQL database. The value should be postgresql.

database: The name of the database that you are attempting to connect to.

username: Optional parameter containing the username of the user as whom you wish to connect to the database.

password: Optional parameter containing the password of the user as whom you wish to connect to the database. This value is provided in plain text.

port: Optional parameter containing the port that the database is available for connections.

host: Optional parameter containing the domain name of the machine that hosts your database.

min_messages: Optional parameter that allows you to set the min_message value within your database for this connection.

schema_search_path: Optional parameter containing a comma-separated list of schema names to use in the schema search path for the connection.

allow_concurrency: Optional parameter that contains either the value true or false. If the value is set to true, the connection uses asynchronous query methods, which will help prevent the Ruby threads from deadlocking. The default value is false, which uses blocking query methods.

encoding: Optional parameter that allows you to specify the encoding to use.

The following example shows how to open an Active Record database connection for PostgreSQL:

```
ActiveRecord::Base.establish_connection(:adapter => "postgresql",
 :database => "test", :username => "kevin", :password => "test")
```

SQLite Parameters

The minimum SQLite requirements are the adapter and database parameters. Here is the complete list of parameters to consider:

adapter: Specifies that this is connection information for a SQLite database. The value should be sqlite.

database: The name of the database that you are attempting to connect to.

The following example shows how to open an Active Record database connection for SQLite:

```
ActiveRecord::Base.establish_connection(:adapter => "sqlite", :database => "test")
```

SQL Server Parameters

The minimum SQL Server requirements are the adapter and the database parameters. Here is the complete list of parameters to consider:

adapter: Specifies that this is connection information for a Microsoft SQL Server database. The value should be sqlserver.

mode: Optional parameter containing the mode in which you wish to make the connection. Valid values are ado or odbc. If this parameter is omitted, the adapter defaults to the ADO mode.

database: The name of the database that you are attempting to connect to.

host: Optional parameter containing the domain name of the machine that hosts your database.

dsn: Required parameter if the mode is odbc. This parameter references the name of your data source set up in your ODBC settings.

username: Optional parameter containing the username of the user as whom you wish to connect to the database.

password: Optional parameter containing the password of the user as whom you wish to connect to the database. This value is provided in plain text.

port: Optional parameter containing the port on which the database is available for connections.

autocommit: Optional parameter to turn the `autocommit` feature of SQL Server on or off. Valid values are `true` and `false`. If this parameter is omitted, the adapter defaults to `true`.

The following example shows how to open an Active Record database connection for SQL Server:

```
ActiveRecord::Base.establish_connection(:adapter => "sqlserver",
:database => "test", :username => "kevin", :password => "test",
 :host => "www.yourdbserver.com")
```

Sybase Parameters

The minimum Sybase requirements are the adapter and the database parameters. Here is the complete list of parameters to consider:

adapter: Specifies that this is connection information for a Sybase database. The value should be `sybase`.

database: The name of the database that you are attempting to connect to.

host: Optional parameter containing the domain name of the machine that hosts your database.

username: Optional parameter containing the username of the user as whom you wish to connect to the database.

password: Optional parameter containing the password of the user as whom you wish to connect to the database. This value is provided in plain text.

The following example shows how to open an Active Record database connection for Sybase:

```
ActiveRecord::Base.establish_connection(:adapter => "sybase",
:database => "test", :host => "www.yourdbserver.com",
:usrname => "kevin", :password => "test")
```

Learning More

By design, Active Record abstracts many of the details of each database, leaving the developer free to focus on the details of coding the application. Switching from one backend database to another, from an Active Record view, generally requires little more than changing your connection information. For the most part, Active Record developers are shielded from having to learn the specifics of any one database implementation—or even most of ANSI SQL for that matter.

Still, each database is fundamentally different and will provide varying levels of support for features and data types. Some will readily support triggers, sequences, and stored procedures; others will not. Some will have elegant ways of dealing with CLOB and BLOB data types; others will not. Each ActiveRecord adapter does its best to create a common denominator for each of these issues, so that nearly all Active Record methods, techniques, and data types are available for each type of database. But as you can imagine, this is a difficult goal to achieve. Databases, like any software application, continue to grow more and more complex and add new features all the time.

With all this in mind, I recommend that you become as familiar as you can with the specific database application you intend to use. I also highly recommend that you learn at least the basics of ANSI SQL. These two chores will help you tremendously throughout your career in debugging and developing even the most advanced Active Record programs. The following list is a rundown of the most common databases available today and some good starting points for learning more about each:

DbB2: DB2 has been around for a very long time, and some even consider it to be the first database product to use SQL. DB2 is a commercial product provided by IBM and comes in a variety of forms for a variety of platforms. For more information about DB2 you should visit `www-306.ibm.com/software/data/db2`.

Firebird: Firebird is a free-of-charge relational database that runs on Linux, Windows, and a variety of Unix platforms. It is based on the source code released by Inprise Corporation on July 25, 2000. For more information and to download Firebird, you should visit `www.firebirdsql.org`.

FrontBase: FrontBase is a relational database primarily designed for Mac OS X. Licenses for FrontBase are now free. For more information, you should visit `www.frontbase.com`.

MySQL: MySQL is an open source relational database developed and primarily maintained by MySQL AB. There are MySQL versions for most all platforms. For more information, you should visit `www.mysql.com`.

OpenBase: OpenBase is a commercial relational database that has been around since 1991. It is provided by OpenBase International and is available for a variety of platforms including Max OS X, Linux, and Microsoft Windows. For more information on OpenBase, you should visit `www.openbase.com`.

Oracle: Oracle is a commercial relational database provided by Oracle Corporation. There are Oracle versions for most all platforms. For more information, you should visit `www.oracle.com`.

PostgreSQL: PostgreSQL is an open source, object-relational database. PostgreSQL is available for various platforms. For more information, you should visit `www.postgresql.org`.

SQLite: SQLite is a public domain C library that implements a SQL database engine. You can run SQLite on most platforms. For more information, you should visit `www.sqlite.org`.

SQL Server: SQL Server is a commercial relational database provided by Microsoft. SQL Server is primarily designed for the Microsoft platform. For more information, you should visit `www.microsoft.com/sql`.

Sybase: Sybase is a commercial relational database provided by Sybase Corporation. Sybase versions are available for a variety of platforms. For more information, you should visit `www.sybase.com`.

Building Your First Active Record Program

This section will walk you through writing your first Active Record program. It will explain the core concepts of Active Record, including the assumptions it makes in order to dramatically simplify development. Finally, we'll begin to explore the ways you can change these assumptions (a topic which we'll dig deeper into later on in the book).

As previously mentioned, Active Record is an ORM library. ORM is a way of persisting objects to and from relational databases. Recall that, with ORM, an object is analogous to a database table, and individual instances of that object are represented as rows in the table. Finally, the individual member variables of an object are represented as columns in the table.

The elements of a standard Active Record program follow:

1. Include or require the Active Record gem.

2. Establish a connection to your database using the appropriate adapter.

3. Define your Active Record classes by extending the `ActiveRecord::Base` class.

4. CRUD away.

Recall the accounts table from earlier in this chapter:

```
Accounts table
    id field (integer; auto-incremented; primary key)
    username field (text type field)
    password field (text type field)
```

We'll use this accounts table in our examples throughout the rest of this chapter.

Your First Example

Below is the source code for your first Ruby program that uses the Active Record library. The program simply establishes a connection, creates an account object, and stores the attributes of that account object in the database as a new record:

```
require "rubygems"
require_gem "activerecord"

ActiveRecord::Base.establish_connection(
  :adapter => "mysql",
  :host => "localhost",
  :username => "project",
  :database => "project_development")

class Account < ActiveRecord::Base
end

account = Account.new
account.username = "cpytel"
account.save
```

This simple Active Record program includes the Active Record gem, which you installed previously. It establishes a connection to the `project_development` database with username project.

Next, the `Account` class is defined. Notice that there is nothing in the class. Our Active Record objects will eventually have stuff in them, but for now, its important to note that no configuration is needed to get up and running with basic functionality. We've merely supplied the database connection parameters.

Finally, we instantiate a new `Account` object, set the username member variable, and save the instance of the object back to the database.

It's possible to merely connect to the database and be up and running because of the assumptions that Active Record is making and because Active Record gets the rest of its configuration from the database itself.

Active Record Assumptions and Conventions

Our first Active Record program example makes full use of Active Record assumptions and coding conventions. This speeds our development, eases our typing workload, and makes our example seem almost magical. Active Record makes the following assumptions:

- It infers database table names based on class names.

- It assumes the existence of certain database columns.

The first assumption of an Active Record class is the table name. In the case of our `Account` class, the table Active Record assumes is `accounts`. It makes this assumption based on the following guidelines:

- The name of the table within the database is the pluralized name of the class defined in your Active Record program. In our experience, this assumption turns out to be one of the large productivity boosts you'll recognize with Active Record once you get used to it, because it enables the developer to gloss over the naming conventions and instead concentrate on the programming aspects.

- The table name is in lowercase. This is important to note because each database may support case in a variety of ways. Since Ruby variables start with lowercase characters and constants start with uppercase characters, Active Record prefers to force all table and column names to lowercase (via a `downcase` method call). In many of the database systems, case does not really matter when referring to a table or column, so the Active Record downcasing should not cause a problem. For the select few in which case is important, Active Record jumps through as many hoops for you as it can to keep its lowercase preference in line with the specific adapter code for that database.

- If the class name includes multiple words that begin with capital letters, the words will be separated by underscores in the table name.

Table 3-1 lists some examples of assumptions Active Record would make based on the guidelines we've just outlined.

Table 3-1. *Examples of Active Record Table Pluralization*

Class Name	Table Name
Account	accounts
Person	people
UserImage	user_images
Address	addresses
Currency	currencies
Mouse	mice

As you can see from the Table 3-1, Active Record is intelligent about pluralizing the class names. In addition, Active Record also assumes that each table has an automatically incremented integer primary key column named id.

When an Active Record class is instantiated and any data is accessed within the class, Active Record reads the columns of the table and maps these to the class's attributes. While there aren't formal conventions for the naming of columns, since Active Record only creates an attribute in the Active Record class that matches the name of the column, many of the Ruby and Rails naming conventions are seen in a typical Active Record table, including the liberal doses of underscores.

When Active Record reads the columns of the database table and creates the attribute mappings, it also reads the data types of those columns and makes sensible mappings among the attribute types and the database column types, as you might expect. However, the boolean attribute type is a little different for two reasons. First, a boolean type is not supported in all databases supported by Active Record. Second, in Ruby only the false constant and the value nil are considered false. As a workaround, Active Record attribute methods expand the values considered false to include an empty string, 0, "0", "false", and "f". Conversely, the values 1, "1", "true", and "t" are considered true.

These few assumptions, coupled with the dynamic language features provided by Ruby (such as duck typing), provide a foundation that makes it possible to provide an incredibly powerful, yet straightforward, feature set.

■**Note** Duck typing is a form of dynamic typing in which the type of an object is not determined strictly by its class but by its capabilities. This term comes from the idea that if it walks like a duck, and quacks like a duck, it must be a duck. You can read more about duck typing at http://en.wikipedia.org/wiki/Duck_typing.

Overriding the Assumptions

While staying true to the Active Record way of doing things can free you up to worry about other things during application development, obviously your application may have some constraints that require you to override some of the assumptions that Active Record is making, particularly if you are working with a legacy database.

If you want table names to be singular instead of plural, you can set the configuration parameter `pluralize_table_names`:

```
ActiveRecord::Base.pluralize_table_names = false
```

If, instead, you need to override a table name completely, you specify this in the Active Record class itself. For instance, if our `Accounts` class should persist to a table named `AccountBean`, we would specify the `Account` class as follows:

```
class Account < ActiveRecord::Base
  set_table_name "AccountBean"
end
```

Additionally, if your primary key column is not named simply `id`, you can override this from within the class definition as well:

```
class Account < ActiveRecord::Base
  set_primary_key "accountId"
end
```

If you want to use a primary key other than an automatically incremented integer, you must set the value of the primary key yourself, and you must still use the `id` attribute to do so. Additionally, you should only use the `id` attribute to *set* the primary key. To retrieve the value of the primary key, you must use your overridden attribute name.

For example, if we've overridden the account primary key to be `account_number`, and we want to use a custom key format, our `Account` creation code would need to be as follows:

```
account = Account.new
account.id = "X5476"
account.save
```

And to retrieve the `account_number` of an account, you would use this:

```
puts account.account_number #=> X5476
```

Retrieving Objects from the Database

With the groundwork laid regarding Active Record knowledge about our database, the dynamic nature of Ruby Active Record is able to help us work with our objects. For instance, to retrieve objects from the database we have a core method `find`. If we know the value of the primary key that we want, for instance 1, we can simply call it:

```
Account.find(1)
```

In addition, it is possible to use a feature of Active Record called dynamic finders. These allow you to easily find records by their attribute values. For example, if you wish to find the account with the username equal to `cpytel` you can simply write:

```
Account.find_by_username("cpytel")
```

While dynamic finders are fun magic, let's be sure not to get ahead of ourselves. Using the normal `find` method, the following code would return the same result as the dynamic finder:

```
Account.find(:all, :conditions => ["username = ?", "cpytel"])
```

> **■Note** A lot of Active Record magic, such as dynamic finders, is made possible by using the Ruby's
> `method_missing` function; `method_missing` allows you to handle situations when a message is sent to an
> object for which it doesn't have a method. The method `find_by_username` doesn't exist in the code anywhere,
> so it is being handled by `method_missing`.

Once we've retrieved an Active Record object, say with

```
account = Account.find_by_username("cpytel")
```

we can delete the associated record from the database by calling this method:

```
account.destroy
```

When you use the destroy method listed here, you are really only executing a SQL delete statement within your database. The record will no longer be available within your database, but your Active Record object, whose attributes were populated with data from that record, will still be available to you as a read-only instance of the object. This object will persist until it goes out of scope within your application or you specifically delete that instance. This turns out to be a handy feature when you want to report on the deletion of data, as the following code snippet shows:

```
account = Account.find(1)
# do a variety of things within your application...
account.destroy
puts "we just deleted the record with id of #{account.id} from the database"
```

We go into more detail on the various CRUD actions you can perform with Active Record in Chapter 2.

Exploring Active Record Relationships

Relationships among objects, that is, when one or more objects are associated with one another, are not only an incredibly important part of the functionality of the Active Record library, but also of any real-world application. There are several types of relationships, and we'll cover them all in detail in Chapter 4.

All configuration options for a relationship occur within the Active Record class definitions themselves. For our `Account` class, we want to add a relationship to a `Role` object, so we can tell what type of account we have on our hands. We start off by manually defining our roles table within our database:

```
Roles table
    id field (integer; auto-incremented; primary key)
    name field (text type field)
    description field (text type field)
```

We want our account class to hold the reference to the account's role, and we want the foreign key (the column in one table that points to the ID of a row in another) to be in the accounts table. So we define this relationship of roles to accounts in our account model with the `belongs_to` method. First, we add our `Role` class definition:

```
class Role < ActiveRecord::Base
end
```

Next, we modify our definition of the Account class as follows:

```
class Account < ActiveRecord::Base
  belongs_to :role
end
```

With those new class definitions we now have a unidirectional relationship between Account and Role. This relationship is unidirectional, because Account knows what role it has, but Role does not know what Account class instances have it.

With this relationship in place, we now have an attribute for the role relationship of our account objects. However, we first need to make sure that we have a role to work with.

Along with the dynamic finder methods we've already seen, Active Record also has a find_or_create_by_* dynamic finder. This finder works just like the normal find_by_* method, but if a matching object is not found, one will be created for you. We'll use this method to make sure that our desired role exists:

```
admin_role = Role.find_or_create_by_name("Administrator")
```

We can then assign our administrator role to our account:

```
account.role = admin_role
```

Putting the pieces together, we can now show a more complete and realistic example of an Active Record program. Here we set up our connection, define two models that have a one-to-many relationship, and perform a number of basic CRUD operations:

```
require "rubygems"
require_gem "activerecord"

ActiveRecord::Base.establish_connection(
  :adapter => "mysql",
  :host => "localhost",
  :username => "project",
  :database => "project_development")

class Role < ActiveRecord::Base
end

class Account < ActiveRecord::Base
  belongs_to :role
end

admin_role = Role.find_or_create_by_name("Administrator")

account = Account.new
account.username = "cpytel"
account.role = admin_role
account.save
```

```
puts "#{account.username} (#{account.id}) is a(n) #{account.role.name}"
# cpytel (1) is a(n) Administrator

# comment out the following line to avoid deleting the created account
account.destroy
puts "We have just deleted the #{account.username} account!"
```

Them's the Basics!

Believe it or not, in just one chapter, we've introduced you to Active Record and walked you completely through installing and configuration; plus, we've built and explained complete working programs showing the basic CRUD operations. It really is amazing how little you need to do to get started with Active Record!

Of course, there's a lot more to Active Record than just the basics we've covered here (otherwise, this would be a *very* short book!). In the next few chapters, we'll dig into the guts of Active Record and show you how to take full advantage of the Active Record feature set. Before you know it, you'll go beyond building simple CRUD programs and start building full-featured applications with complex business logic seamlessly integrated with your database via Active Record!

CHAPTER 2

███

Active Record and SQL

Active Record interacts with SQL primarily on a CRUD (create, read, update, delete) basis. Those are the only actions that happen to model objects, and there are a number of ways that Active Record makes their use much easier on programmers. In this chapter, we're going to go over how each of these actions translates to the SQL you would normally use to accomplish the same tasks. Then, we'll show you how you can accomplish other common SQL functions, such as locking and transactions.

Creating a Record

Creating an object inserts it into its table in the database. In SQL, this would happen with an `INSERT` statement. With Active Record, this happens with the `save` method. From this angle, both creating and updating a record look the same. The `save` method will create new records and update old ones with equal ease and transparency.

Recall the example from the previous chapter:

```
account = Account.new
account.username = "cpytel"
account.password = "secret"
account.save
```

Assuming that you are saving a new object, the foregoing code would translate into the following SQL:

```
INSERT INTO accounts ('username', 'password') VALUES ('cpytel', 'secret')
```

Note The `id` column is not specified in the `INSERT` preceding statement. Active Record knows the primary key column is special and leaves it out. Normally, you would make the `id` automatically increment in a manner that's appropriate to your database, which keeps the rows individually accessible.

If the creation of the object is successful, the values will be inserted into the database. However, if the save is unsuccessful, the `save` method will return `false`. Then too, there is an alternative `save` method called `save!`. The `save!` method will raise a `RecordNotSaved` exception if the save was not successful.

It's also possible to create objects in one swift stroke using the create method. This method works almost exactly like new plus save. If it is possible for Active Record to save the object with the attributes you've passed in, it will. If it can't, it won't. In either case, the object is returned and ready for normal use. This is useful if you have an object that can easily be instantiated in one line, for example:

```
bookmark = Bookmark.create(:url => "http://www.apress.com", :name => "Apress")
```

There are also some dynamic methods for creating objects, but we'll discuss those when we get to the finder methods.

■**Note** When Active Record translates the value of an attribute into the data that will be used in the SQL query, the value is given to the connection-specific adapter for translation into the format that the database expects. For example, giving a date or time field a Ruby Time object will convert the value into YYYYMMDD hh:mm:ss format when used with a MySQL database. Each type of value is converted in the same way. The values are also escaped by the adapter so that errant quotation marks or comment sections do not accidentally trip up the database and cause it to do something it wasn't meant to do.

Active Record also allows you to create multiple objects across associations. For example, if you had the following object

```
class Person < ActiveRecord::Base
  belongs_to :parent, :class_name => "Person"
  has_many :children, :class_name => "Person", :foreign_key => :parent_id
end
```

you could perform the following actions to create a parent and its children all at once:

```
person_1 = Person.new :first_name => 'Bonnie', :last_name => 'Pytel'
person_2 = Person.new :first_name => 'Chad', :last_name => 'Pytel'
person_1.children << person_2
person_1.save
```

The preceding code will result in the following SQL statements, assuming that the first record inserted will be given the id of 1:

```
INSERT
  INTO people (`first_name`, `last_name`)
  VALUES (`Bonnie`,`Pytel`);
INSERT
  INTO people (`first_name`, `last_name`, `parent_id`)
  VALUES (`Chad`, `Pytel`, 1);
```

Reading a Record

Once you've saved your records to the database, you're going to need a way to get them back. In SQL, this would happen with the SELECT statement, and with Active Record, you use the find method. The definition of the find method is rather ambiguous, so looking at the names of the arguments isn't going to help. As it turns out, find has a few different ways of getting your data back to you.

It's probably best if we deal with find as acting like two different methods: one that will retrieve objects with the specified IDs (which is simple) and one that will find objects with a more complicated set of criteria. The first form of the find method takes a list of one or more integers:

```
book = Book.find 5
```

This invocation of find will query the database for the row that has an ID column equal to 5. Specifically, it is equivalent to

```
SELECT* FROM books WHERE (id = 5)
```

Similarly, you can give an array of integers to this form of find, and it will return all of the corresponding rows. For example, the following invocation of find

```
books = Book.find 1, 3, 5, 7, 9
```

will generate the equivalent of the following SQL statement:

```
SELECT * FROM books WHERE (id IN ( 1, 3, 5, 7, 9 ))
```

The find method possesses quite a lot more power than simply fetching a list of IDs. We have a whole relational database at our disposal, so we'd better use it for something more than a glorified hash table, right? As it turns out, find's other syntax has a much longer list of available options.

This second version of find takes two arguments. The first controls how many results will be returned. It can be either :first or :all. Using :first is the same as tacking LIMIT 1 to the end of the equivalent SQL. Using :all does what you'd expect; it selects over the entire table; an example follows:

```
Account.find :all
# SELECT * FROM accounts
Account.find :first
# SELECT * FROM accounts LIMIT 1
```

The last argument to find can be a hash of options; this is where the real fun happens. The list contains a number of possible options, each of which roughly correspond to some part of a normal SQL SELECT statement. The valid keys for the options hash are :conditions, :include, :order, :select, :group, :joins, :from, :limit, :offset, :readonly, and :lock. Each of the following sections will present these different values, and offer instructions for their use.

:conditions

The :conditions options supplied to the find method will be converted into the WHERE clause of the SQL statement. Like the find method itself, there are a number of ways you can properly pass it in. You can pass a string or a hash of column names and values, or you can specify a more complex string of SQL along with values to interpolate inside an array, as follows:

```
Account.find :all, :conditions => "keyword = 'ruby'"
Account.find :all, :conditions => { :keyword => 'ruby' }
Account.find :all, :conditions => [ "keyword = ?", 'ruby' ]
```

These statements will all generate the following WHERE clause:

```
SELECT * FROM accounts WHERE keyword = 'ruby'
```

You can also do more interesting things like find all accounts named John Doe who have no favorite band:

```
Account.find :all, :conditions => { :first_name =>  @first_name,
                                     :last_name => @last_name,
                                     :favorite_band_id => nil }
```

which would result in the following SQL query:

```
SELECT *
  FROM accounts
  WHERE
    first_name = 'John'
    AND last_name = 'Doe'
    AND favorite_band_id IS NULL
```

You can also have full control over the content of the WHERE clause, because in the Array form of the conditions parameter, you can specify full SQL instead of having it generated for you. This SQL is grouped inside parentheses in the final query, so you don't have to worry about a stray OR statement ruining your results. In the following example, the Array form of the conditions parameter is used in a query to find the records that have been recently updated, or those in the included set of IDs:

```
Account.find :all, :conditions => [ "updated_on > ? OR id IN (?)",
                                     @last_update,
                                     [ 2, 3, 5, 7, 11 ] ]
```

It will result in the following SQL:

```
SELECT *
  FROM accounts
  WHERE
    updated_on > '20061214 15:29:12'
    OR id IN (2, 3, 5, 7, 11)
```

As mentioned earlier, Active Record will interpolate the values supplied as conditions for you, making sure that they are quoted properly to avoid any potential issues, both accidental and intentional. It will also make sure to properly convert data types, like the date used in the previous example, into whatever format your database expects.

:include

Here, we have the FROM clause in your SQL statement. The :include parameter will take a (potentially very) nested hash of symbols that corresponds to the names of relationships you've defined for your model, and add them as joining conditions. For example, assume that, in your social network, you have the following classes:

```
class Person < ActiveRecord::Base
  has_many :favorites
end

class Favorite < ActiveRecord::Base
  belongs_to :person
  belongs_to :band
end

class Band < ActiveRecord::Base
  belongs_to :location
end

class Location < ActiveRecord::Base
end
```

If you wish to find people who like bands that are based in a particular city, you can use the :include hash as follows:

```
city = 'Boston'
Person.find :all, :include => { :favorites => { :bands => { :location => {} } } },
                  :conditions => ["locations.city = ?", city]
```

The generated SQL would be

```
SELECT *
  FROM people
  LEFT OUTER JOIN favorites
    ON people.id=favorites.person_id
  LEFT OUTER JOIN bands
    ON favorites.band_id=bands.id
  LEFT OUTER JOIN locations
    ON bands.location_id=locations.id
  WHERE locations.city = `Boston`
```

The SQL will look like the preceding statement under most circumstances. However, if the tables included loop back on themselves, the table names will need to be relabeled. Therefore, if we had the following class

```
class Person < ActiveRecord::Base
  belongs_to :parent, :class_name => "Person"
  has_many :children, :class_name => "Person", :foreign_key => :parent_id
end
```

we would need to use the following statement to find people who have a child with a particular name:

```
Person.find :all, :include => {:children => {}},
                  :conditions => ["children_people.name = ?", name]
```

If Active Record finds that it's trying to join back to a table it has already included, it will change the name of the table to eliminate ambiguity. It does this using a breadth-first search of all the keys in the hash table, so in the rather contrived example of

```
:include => { :parent => { :parent => {}}, :children => {}}
```

the parent can be referenced via parents_people, but the parent's parent must be referenced via parents_people_2. The full method call for obtaining all the people whose grandparents have a specific name is

```
Person.find :all, :include => { :parent => { :parent => {} },
                  :conditions => ["parents_people_2.name = ?", name ]
```

This would generate the following SQL clause:

```
SELECT *
  FROM people
  LEFT OUTER JOIN people AS parents_people
    ON parents_people.id = people.person_id
  LEFT OUTER JOIN people AS parents_people_2
    ON parents_people_2.id = parents_people.person_id
```

When there are no includes specified—so there is only one table involved in the query—the SELECT clause is an asterisk (*) for simplicity. However, once you include other models into your find call, the columns become specified and are aliased so Active Record can tell them apart. For example, the actual SELECT clause from the preceding query looks like this:

```
SELECT
  people.`id` AS t0_r0,
  people.`person_id` AS t0_r1,
  people.`name` AS t0_r2,
  parents_people.`id` AS t1_r0,
  parents_people.`person_id` AS t1_r1,
  parents_people.`name` AS t1_r2,
  parents_people_2.`id` AS t2_r0,
  parents_people_2.`person_id` AS t2_r1,
  parents_people_2.`name` AS t2_r2
  FROM
    ...
```

This way, all of the fields can be differentiated and placed into their proper objects before being given back to you.

:order

The :order parameter is where you define the sorting order that would normally appear in the ORDER clause.

```
Account.find :all, :order => "created_on DESC, last_name, first_name"
```

As you can see this example, the format for the order string is the same as the ORDER BY clause in SQL. Therefore, the SQL generated from the preceding example is

```
SELECT * FROM accounts ORDER BY created_on DESC, last_name, first_name
```

When you specify the :order option, you are literally specifying a snippet of the SQL statement that will be sent to your database server. Therefore, the naming rules described in the previous section, which come as a result of using the :include option, apply to the columns specified in the :order parameter as well.

:select

You can use the :select option to specify some extra columns in the SELECT clause. Any extra columns will be added as additional attributes on the returned objects. However, because Active Record doesn't know how to save these extra attributes, the objects it returns will automatically be marked as read only, so they cannot be saved.

The :select option is most often used together with the :group or :joins options, both of which are described in the following subsections. For now, let's do something simple and add an extra string to our returned objects, as shown in the following SQL statement:

```
SELECT accounts.*, "extra data" FROM accounts
```

The Active Record equivalent would be

```
Account.find "all", :select => "accounts.*, 'extra data'"
```

:group

Much like the :order option described earlier, what you specify in the :group option directly translates to a portion of the SQL query to be performed. In this case, it is the GROUP BY clause of the SQL statement. The Active Record find call

```
Account.find :all, :group => "last_name"
```

will result in the following SQL:

```
SELECT * FROM accounts GROUP BY last_name
```

It will most often be the case that you will use the :group option in concert with the :select option to define some additional grouped parameters. For instance, if you wanted to find the number of people who have the same last name, you could do the following

```
Account.find :all, :select => "COUNT(last_name) AS total, *", :group => "last_name"
```

which would result in the following SQL:

```
SELECT COUNT(last_name) AS total, * FROM accounts GROUP BY last_name
```

:joins

While the join parameter is similar in function to the :include option, it works on a lower level in the resulting SQL statement. The value given to the :joins option is a string that will get added to the FROM clause of the SQL statement. You can use this to perform a join on tables to which you don't have a defined Active Record relationship. While such a join may not be something that you will use on a normal basis, it can be very powerful in the situations where you do need it.

For example, if you have a legacy table named visits that does not have a defined relationship to your Active Record model's table and you need to join against and select out of visits, your code might look something like the following:

```
Account.find :all,
            :joins => "LEFT JOIN visits ON accounts.id=visits.account"
```

The result will be the following SQL query:

```
SELECT * FROM accounts LEFT JOIN visits ON accounts.id=visits.account_id
```

As you can see, the value given to the :joins option is *appended* to the FROM portion of the SQL; it does not replace it. Therefore, your model's table, in this case accounts, will always be included in the FROM clause. If you don't want your model's table to be included, you can use the :from option, described next—but, in that case, you also should probably consider just querying the database directly, using either the find_by_sql or execute methods, described later in this chapter.

:from

Whereas the :joins option will let you specify extra tables to join to in the FROM clause, the :from option allows you to specify the entire contents of the FROM clause of the SQL statement. For example, given the same visits table mentioned in the :joins example, we can reverse the query to stem from visits:

```
Account.find :all,
            :from => "visits LEFT JOIN accounts ON visits.account=accounts.id"
```

And the following SQL query will result:

```
SELECT * FROM visits LEFT JOIN accounts ON visits.account=accounts.id
```

:limit and :offset

The :limit and :offset options both take an integer and correspond directly with the LIMIT and OFFSET clauses in SQL. For example, the following statement:

```
Account.find :all, :limit => 10, :offset => 20
```

will find you the twenty-first to thirtieth people in the people database, using the following SQL query:

```
SELECT * FROM accounts LIMIT 10 OFFSET 20
```

:readonly

As previously mentioned, when a query returns data columns that don't correspond to columns in a table, for example, manually added joins using the `:joins` option or grouped columns using `:select` and `:group`, Active Record will mark the each record returned as read only, as it won't know what to do with those columns. You can override that behavior by passing `:readonly => false` as an option.

Likewise, sometimes you just don't want your data to be changed. For security purposes, you can add `:readonly => true` to your options, and you won't be able to save the records that come out of that particular find call.

:lock

You can use the `:lock` option to have the database lock the selected rows. The value given for the lock option is either the Boolean `true` or an SQL fragment like `LOCK IN SHARE MODE`. If you pass in `true`, Active Record will use the default locking syntax for your connection. For a complete discussion of the locking features of Active Record, see the "Locking" section later in this chapter.

Dynamic Finders

It just wouldn't be Ruby if we didn't have a cleaner, easier way to access data. The normal `find` method works well, but it can get unwieldy if you're not careful. Thankfully, Active Record provides dynamic finders that can find your data while still looking clean.

You can use these dynamic finders by starting a method call with `find_by_` or `find_all_by_` and adding in the columns you want to search on, as shown in the following example:

```
Person.find_by_username @username
```

You can also search on multiple columns by separating them with `_and_`:

```
Song.find_all_by_artist_id_and_genre @artist.id, @genre
```

These uses of the dynamic finder methods are the same as the detailed `find` calls:

```
Person.find :first, :conditions => { :username => @username }
Song.find :all, :conditions => { :artist_id => @artist.id, :genre => @genre }
```

Like all of the different `find` variations, the dynamic finders also take an options parameter as their last argument, so you can `:limit`, `:order`, `:group`, `:lock`, and so on, just as you would with the normal syntax.

Additionally, if you find yourself in a scenario where you want to search for an object and create it if it does not exists, you can use the dynamic finder `find_or_create_by_`, which works just like the `find_by_` method but with one exception: instead of returning `nil` if a matching object is not found, that object will be created. `find_or_create_by` can come in handy during legacy data importing, for instance, if you have a list of categories to which a product could belong. Assume you're given a text file that tells you the product and to which category it belongs, as shown here:

```
HTW2, Dairy
HTZ3, Meat
HTW3, Dairy
HTH9, Product
```

In this example data set, you know each product is unique, and therefore, you could loop through each line of the file, creating the product. However, you know that the categories can be repeated, as shown with the Dairy category above. You wouldn't want to create the Dairy category twice. This is an ideal scenario for find_or_create_by_, as follows:

```
p = Product.new(:number => @product_number)
p.category = Category.find_or_create_by_name(@category_name)
p.save
```

This code will appear inside a loop and assumes that the product number and category name have been placed inside the @product_number and @category_name, respectively. The category on the product can safely be set, without fear of duplication, because that category has either been found or was created based on the category name.

Updating a Record

Updating a record looks a lot like creating a record, at least with save. Like creating, though, there are a few other methods for updating one or more attributes besides the normal save method. For example, the use of the save, update_attribute, and update_attributes methods will all generate the same SQL statement in the end:

```
song.name = "Ruby Dear"
song.save

song.update_attribute :name, "Ruby Dear"
song.update_attributes :name => "Ruby Dear"
```

The resulting update statement would look as follows:

```
UPDATE songs SET `name` = 'Ruby Dear', `artist` = 'Talking Heads' WHERE id = 2
```

The update_attribute method only works on a single attribute. It takes two parameters, the name of the column and the new value to save. The update_attributes method takes in only one parameter, a hash containing the pairings of names and values that should be saved.

■**Note** When you call update_attributes (and update_attribute), Active Record basically sets the attributes you specify and calls save, so any other changes you've made to attributes will be saved along with the arguments to update_attributes.

It's important to note that when a record is saved because of update_attributes, that save is *not* subject to validation checks. If you have an invalid record for whatever reason, the attributes *will* be updated anyway. This is important to know, because if you're ever in a situation in which you have an invalid object but still need to toggle a flag or set a status, you can.

While creation of related objects will occur when your object is created, as described in the "Creating a Record" section earlier, it is important to note that associated objects do not behave similarly when updates are performed. For example, in the following code, the modification to the Category model will not be saved:

```
p = Product.find 1
p.category.name = "Changed"
p.save
```

Therefore, you must explicitly call save on associated objects, for example:

```
p = Product.find 1
p.category.name = "Changed"
p.category.save
```

That being said, it is not necessarily commonplace to perform the type of operation illustrated here, especially in a web-based application.

Deleting a Record

Sometimes, data has to go away. We know, it's not always a pleasant thought, but not all data is useful all the time. Sometimes the user makes a mistake; sometimes data is past its prime and needs to get put out to pasture. Regardless of the reason, Active Record is capable of handling the deletion of rows from the database using several different methods: destroy, destroy_all, delete, and delete_all.

Calling destroy on an object will delete it from the database keyed on its primary key. For example, the following call

```
song = Song.find(3)
song.destroy
```

would be the same as this one:

```
DELETE FROM songs WHERE id = 3
```

Similarly, you can use the destroy class method like you can use find and pass in one or more IDs, which will be instantiated and then have the destroy method called on them. For example

```
Song.destroy( 10, 11, 20 )
```

would be the same as

```
DELETE FROM songs WHERE id IN (10,11,20)
```

Calling destroy (and also passing an ID to the class's destroy method) means that any deletion-triggered callbacks that the model might have instantiated, such as a cascading delete or a cascading nullify on its relationships, will be called. If you would prefer to delete something without calling all the callbacks or instantiating the objects, you can call delete. It works exactly the same way as destroy but does not call the callbacks.

You can also delete_all and destroy_all. These two methods work the same way as the destroy and delete methods do, except they delete all of the records of the Active Record class on which they are called. Additionally, they optionally take a hash of options that will be used to construct the WHERE clause of the SQL statement as a parameter. This options hash works in exactly the same way as the :conditions option does for the find method. The following example

```
Song.destroy_all :artist => "Garth Brooks"
```

is the same as this:

```
DELETE FROM songs WHERE artist = "Garth Brooks"
```

When you have associated models that should not exist without each other being present, such as the person models used previously in the chapter, you may want to ensure that when one object is deleted, the others are deleted as well. You can accomplish that using the :dependent option on the relationship definition, as shown here:

```
class Person < ActiveRecord::Base
  belongs_to :parent, :class_name => "Person"
  has_many   :children,
             :class_name => "Person",
             :foreign_key => :parent_id,
             :dependent => :destroy
end
```

With the :dependent => :destroy option on the :children association, if the object is deleted, then the associated children objects will also be deleted, for example:

```
bm = Person.new(:first_name => "Bob", :last_name => "McCracken")
pm = Person.new(:first_name => "Pam", :last_name => "McCracken")
jm = Person.new(:first_name => "Joey", :last_name => "McCracken")

bm.children << pm
bm.children << jm
bm.save
```

This code executes the corresponding SQL statements:

```
BEGIN;
  INSERT
    INTO people (`first_name`, `last_name`, `parent_id`)
    VALUES ('Bob', 'McCracken', 0);
  INSERT
    INTO people (`first_name`, `last_name`, `parent_id`)
    VALUES ('Pam', 'McCracken', 1);
  INSERT
    INTO people (`first_name`, `last_name`, `parent_id`)
    VALUES ('Joey', 'McCracken', 1);
COMMIT;
```

Afterward, the people table would have the following entries:

```
+----+-----------+------------+-----------+
| id | parent_id | first_name | last_name |
+----+-----------+------------+-----------+
| 1  | 0         | Bob        | McCracken |
| 2  | 1         | Pam        | McCracken |
| 3  | 1         | Joey       | McCracken |
+----+-----------+------------+-----------+
```

Now, if you subsequently execute the following code

```
bm = People.find_by_first_name_and_last_name("Bob", "McCracken")
bm.destroy
```

it will result in the following SQL statements being executed:

```
SELECT * FROM people WHERE (people.parent_id = 1)
BEGIN
  SELECT * FROM people WHERE (people.parent_id = 2)
  DELETE FROM people WHERE `id` = 2
  SELECT * FROM people WHERE (people.parent_id = 3)
  DELETE FROM people WHERE `id` = 3
  DELETE FROM people WHERE `id` = 1
COMMIT
```

As you can see in these SQL statements, each of the children is loaded and deleted, and then the parent object is deleted as well. Each of the objects is loaded because each is literally having destroy called on it, which means that all of the callbacks are called as with a normal destroy call. If you do not wish for all of the callbacks on the children to be called, you can change :dependent => :destroy to :dependent => :delete_all. If you do this, the call to bm.destroy will result in the following SQL statements being called:

```
BEGIN
DELETE FROM people WHERE (parent_id = 1)
DELETE FROM people WHERE `id` = 1
COMMIT
```

You can see from this SQL that when :dependent => :delete_all is used on the children's relationship, the children are not loaded. Rather, a normal delete_all is performed. This means that any destroy callbacks on the children will not be executed.

Completely Nondynamic Finders

It should be mentioned that Active Record, in the end, works by passing an SQL string to the database through an adapter. Since Active Record doesn't deny its roots, you are also able to access the database in a more direct fashion. To this end, Active Record supplies a find_by_sql method as well as the execute method.

You can use the find_by_sql method to pass in a string of SQL and obtain an object that contains the attributes you specify in the SELECT clause. The useful thing about find_by_sql is that Active Record will still return an array of objects, saving you the tedium of having to parse through everything yourself. The type of object that gets returned is the same as the class that find_by_sql was called on. That this means if you call

```
Song.find_by_sql("SELECT users.* FROM users")
```

you'll have an array of Song objects that contain User data. So be careful about what data you're expecting to return.

Because the find_by_sql method will create objects from the return value of the SQL, you cannot use it to execute any bit of arbitrary SQL. Therefore, if you are seeking to execute truly custom SQL statements, including INSERT and UPDATE statements, the execute method is what you'd want to use. You can do anything with the database that you'd need to (except, of course, return fields) through this function.

Transactions

Many databases support the idea of transactions, that is, if there is an error performing a statement, which occurs within a specified block, the database will be rolled back to the state it was in before the block of statements.

A simple example for transactions is when you need to perform two actions, the second of which should not occur if there is a problem performing the first. The classic example is a bank account transfer. In SQL, an account transfer would be performed in the following manner:

```
UPDATE accounts SET balance=balance-300.00 WHERE id=3;
UPDATE accounts SET balance=balance+300.00 WHERE id=4
```

In this example, $300.00 is being transferred from account number 3 to account number 4. If something were to go wrong with removing the $300.00 from account number 3, the addition of $300.00 to account number 4 would still occur. While that might make account holders happy, it certainly doesn't make the bank happy. The solution to the problem is to wrap the SQL statements in a transaction. With most databases that support transactions, you demarcate a transaction using the BEGIN and COMMIT (or ROLLBACK) statements, as follows:

```
BEGIN
  UPDATE accounts SET balance=balance-300.00 WHERE id=3
  UPDATE accounts SET balance=balance+300.00 WHERE id=4
COMMIT
```

With the BEGIN and COMMIT (or ROLLBACK) statements now enclosing the SQL commands, if something goes wrong, the database will be returned to the state it was in before the operations were performed. In other words, any failure will cause the database to be *rolled back* to before the transaction began.

Fortunately, Active Record fully supports transactions. In fact, all save and destroy method calls are wrapped in transactions by default, to ensure that all save and destroy procedures, including the callbacks, are atomic.

However, the transactions in Active Record really just result in the BEGIN, COMMIT, and ROLLBACK statements being used (or the corresponding statements specific to the database you are using). Therefore, if your underlying database does not support transactions (such as the MyISAM table format in MySQL), then the transaction code will have no effect. Fortunately, you can use the transaction code without error on databases that don't support transactions, but this may result in a false sense of security.

Our simple update statements for transferring the money, like the previous SQL statements, follow:

```
my_account.update_attribute(:balance, my_account.balance-300.00)
your_account.update_attribute(:balance, your_account.balance+300.00)
```

To wrap this code in a transaction, you use the transaction class-level method on the Active Record model, which would look like the following:

```
my_account = Account.find 3
your_account = Account.find 4
Account.transaction do
  my_account.update_attribute(:balance, my_account.balance-300.00)
  your_account.update_attribute(:balance, your_account.balance+300.00)
end
```

The SQL generated from these statements will be very similar to the SQL statements that added and subtracted from the account balance previously, but the computation of the new balance was performed in Ruby (i.e., my_account..balance-300.00). The resulting SQL statements from the Active Record preceding update_attributes calls are shown following:

```
SELECT * FROM accounts WHERE id=3;
SELECT * FROM accounts WHERE id=4;
BEGIN;
  UPDATE accounts SET balance=20.00 WHERE id=3;
  UPDATE accounts SET balance=340.00 WHERE id=4;
COMMIT;
```

It's important to note that a transaction will not only be rolled back if something wrong occurs at just the database level. When using an Active Record transaction, if any exception is raised, the transaction will automatically be rolled back by Active Record. To take advantage of this rollback, the preceding Ruby code that modifies the account balances can be refactored to ensure that no account will contain less than $0.00. Because additional code will be added, the existing Account model will be refactored to have withdraw and deposit methods, as follows:

```
class Account < ActiveRecord::Base
  def withdraw amount
    update_attribute(:balance, balance-amount)
    if balance < 0
      raise
    end
  end

  def deposit amount
    update_attribute(:balance, balance+amount)
  end
end
```

Now, given the preceding Account class, you can perform the following actions:

```
my_account = Account.find 3
your_account = Account.find 4
Account.transaction do
  my_account.withdraw(300.00)
  your_account.update_attribute(300.00)
end
```

If subtracting $300.00 from my_account will result in a negative balance, an exception will be raised, and the transactions will be rolled back. In the preceding scenario, if the beginning balance of account number 3 is only $20.00, which would result in a negative balance, then the SQL for the Ruby code would actually look like this:

```
SELECT * FROM accounts WHERE id=3;
SELECT * FROM accounts WHERE id=4;
BEGIN;
  UPDATE accounts SET balance=-280.00 WHERE id=3;
ROLLBACK;
```

Because the balance of the account is negative, COMMIT is not called at the end of the transaction block; rather, the ROLLBACK statement is called.

Note If you need to do transactions across multiple databases, you can nest transactions. For an example of how to do this, see the "Common Active Record Questions" section in Chapter 5.

It is important to note that the value of my_account.balance at the end of the previous actions will still be -$190.00. Because the transaction rollback occurs at the database level, not at the object level, the objects themselves will not be returned to their original state. Currently, Active Record does support object-level transactions, but they are deprecated. They are not commonly needed and will be removed from the release of Active Record included in Rails 2.0; therefore, they will not be covered here. If you do, in fact, need this functionality, it is available in the object_transactions plug-in from Jeremy Kemper (also known as bitsweat) at http:// code.bitsweat.net/svn/object_transactions.

Locking

Active Record supports two forms of locking, optimistic and pessimistic. In Active Record, optimistic locking means that the database records are versioned, and before an objects is actually saved back to the database record, the version you are saving is checked against the version in the database to make sure the model was not otherwise modified while you were working on it. If it was modified, an exception is raised. The other type of locking in Active Record, pessimistic locking, is simply row-level locking, as supported by the database.

Optimistic Locking

As previously mentioned, optimistic locking in Active Record is accomplished by keeping track of which version of a model you are working with. The use of optimistic locking is triggered simply by adding a column named `lock_version` to your model's database table.

Tip You are responsible for ensuring that the database schema defaults the `lock_version` column to 0. Additionally, you can use a different column name by calling the `set_locking_column` method in your model.

If the version of the object you are working on is out of date, when you attempt to save your object, an `ActiveRecord::StaleObjectError` exception will be raised. It is your responsibility to handle this error by either rolling back or providing the logic needed to resolve the possible conflict. Because of this, it is very common to use transactions along with locking.

To further illustrate optimistic locking, it can be used to ensure that the `Account` records are not modified by multiple processes, thereby ensuring that your account data remains consistent. Here's our trusty `Account` model, repeated here for your reference:

```
class Account < ActiveRecord::Base
  def withdraw amount
    update_attribute(:balance, balance-amount)
    if balance < 0
      raise
    end
  end

  def deposit amount
    update_attribute(:balance, balance+amount)
  end
end
```

If optimistic locking is enabled on the `Account` model by including a `lock_version` column in your accounts table, the following code will cause an `ActiveRecord::StaleObjectError` to be raised:

```
my_account1 = Account.find 3
my_account2 = Account.find 3

my_account1.withdraw 20
my_account1.save

my_account2.withdraw 40
my_account2.save # This line raises an ActiveRecord::StaleObjectError
```

The exception was raised, because the object was previously modified. This example is somewhat contrived, but hopefully, you can envision that the modification of the `Account` object might take place in another process or web request, and in that case, knowing that your underlying record has changed before attempting to save it would be very important.

Pessimistic Locking

The second form of locking that Active Record is capable of is pessimistic locking. Active Record's implementation of pessimistic locking is simply row-level locking as supported by your database. Therefore, if your underlying database does not support locking, neither will Active Record.

There are two different ways to invoke a row-level lock on your data. The first is by using the `:lock` option of the `find` method. As described when we introduced the `find` method, the `:lock` option to `find` takes either the Boolean `true` or a string that is a database-specific locking statement. If you give the option the Boolean `true`, the locking statement will default to `FOR UPDATE`. For example, the following statement

```
Account.find 3, :lock => true
```

will result in this SQL statement, with the row for the account with an ID of 3 locked for updating:

```
SELECT * FROM accounts WHERE id=3 FOR UPDATE
```

And this Active Record code

```
Account.find 3, :lock => "LOCK IN SHARE MODE"
```

will result in the following SQL statement, with the row for the account with the ID of 3 locked in share mode:

```
SELECT * FROM accounts WHERE id=3 LOCK IN SHARE MODE
```

You can also use the instance method `lock!`, which will reload your row with locking for just that row. For example, the following method call

```
my_account = Account.find 3
my_account.lock!
```

results in the following SQL statements:

```
SELECT * FROM accounts WHERE id=3
SELECT * FROM accounts WHERE id=3 FOR UPDATE
```

CRUD Isn't Cruddy

Now that you've explored how Active Record relates to the underlying SQL statements it creates, you have a better appreciation for the power of Active Record, as well a more complete understanding of what Active Record does and how it works. In addition, hopefully you've begun to understand how to think about the basic Active Record operations in the context of the four basic CRUD operations. If you're using Active Record in the context of Ruby on Rails, thinking about Active Record this way will be especially helpful.

You may have also started to notice recurring patterns in the way names of Active Record classes and attributes relate to the generated SQL. In the next chapter, we'll explain how to set up and maintain your database using standard Active Record naming conventions and tools. And of course, we'll show you how to break these conventions for your own twisted uses.

CHAPTER 3

■■■

Setting Up Your Database

If you've been reading through this book from the start, you should now be pretty comfortable with the basic idea of Active Record and how to write create, update, read, and delete operations. So you're just about ready to start digging into all the juicy details and extras that Active Record brings to the table. There is just one last detail to get out of the way, and that's the process of actually setting up our database.

Designing Active Record–Friendly Tables

Later in this chapter, you will be introduced to Active Record migrations, a powerful way to set up and maintain your database schema with nothing more than simple Ruby code. Before we get into that though, let's take a quick minute to review the things you should keep in mind when designing tables for use with Active Record. Most of these things were covered in Chapter 1 when we talked about Active Record assumptions, but as these assumptions are especially important to keep in mind when you are designing your tables, they're worth a quick review here as well. Ready?

Every table should have an automatically incrementing primary key called id. If you chose not to follow this rule, you will have to specifically define your primary keys within your models with the set_primary_key method and specifically define your foreign keys for each of your associations.

Table names should be plural. If you choose not to follow this rule, you will have to specifically define your table names from within your models with the set_table_name method.

Tables and fields should stick to lowercase letters. Ruby is a case-sensitive language, so it stands to reason that Active Record objects are also case sensitive. For example, assume you have an account table with a field labeled account_username. From within your Ruby code, you would be able to access the data from an Active Record object (account in this example) as account.account_username but not as account.Account_Username or any other case variation (this would throw a method_missing error). We will revisit this issue when we talk about legacy systems and especially the find_by_sql method in Chapter 7.

To track record additions and updates, tables should have fields called `created_on` *or* `created_at` *and* `updated_on` *or* `updated_at`. If these fields exist within your table, Active Record will automatically populate them with the timestamp when records are created for the `created_on` or `created_at` field or when records are updated for the `updated_on` or `updated_at` field. If you prefer to use another field name for either of these, you can just use callbacks to keep these fields properly updated. We cover the details of callbacks in Chapter 4.

Foreign keys should be of the structure `tablename_id`. If you choose not to follow this rule, you will have to specifically define what field to use for each of your associations.

Active Record treats `0`, `"0"`, `"false"`, *and* `"f"` *as* `false` *for Boolean field types, whereas in general Ruby syntax, all those values evaluate to* `true`. Each database implements Boolean data types a little bit differently, and some don't support them at all. As an attempt to work properly in as many cases as possible, Active Record will convert values to Ruby `true` or `false` values for most Boolean field types. Just keep in mind that this conversion to Boolean types is done by Active Record magic to work around a Ruby design issue. If you find that you are having problems with Booleans in your Active Record programs, you should check how the specific adaptor for your database implements Boolean types. We talk more about Booleans and other data types in Chapter 7.

Active Record assigns values to all fields within a table. When you save a new Active Record object or do an update on an Active Record object, Active Record actually assigns a value to every field within the table in the database. If you haven't set a value for a given field, the field will be set to `nil`. This is important to remember, because it means default values set up within your database (like a timestamp) will most likely not be triggered since a specific value is provided (`nil`) for the field. We covered this issue in Chapter 2 with create and update statements and will speak about it again in Chapter 7, when we deal with legacy database systems.

The items in this list are the key things you should keep in mind when designing your database tables. You can ignore each as you see fit for your specific needs, but doing so generally means more typing and more work for you as a developer. So, all things being equal, we believe you're better off making your database conform to the way that Active Record is designed to work.

Traditional Database Management

Now that you recall the basic naming conventions and design rules we should follow when defining our tables, it's finally time to start building our real tables. If you are coming from a development background in another language such as Java, PHP, Perl, or Active Server Pages (ASP), it's likely that you've been building database-driven applications in the traditional manner. That is, every time you build an application, you go through steps like these:

1. Define and design your tables in a database management program such as SQL Server Enterprise Manager, TOAD for Oracle, MySQL Administrator, or even in something like batch SQL scripts.

2. Configure your development environment to work with the database details you have just defined and set up, generally with configuration files (XML, properties, or simply text files).

3. Start writing your application logic.

4. Load data into your testing database manually with your database administration program, through some batch SQL scripts, or through a custom-built web or application administration tool.

5. Test, release, repeat.

While your specific situation may vary from project to project, the previous steps are the common and general things we programmers do when we build an application. And while they are a proven and tested approach, there are some common problems that most of us have just learned to accept.

Common Problems with the Traditional Approach

Admittedly building database-dependent web sites and applications with the traditional approach is not too complex of a process. We've all been using that same process for years, and many successful projects have been built using it. Still, if you take a minute to think about the process itself, there are a few common problems that come into focus:

- You need to do a lot of jumping back and forth between your database application and your code environment. This means a slower development time and a higher potential for error. Each environment also comes with its own set of knowledge requirements, and that means you have to learn a lot to do even the simplest of projects.

- You need to know how to work within your specific database environment, which often includes having to know the ins and outs of the specific SQL syntax your database engine supports. Dealing with the various SQL syntax gets worse if you intend to develop against one database backend but release to production on another

---

■**Note** Switching from one database backend to another is common in Rails development, because it's usually easier to work locally with a database like MySQL, but many people prefer the higher performance of an Oracle or SQL Server for production environments.

- As you make updates and changes to your database, you must maintain those changes across all of your environments—and often there is no easy way of rolling back or undoing those changes if errors occur.

While none of these problems are show stoppers on their own, it certainly seems like there should be an easier way to do things. And, as you probably guessed by now, Active Record does have another option for you—migrations.

Managing Your Database with Migrations

Before we get into the details of using Active Record migrations and show you some example code, we need to get a few key definitions out of the way. First, just what are Active Record migrations? The following is our plain English base definition: Active Record migrations offer a pure Ruby solution to managing the creation and evolution of database schema.

From a more technical point of view, migrations come in the form of a Domain Specific Language (DSL) that is expressly created for abstracting out the differences in database definitions and managing changes of the database and its tables. In case you are not familiar with what a DSL is, Wikipedia defines DSL as "a programming language designed for, and intended to be used for, a specific kind of task" (see http://en.wikipedia.org/wiki/Domain_Specific_Language for more Wikipedia information on DSL).

We think that's a pretty clear definition, but we'll take it a few steps further to be specific within our realm. As Active Record developers, our migration DSL is a set of Ruby instructions or modules that allow us to create more Ruby programs that we use to build and manage our database schema. The migration DSL is like a language within a language. It is how we interact with our database without having to actually learn everything about our database environment and without having to do anything directly within our database application.

For us, the key to working with our migration DSL is to learn the keywords and their related actions. The rest is all Ruby syntax (which you already know) and database design theory (we covered the basic rules for this at the start of this chapter and have hopefully defined it in more detail as part of our application specifications before we sat down and started to write any code).

How the DSL Works

The DSL essentially enables us to map our database schema to an Active Record schema. The documentation for Active Record Schema states this:

> *Active Record Schema allows programmers to programmatically define a schema in a portable DSL. This means you can define tables, indexes, etc. without using SQL directly, so your applications can more easily support multiple databases.*

What this really means is that the `ActiveRecord::Schema` class is where all the real action of your database schema definitions and maintenance happens. As we build our migrations, we will be continuously switching between our database schema and our Active Record schema. While this switching back and forth between database and Active Record schema will often be transparent to you, the developer, it nonetheless occurs quite often and is accomplished primarily through the `ActiveRecord::SchemaDumper` class.

> **■Note** We'll use `ActiveRecord::SchemaDumper` at various points in our examples later in the chapter to show just in what state our database schema is at a given time.

Finally, we have the actual migration wrapper class. This is where all the parts we've talked about previously come together and our scripts come to life.

The important thing to remember is that migrations involve a DSL and act as a wrapper, or glue, for the other pieces of our database to set up the code and DSL we've mentioned previously. We should also mention that, because migrations abstract the details of working with your specific database, they rely heavily on each database adapter to perform many of the database-specific functions (that is, to do the actual conversion from the migration DSL to the database-specific SQL that will be executed against the database). If you find that you are having trouble with a specific migration situation, you will likely want to refer to your adapter code and documentation first.

It's also important to remember that with migrations you're actually just working with Ruby code. Migrations can perform calculations, manipulate data, and do anything that you'd normally be able to do within Ruby. Because of this, migrations can prove to be a very, very powerful tool in the Ruby programmer's arsenal.

In the end, using migrations means that, as a developer, you can work strictly in Ruby code to set up and manage your database. And you can more easily switch among database backends as you like, because all of the database SQL specifics have been abstracted for you!

Migrations are also an important part of making sure you and your development team keep your databases in sync from revision to revision and to make sure that everything goes as planned when you're deploying your applications to a different database or machine. That sounds pretty exciting, doesn't it? And, believe it or not, migrations are not even all that hard to learn or use!

Using Migrations

We've mentioned the traditional steps that programmers go through when building database applications. Now, let's compare that process to the steps that a programmer goes through using Active Record migrations:

1. Create a connection for your Active Record program to your database. This is generally done through a YAML configuration file or through the `ActiveRecord::Base.establish_connection` method.

2. Create and execute Ruby scripts using the Active Record migration DSL syntax and rules.

3. Start writing your application logic.

4. Load data into your testing database manually with your database administration program, through some batch SQL scripts, through custom-built web or application administration tool, or via fixtures with your migration scripts.

5. Test, release, repeat.

At first glance, this process may not seem that much different than the traditional approach. However, after closer examination, you will see the following key differences and that those differences directly address the common problems with the traditional approach:

- Everything is done from within Ruby scripts. There is no switching among environments or wasting time learning the ins and outs of multiple environments.

- The migration DSL abstracts the database-specific details for you, so you no longer need to know the ins and outs of your specific database. Oftentimes, you don't even need to know anything about the specific SQL that your database engine supports. You can now switch among database engines with almost no extra effort (as long as the Active Record database adapter supports migrations).

- Since all of your database schema changes are now stored in migration scripts (which should be versioned), you now have an audit trail of all your actions. The biggest advantage to this is that you can rebuild your database from scratch regardless of the database backend by simply running your migration scripts in sequential version order! If your database supports the related database management SQL syntax, such as rollback statements, you can also roll back from a given state to any previous state by simply executing your migration scripts in reverse version number order.

If you aren't excited by now about working with Active Record migrations, then you're either in the wrong profession or you just haven't suffered through the traditional approach enough yet (build a few more midsized Java applications and then come check out Ruby and Active Record)! For the rest of us who can't wait any longer, let's get into the details of actually using migrations—and what better place to start then with how to execute your migration scripts.

Executing Migration Scripts

Migrations, like Active Record itself, evolved out of the Rails framework, so migrations are still somewhat tightly coupled with the Ruby on Rails framework. If you want to run migrations outside of the Rails framework, it's very feasible, but you will need to do just a little bit more work than if you want to run migrations within your Rails framework. To be thorough, we'll explain how to execute migrations in both situations, starting with the Ruby on Rails framework.

Executing Migrations Within Ruby on Rails

Within a Ruby on Rails project, migrations are stored in the db/migrations folder and are named by prepending numbers, in sequential order, to the script name. When you run script/generate migration from your Rails root and give it a name, it will generate a file using the next number available. For example, executing the command script/generate migration create_users_table will make a file in db/migrate called 001_create_users_table.rb.

Running the migrations to apply the Active Record schema to your database schema within the Rails framework is done with a Ruby on Rails rake task and can move the migration version up or down to any specific revision using a command like rake db:migrate [VERSION=X].

■**Note** If you leave off the `VERSION` parameter, it will attempt to migrate the database as high as it can go by adding one to the highest version number found in the `schema_info` table.

Executing Migrations Outside of Ruby on Rails

The `rake` method for generating and running migrations described previously is only valid if you are working from within the Ruby on Rails framework. As we mentioned, though, you can still use migrations outside of the Rails framework, you will just need to create your own script to run the migrations. Lucky for you, we're going to get you started on that task.

The following script assumes that you will be storing your database configuration details in a YAML file called `database.yml`. For simplicity, the following script, the YAML file, and your migrations are assumed to all be located in the same directory.

```
require 'rubygems'
require_gem 'activerecord'

if ARGV[0] =~ /VERSION=\d+/
  version = ARGV[0].split('=')[1].to_i
else
  version = nil
end

@logger = Logger.new $stderr
ActiveRecord::Base.logger = @logger
ActiveRecord::Base.colorize_logging = false

@config = YAML.load_file(File.join(File.dirname(__FILE__), 'database.yml'))
ActiveRecord::Base.establish_connection(@config["development"])
ActiveRecord::Migrator.migrate("", version)
```

Assuming you place the preceding script in a file called `migrate.rb`, you can run your sequentially numbered migrations with the command `ruby migrate.rb`.

■**Note** This script does not generate the migration files. You'll still need to create and populate the files by hand (or write another script to generate them).

Finally, executing a migration will create (or update depending on the project life cycle) a table in your database called `schema_info` that contains the number of the latest run migration file. The `schema_info` table is used to determine which migration script to start with the next time you run a migration process as well as what number to prepend to any new migration scripts.

■**Note** You should always be able to run your migrations back and forth from version zero to wherever you are at any time. It's not mandatory to be able to do that, but it's sound migration practice, because it lets you make sure your database is in a sane state at all times. If you can't bring your database from migration zero to your latest state, then migrations really haven't allowed you to automate or simplify the management of your database schema. Therefore, you should avoid using model class names inside migration files, because if you remove one of those classes later on, you won't be able to do a clean migration from zero forward. Stepping through your scripts will, instead, throw an error when older versions of your script can't find the referenced class.

The Anatomy of a Migration File

Regardless of how you create your migration scripts (either via the Rails generate command or simply by hand), they all should start out with a basic structure that looks something like the following:

```
class CreateUsersTable < ActiveRecord::Migration
    def self.up
    end

    def self.down
    end
end
```

In this structure, the up method will get called when you're migrating up to the latest version (i.e., when you are releasing new code and updates) and down will get called when you're migrating down to a previous version (i.e., when you are rolling back because of unexpected errors or problems).

The up and down methods are each run inside of a transaction. This means that if an exception occurs during migration execution, the transaction will be rolled back, and the schema_info version number will not be updated.

■**Caution** At the time of this writing, MySQL could not successfully roll back ALTER TABLE statements, so despite the fact that a migration is run in a transaction, if an exception occurs, the MySQL database will likely be left in the state just prior to the occurrence of the exception. This situation is a good reason to get very comfortable with the ActiveRecord::SchemaDumper class, as it will allow us to check just what state our database is in at any given time (and act accordingly). We'll show the SchemaDumper in action within our example code in a minute.

Migrations in Action

Because the concept of migrations is somewhat of a paradigm shift for most of us traditional developer types (those of us coming from a background other than Ruby or Ruby on Rails), we've found that some examples can make learning migrations easier. Examples go a long way in helping to point out the specific details and situations involved in implementing migrations.

Let's pretend that we need to build an application that is going to track information about milk production. We'll have information about farmers, cows, milk, and various other milk production issues (some of which we will recognize and retrofit as needed). The overall basic concept of our example will be to report on how much a given farmer sells milk to various stores for.

With all of this in mind, we are finally ready to start coding our migrations! Throughout the rest of this chapter, we'll walk you through the various CRUD operations as they relate to migrations, and where possible, we'll compare and contrast the migration approach to that of the traditional database development approach.

Creating Tables

The first thing you're going to want to do when you start using migrations is create the tables that you're going to be using for your application.

Since this is our first migration and we want to move forward with our development process, we'll be using the up method. And since we want to create our first table, we'll be using the create_table method to give the table its definition. In the following code we create a cows table:

```
# Script to create the first version of a cows table
def self.up
    create_table :cows do |t|
        t.column :name, :string
        t.column :breed, :string
        t.column :born_on, :datetime
        t.column :milkable, :boolean
    end
end
```

Before the code is run, your application database should be empty. Here's how to check on that:

```
mysql> show tables;
Empty set (0.12 sec)
```

The migration code is run when you run rake db:migrate, resulting in the cows table being created with the following columns:

```
mysql> describe cows;
+----------+--------------+------+-----+---------+----------------+
| Field    | Type         | Null | Key | Default | Extra          |
+----------+--------------+------+-----+---------+----------------+
| id       | int(11)      | NO   | PRI | NULL    | auto_increment |
| name     | varchar(255) | YES  |     | NULL    |                |
| breed    | varchar(255) | YES  |     | NULL    |                |
| born_on  | datetime     | YES  |     | NULL    |                |
| milkable | tinyint(1)   | YES  |     | NULL    |                |
+----------+--------------+------+-----+---------+----------------+
```

Additionally, if you now list the tables in your database, you can see that not only has the cows table been created but an additional table as well:

```
mysql> show tables;
+----------------------------+
| Tables_in_test2_development |
+----------------------------+
| cows                       |
| schema_info                |
+----------------------------+
```

The schema_info table is a table used internally by the Active Record migrator. It has a single integer column named version that is updated with the number of the migration that was last run. If migrations are run and this table does not yet exist, the Active Record migration process we are executing will create it. If you select from the table, you can see that there is a single row, and the value of the version column is 1.

```
mysql> select * from schema_info;
+---------+
| version |
+---------+
|       1 |
+---------+
1 row in set (0.00 sec)
```

Referring to the original migration code, you can see the create_table method takes the block form endemic to most DSLs. You can pass a few different options to the create_table method itself to change the way the table works. You can specify the name of the primary key column with the :primary_key option. You can turn off a default primary key completely by adding :id => false; this is most useful when you're creating a join table for HABTM relationships, which don't typically have a normal id column. Supplying :temporary => true will create a temporary table. The :options option will add a free-form string after the definition, allowing you to specify things like the charset or the database engine in MySQL. Finally, if you want the table to be created regardless of its current existence, you should use :force => true.

The column method also has a nonblock counterpart, add_column. The difference between the two is that add_column takes the name of the table it operates on. Aside from that, they're the same. Both methods take the name of the column you want to create and the data type. The possible data types are :primary_key, :string, :text, :integer, :float, :decimal, :datetime, :timestamp, :time, :date, :binary, and :boolean, and each corresponds to its database-specific counterpart when the table is generated. Additionally, the add_column and column methods take a third argument that is a hash of options that define column configuration. The available options are :limit, :default, :null, :precision, and :scale. For more information on the add_column and column methods and their arguments, including database-specific consideration regarding of each of the configuration options, see TableDefinition#column in Appendix A.

Now that you've provided the self.up method, it will be executed when we run rake db:migrate from the command line. But what happens if you run rake db:migrate VERSION=0? If you did that right now, the cows table would still be in the database, which isn't the state you might expect it to be in. You might expect, naturally, that version zero of the database is completely empty. That is what the self.down method is for. The self.down method should always reverse the action performed in self.up.

Of course, there will be times where a destructive action will have consequences that you cannot reverse, such as the deletion of data. However, it's still best to think of migrations as primarily maintaining the *structure* of the application's database, and therefore, self.down should do its best to maintain structure both in forward and reverse. In this case, you need to remove the table in the self.down method.

You can remove a table with the predictably named drop_table method. This method actually takes an options hash, but it doesn't use anything in there as of this writing. Simply pass it the name of the table you want to drop, and it's dropped.

```
def self.down
    drop_table :cows
end
```

It's that simple. Now, migrating from zero to the most current schema, as defined by our most recent migration script, and back will keep our database in a consistent state, as shown following:

```
mysql> show tables;
+----------------------------+
| Tables_in_test2_development |
+----------------------------+
| schema_info                |
+----------------------------+
```

Adding, Removing, and Changing Database Columns

There's more to migrations than simply creating and dropping tables. They let you deal with any part of database management in an abstract way. If you look at our previous cows table, you may notice that we forgot to add the farmer_id column. Since a Cow belongs to a Farmer, the foreign key farmer_id is an important field. What's more, we've already committed the migration to source control, so we should assume that someone else has already run it.

■**Note** Once you've committed a migration file, you need to assume that someone else on your project has obtained the file and run it. This means that you cannot make changes to that file, since the migrator will assume that the file has already been run and completely ignore your changes, making the database inconsistent with the code. It's completely acceptable to have a lot of little migration files that make small changes, because it keeps everyone working together and unconfused. Migration errors and consistency problems are some of the most annoying to clean up.

Since we need to add the farmer_id column to the table, we create another migration with script/generate migration add_farmer_id_column. This command will make the file db/migrate/002_add_farmer_id_column.

To add a single column, we use the add_column method, as we described previously. It works just the same as the column method in create_table's block form, only now you must supply the name of the table you're working on:

```
def self.up
    add_column :cows, :farmer_id, :integer
end
```

And for reversibility we define the following down method:

```
def self.down
    remove_column :cows, :farmer_id
end
```

Note that the method is remove_column, which may be different from what you'd expect from the command your DBMS would use.

Now that your migration to add the farmer_id column is finished, you should run rake db:migrate to make sure that our Cows can see our Farmers. If you go into the mysql console, you can see that the changes are immediate:

```
mysql> describe cows;
+-----------+--------------+------+-----+---------+----------------+
| Field     | Type         | Null | Key | Default | Extra          |
+-----------+--------------+------+-----+---------+----------------+
| id        | int(11)      | NO   | PRI | NULL    | auto_increment |
| name      | varchar(255) | YES  |     | NULL    |                |
| breed     | varchar(255) | YES  |     | NULL    |                |
| born_on   | datetime     | YES  |     | NULL    |                |
| milkable  | tinyint(1)   | YES  |     | NULL    |                |
| farmer_id | int(11)      | YES  |     | NULL    |                |
+-----------+--------------+------+-----+---------+----------------+
```

You can also rename columns using the rename_column method, which takes as arguments the table name and the old and new names of the column you want to rename:

```
rename_column :cows, :born_on, :created_on
```

Finally, you can also change columns with the change_column method. The change_column method works just like the add_column method, except that it works on existing columns and will change their data types instead of creating a new column. Most database engines will preserve the existing data in a column, if it's possible.

```
change_column :address, :postal_code, :string
```

Indexing Columns

One of the important things that developers often forget to do is create indexes on their tables. Indexes can dramatically decrease query times and should always be in place on often-queried columns or groups of columns. Especially important are indexes on foreign keys, join tables, type columns, and compound keys from polymorphic associations. They often go overlooked, which adds a great deal of overhead to traversing relationships.

You can add an index with the add_index method. Indexes are placed on a table over one or more columns. The add_index method takes a table name and either a column name or an array of column names.

```
add_index :cows, :farmer_id, :name => "index_on_cows_for_farmers"
add_index :ownerships, [:farmer_id, :tractor_id], :unique => true
```

Notice the :unique => true option. This makes the index a unique index, which will allow only one instance of any combination of tractor_id and farmer_id.

By default, the name of the index is tablename_allcolumnnames_index. If you didn't want the index on the cows table to be named cows_farmer_id_index, you could specify the :name option (as has been done in the preceding example). However, since Active Record doesn't really care about the name of the index, it's not terribly important to have a nice name on it.

The syntax for removing the index depends on how it was named in the first place. If you let the standard Active Record index naming take place, then you do not need to specify the index name, as it will be assumed:

```
remove_index :ownerships, :column => [:farmer_id, :tractor_id]
```

However, if you did not take the standard Active Record name, you will need to explicitly specify the index name in order to successfully remove it:

```
remove_index :cows, :name => "index_on_cows_for_farmers"
```

You should note that if you're going to remove an index and a table at the same time, it's important to remove the index first.

Managing Application Data

As mentioned previously, you can use any Ruby code within your migrations. Additionally, when working within the Ruby on Rails framework, you're migrations will have full access to all your models (and anything else in the base environment).

When the need arises to manipulate data in your application, such as the need to prepopulate a new column with computed date (e.g., a column called total on a model Order that holds the precomputed total of all of Order's LineItems), your first instinct may be to use your models directly within the migrations to populate this new column. However, it is strongly recommended that you not use your models directly inside your migrations. This is because migrations are all about mitigating the problems that come from the differences among databases, developers, and even the times in the same project.

Strictly speaking, you don't know when you'll need to change your models, so referencing them in your migrations, while it could work out perfectly, may end up breaking the migration process. The ways that your models can change are many, from renaming a method to removing an entire model altogether. You may not notice that a change has made it impossible to migrate from migration zero to the latest one (e.g., if your database is at revision thirty and you changed the model back around revision eight or nine), but you will notice when it comes time to deploy to the production environment and an empty database.

As we mentioned, you might be inclined to create a migration like the following one to populate the total column for our Orders model:

```
def self.up
  add_column :orders, :total, :decimal

  orders = Order.find(:all)
  orders.each do |order|
```

```
      subtotal = 0
      order.line_items.each do |line_item|
        subtotal += line_item.quantity * line_item.price
      end
      order.total = subtotal
    end
  end

  def self.down
    remove_column :orders, :total
  end
```

While this migration will work just fine, it is brittle. If the relationship between the Order and LineItem models were to change or the quantity or price methods were to be removed, the migration would not run. Therefore, rather than using models directly in your migrations, it is recommended that you use the execute method and ANSI-compliant SQL to perform manipulations on the data directly, as shown in the following migration code:

```
  def self.up
    add_column :orders, :total, :decimal
    ActiveRecord.execute("UPDATE orders LEFT OUTER JOIN line_items
      SET orders.total=SUM(line_items.quantity * line_items.price) ON
      orders.id=line_items.order_id")
  end

  def self.down
    remove_column :orders, :total
  end
```

Additionally, if your data manipulations rely on logic contained within your model, you might go so far as to copy this logic directly into the migration file as a separate method. This is because you *cannot* guarantee that that same code will still be present within the model the next time that migration is run.

■**Note** At the start of this chapter, we talked about migrations being a great, database-independent Active Record feature, but here we seem to be going against that statement by including raw SQL into our migration scripts. The difference is that, in our current example, we are using migrations not only to manage our schema but also to populate various tables within our schema. When you use migrations in this dual-purpose way, it is better to give up some of the abstraction by using direct SQL rather than give up the ability to move from one version to another because of the use of models within your scripts.

Another common scenario where you may be tempted to reference your models within migrations is when you need to load static data into the database. It is much better to use YAML files (i.e., fixtures within Rails) to perform load operations. Fortunately, Ruby on Rails has a rake task specifically for data loading chores, available at db:bootstrap. Again, if you are working outside of Ruby on Rails, we still recommend writing a script to load YAML files or another data format to store and load your basic set of application data into your database, rather than using migrations.

Migrations Are Easier Than They Sound

Migrations are one of the hardest concepts for new Active Record programmers to truly grasp, because the concept goes somewhat against the SQL-heavy traditional development process most of us have been successfully using for years. But if you take a second to step back and think about what migrations really provide by abstracting much of the database-specific SQL and adding a sense of version control, you'll see the true advantages of speed and simplicity of development.

By learning the simple migration DSL and using normal Ruby syntax, Active Record migrations allow you to spend less time thinking about how to create or manage your schema and more time actually doing it.

■ ■ ■

Core Features of Active Record

Kevin's a strange bird. Outside of technical books like this one, the books he likes to read most are marketing- and sales-related. He always tells us that after you've read a few of those types of books, you'll notice a strong theme of advice that basically boils down to one simple, golden rule: Get to the core of what you've got and focus relentlessly on it. As it turns out, it's great advice for more than just marketing, so without further ado, let's get to the core of what really makes Active Record a "wow" library. If you aren't impressed with what Active Record provides after this chapter, you're just not passionate enough about coding!

There are three main features of Active Record that are at the real core: callbacks, associations, and validations. Callbacks are hooks into various logic points of the Active Record life cycle. Associations provide a means to handle SQL and link together your Active Record models, and validations allow you to do some basic checks and balances on your data via code. Throughout this chapter, we'll take a deeper look at each of these features, and since callbacks directly relate to the life cycle of Active Record objects, we'll start by focusing on them and cover validations and associations later in this chapter.

Callbacks

When initially trying to learn Ruby and Active Record, we all found the term "callbacks" confusing. The documentation's definition of callbacks didn't really help much, and we needed to play around with real code a while before we felt like we really got the concept. Still, we need a definition to build from, so here's a plain English explanation of callbacks:

> *Active Record objects can perform a large number of methods or actions throughout their existence; callbacks allow you to insert your business logic before or after many of these actions.*

As we've mentioned previously, some plain English examples of tasks accomplished by callbacks may also help you to visualize the concept:

- Before you save an update to the Account table, set the last updated field to the current time.

- Before you delete a record from the Account table, make sure you delete records from the contact table that have the deleted record's account_id.

- After you find a promotional code record, calculate the current subscription cost.

As these examples show, callbacks are really just a nice and simple way to add some potentially complex business logic right into the process of communicating with your database. From a developer's point of view, you can implement callbacks by either manually overwriting the callback method or by using a callback macro. There are a few subtle differences to each approach, so let's look a quick example to explain each.

Implementing Callbacks

The easiest way to implement a callback is to just overwrite the method within your model:

```
class Account < ActiveRecord::Base
    def before_save
        self.Account_Updated = Time.now
    end
end
```

This approach works great for situations like the preceding example, where you want to set values for fields programmatically or when you want each descendant of an inheritance hierarchy to decide if it wants to call the super command and trigger the inherited callbacks—which points out the biggest disadvantage to the overwriting approach: your callbacks are not executed through an inheritance hierarchy. This is probably most important, and obvious, when using callbacks to delete associated records from other tables. Consider this example from the Active Record documentation:

```
class Topic < ActiveRecord::Base
    def before_destroy()
        destroy_author
    end
end
class Reply < Topic
    def before_destroy()
        destroy_readers
    end
end
```

Basically, with this approach, when you delete a reply, the destroy_readers method is called, but the destroy_author method is not. If you want to use this approach and make sure destroy_author is called, you need to update your Reply model to take advantage of the super command:

```
class Reply < Topic
    def before_destroy()
        destroy_readers
        super.destroy_author
    end
end
```

Callback Macros

Of course, there's an easier way to that ensure your callbacks are kept intact down through the inheritance hierarchy—callback macros. Continuing with our example from the Active Record documentation, you could rewrite the example using macros:

```
class Topic < ActiveRecord::Base
    before_destroy :destroy_author
end
class Reply < Topic
    before_destroy :destroy_readers
end
```

Now, when you delete a reply, both the destroy_readers and destroy_author methods are called.

Note If you intend to use callback macros to ensure your callbacks are kept intact down through your inheritance hierarchy, it's important that you define your callback macros in your model *before* you specify your associations. Otherwise, you risk loading your children records before their parent callback, and therefore, the parent callback would not be applied to the children.

As you probably guessed, in most cases, callback macros are the way to go. Because of the inheritance hierarchy, callback macros probably operate like you would intend in most cases, and they give you the most options for implementation. Actually, four types of callbacks are accepted by callback macros: method references, callback objects, inline methods, and inline eval methods (though inline eval methods are now deprecated).

Probably the easiest, and most common, approach you will see is the method reference. You simply define a protected or private method in your model:

```
class Account < ActiveRecord::Base
    before_save :setupdate
private
    def setupdate
        self.Account_Update = Time.now
    end
end
```

Sometimes, you might need to perform a large number of tasks with a callback that you don't want to clutter up you model with or perhaps share some functionality for callbacks across multiple models. These situations are a good times to use objects. There are a couple of steps required to use this approach to creating callbacks:

1. Specify the object you want called by your callback:

```
class Account < ActiveRecord::Base
    before_save AccountChecks.new
end
```

2. Define a method within your object that has the name of the callback and accepts your data record as a parameter:

```
class AccountCheck
    def before_save(record)
        record.Account_Update = Time.now
    end
end
```

The third, and somewhat less common, approach is to use an inline method. To do this, you simply put your code into a single-quoted string:

```
class Account < ActiveRecord::Base
    before_save 'self.Account_Update = Time.now'
end
```

You use single quotation marks so that you can include double-quoted strings inside your inline method; values enclosed in double quotation marks won't be evaluated until the callback is actually triggered:

```
class Account < ActiveRecord::Base
    before_save 'self.Account_Update = "Updated at #{Time.now}"'
end
```

Though the code for this appears to be shorter, it could also be said that it's more obscure and difficult to understand. For this reason, we recommend that, in most cases, you use either the method or object approach when possible.

It should also be mentioned that in all of the cases mentioned, you may assign multiple methods, objects, or inline methods to your callbacks:

```
class Account < ActiveRecord::Base
    before_save :setupdate, :setloggedin
private
    def setupdate
        self.Account_Updated = Time.now
    end
    def setloggedin
        self.Account_LoggedIn = Time.now
    end
end
```

Here's the same example using the inline method approach we outlined previously:

```
class Account < ActiveRecord::Base
    before_save 'self.Account_Update = Time.now', 'self.Account_LoggedIn = Time.now'
end
```

Specific Types of Callbacks

Now that you understand what callbacks are and the basics of implementing them, let's look at the 16 specific types of callbacks we can use. As we mentioned before, we all needed to digest some code with callbacks before we really felt like we understood them, so we'll also examine a working example for each.

after_find

As you would expect, the after_find method is initiated after an ActiveRecord::Base.find operation.

■**Note** To use the after_find method, you must define it as a method in your ActiveRecord class; there is no callback macro for this specific method. The lack of a callback macro for the after_find method is built into the design of Active Record to help improve performance when you use after_find. The method is called once for every record that the find method returns, so executing the method via a macro would be very expensive for your processing resources.

The following example adds a fullname attribute to the account records that are found. Because we are adding an attribute that is not directly derived from the database table, we must use the class attribute accessor method (cattr_accessor) as well. We discuss the details of cattr_accessor in other chapters.

```
class Account < ActiveRecord::Base
    cattr_accessor :Account_fullname
    def after_find
        self.Account_fullname = self.Account_firstname + " " + self.Account_lastname
    end
end
```

With this example, the following code would trigger the after_find method, so each record within the results would now have an Account_fullname attribute, even though your database table does not have that specific field or collection of data:

```
useraccount = Account.find(1)
puts "Found account for #{useraccount.Account_fullname}"
#=> Found account for Kevin Marshall
```

after_initialize

The `after_initialize` method is executed after an `ActiveRecord::Base.new` or `ActiveRecord::Base.create` call. It's important to note that this method is executed before a corresponding record in the database exists for this object.

■ **Note** To use `after_initialize`, you must define the method in your `ActiveRecord`; there is no callback macro for `after_initialize`. This is built into the design to improve performance.

```
class Account < ActiveRecord::Base
    cattr_accessor :Account_initialized
    def after_initialize
        self.Account_initialized = Time.now
    end
end
```

With this example, `Account` objects will now have an `Account_initialized` attribute throughout the object's existence; the attribute contains a time stamp noting when the object was initialized. The following code shows this in action:

```
useraccount = Account.new
puts "Account object created #{useraccount.Account_initialized}"
#=> Account object created Sun Jul 9 10:09:32 Eastern Standard Time 2006
```

before_save

This method is executed before an `ActiveRecord::Base.save` call; it will be executed before creating and saving records with the `ActiveRecord::Base.save` statement:

```
class Account < ActiveRecord::Base
    def before_save
        self.Account_updated = Time.now
    end
end
```

This example ensures that the `account_updated` field always contains the time that the record was last saved (this callback value would overwrite any value that may have been set within your code for the `Account_updated` attribute).

after_save

The `after_save` method is executed after an `ActiveRecord::Base.save` statement for both new records (inserts) and record updates:

```
class Account < ActiveRecord::Base
    cattr_accessor :Account_lastsaved
    def after_save
        self.Account_lastsaved = Time.now
```

```
        end
end
```

This example populates the `Account_lastsaved` attribute with the time just after the record was saved to the database. Again, the following example shows the callback we just defined in action:

```
example = Account.new(:Account_Name => "Kevin")
example.save
puts Account.Account_lastsaved
# Sun Oct 15 21:41:39 Eastern Standard Time 2006
```

before_create

This method is executed before an `ActiveRecord::Base.save` statement when the object does not already have a corresponding record in the database:

```
class Account < ActiveRecord::Base
    def before_create
        self.Account_updated = Time.now
    end
end
```

This example populates the `Account_updated` attribute with the time immediately before an `Account` object is created. The following code shows an example use of this callback:

```
Example = Account.new(:Account_Name => "Kevin")
puts Account_updated      # Sun Oct 15 21:41:39 Eastern Standard Time 2006
```

after_create

This method is executed after an `ActiveRecord::Base.save` statement when the object does not have a corresponding record already in the database.

```
class Account < ActiveRecord::Base
    def after_create
        logger.info( "Account was created at #{Time.now}" )
    end
end
```

This example assumes that we have a logger object to which we are recording certain actions. Here, we log the fact that a new account object was created and the time. Remember that this example logs the object's creation even if a database record is not created (because of, say, failed validations or the lack of an `ActiveRecord::Base.save` call).

before_update

You would execute the `before_update` method before an `ActiveRecord::Base.save` or an `ActiveRecord::Base.update` statement when the object already has a corresponding record in the database.

```
class Account < ActiveRecord::Base
  def before_update
    self.Account_updated = Time.now
  end
end
```

This example ensures that the Account_updated field always has the current time before a record is updated. The following code will use the before_update callback to update the account_updated field within our database:

```
Account.update(1,{:Account_Name => "Kevin Nelson"})
# Account_updated would now have the current time
```

after_update

after_update is executed after an ActiveRecord::Base.save or an ActiveRecord::Base.update statement when the object already has a corresponding record in the database.

```
class Account < ActiveRecord::Base
  def after_update
    logger.info("Account was updated at #{Time.now}")
  end
end
```

This example assumes that we have a logger object to which we are recording certain actions; we log the fact that an account record is updated and the update time:

```
Account.update(1,{:Account_Name => "Kevin Nelson"})
# Logger now has a record and time of our update
```

before_validation

This method is executed before an ActiveRecord::Validations.validate statement (which is itself executed from within an ActiveRecord::Base.save statement).

```
class Account < ActiveRecord::Base
  def before_validation
      logger.info("Account data about to be validated")
  end
end
```

This example also assumes that we have a logger object to which we are recording certain actions. Here, we log the fact that our attribute data is about to be submitted to our validation methods.

after_validation

The after_validation method is executed after an ActiveRecord::Validations.validate statement (which is itself executed from within an ActiveRecord::Base.save statement).

```
class Account < ActiveRecord::Base
  def after_validation
    logger.info("data passed all validations")
  end
end
```

This example assumes that we have a logger object to which we are recording certain actions, and this time, we log the fact that our attribute data has just returned from our validation methods.

before_validation_on_create

This method is executed before an ActiveRecord::Validations.validate_on_create or an ActiveRecord::Validations.validate statement is initiated from an ActiveRecord::Base.save statement on an object that does not yet have a corresponding record in the database.

```
class Account < ActiveRecord::Base
  def before_validation_on_create
    logger.info("Account data about to be validated for new record")
  end
end
```

This example assumes that we have a logger object to which we are recording certain actions. Here, we log the fact that our data is about to be passed to our validation methods before a new database record is created (the new record would be created only if all the validations are passed successfully).

after_validation_on_create

The after_validation_on_create method is executed after an ActiveRecord::Validations.validate_on_create statement or an ActiveRecord::Validations.validate statement is initiated from an ActiveRecord::Base.save statement on an object that does not yet have a corresponding record in the database.

```
class Account < ActiveRecord::Base
  def after_validation_on_create
    logger.info("Account data passed all validations for a new record")
  end
end
```

This example again assumes that we have a logger object to which we are recording certain actions. Here, we log the fact that our data just passed through all of our validation methods.

before_validation_on_update

This method is executed before an ActiveRecord::Validations.validate_on_update statement or an ActiveRecord::Validations.validate statement is initiated from an ActiveRecord::Base.save or ActiveRecord::Base.update statement on an object that already has a corresponding record in the database.

```
class Account < ActiveRecord::Base
  def before_validation_on_update
    logger.info("Account data about to be validated for existing record")
  end
end
```

This example assumes that we have a logger object to which we are recording certain actions; we are logging the fact that our data is about to be passed to our validation methods before executing a SQL update statement.

after_validation_on_update

This method is executed after an `ActiveRecord::Validations.validate_on_update` statement or an `ActiveRecord::Validations.validate` statement is initiated from an `ActiveRecord::Base.save` or `ActiveRecord::Base.update` statement on an object that already has a corresponding record in the database.

```
class Account < ActiveRecord::Base
  def after_validation_on_update
    logger.info("Account data passed all validations for existing record")
  end
end
```

This example assumes that we have a logger object to which we are recording certain actions. Here, we log the fact that our data passed through all of our validation methods before executing a SQL update statement.

before_destroy

`before_destroy` is executed before an `ActiveRecord::Base.destroy`, `ActiveRecord::Base.destroy_all`, `ActiveRecord::Base.delete`, or `ActiveRecord::Base.delete_all` statement is executed.

```
class Account < ActiveRecord::Base
  def before_destroy
    Contacts.delete_all(["Account_ID = ?", self.Account_ID])
  end
end
```

With this example, we are making sure that we delete all contact records that were associated with an account record before we delete the actual account record. This would produce similar results to performing a cascading delete within a database.

after_destroy

This method is executed after an `ActiveRecord::Base.destroy`, `ActiveRecord::Base.destroy_all`, `ActiveRecord::Base.delete`, or `ActiveRecord::Base.delete_all` statement is executed.

```
class Account < ActiveRecord::Base
  def after_destroy
    logger.info("Account record was deleted")
  end
end
```

This example assumes that we have a logger object to which we are recording certain actions; we are logging the fact that an account record was deleted from the database.

One Down, Two to Go

You should now be an expert on Active Record callbacks, or at least well on your way. As we mentioned at the start of this chapter, it sometimes takes a little bit of playing around with real code before you can truly understand callbacks, so we do encourage you to try it. We promise that it can only improve your understanding.

Let's now shift our focus to the second of the three core features we introduced at the start of this chapter, Active Record associations.

Associations

Up until this point, we've pretty much been talking about Active Record objects as stand-alone objects—they're tied to a table in the database, and they can update some records in that table. That's fine, but relational databases can provide so much more than a simple place to mark down some values. One of their strong points is right out in front as part of their name: relationships.

As it you probably guessed, Active Record makes it easy to maintain relationships between your models. You do this by associating each of your Active Record models to one another through various association methods. We'll cover each of these methods in the next section, but first, let's take a minute to talk a little about the idea of associations.

For some reason, associations—or joins, as SQL refers to them—cause a lot of confusion for many developers. The basic idea is actually quite simple. You have two or more tables, and each contains a set of data that is logically associated in some way. You want to grab a collection or subset of that data and treat it as one set of data. Seems simple enough, right?

The confusion generally comes when you start to describe these connections as inner joins, outer joins, left outer joins, and so forth. Oftentimes, expressing what you want to in plain English is easy enough, "Give me a list of cows owned by farmers who live in Ohio." Somehow, though, translating that into proper SQL statement to return the correct set of data gets mucked up. We know we want to join the cow and farmer tables, but do we want to do an inner or outer join on the tables? Should it be a left or full join? How do we know if it's really returning just the data we want without having to manually check all the results?

Farmers, Cows, Milk, and How They Relate

In an attempt to clear things up and to explain how Active Record tackles associations between models, let's take an example to talk about and break down each specific situation. For the remainder of this section, let's say we're writing an application to maintain the books for a cooperative of farmers who raise cattle.

Every farmer needs to keep track of a lot of cows, and all farmers sell their cows' milk to various resellers at their own unique prices. Finally, each reseller and farmer has an address, because the reseller needs to know where to send the checks, and the farmer needs to know where to send the milk. The basics of the tables are laid out as follows (we are using basic migrations for these definitions, for more on migrations refer to the previous chapter):

```
create table :cows do |t|
  t.column :name, :string
  t.column :farmer_id, :integer
end
create table :farmer do |t|
  t.column :name, :string
t.column :address, :string
end
create table :reseller do |t|
  t.column :name, :string
  t.column :address, :string
end
create table :farmers_resellers do |t|
  t.column :resller_id, :integer
  t.column :farmer_id, :integer
end
create table :distributors do |t|
  t.column :reseller_id, :integer
  t.column :farmer_id, :integer
  t.column :milk_price, :float
end
```

This should now give us a good starting point to break down each type of association.

Association Types

Active Record actually has support for a wide variety of different association types. These association types include belongs_to, has_many, has_one, has_and_belongs_to_many, and has_many :through. Along with these association types, there are also a handful of association modifiers that give you full control of your Active Record models.

belongs_to

belongs_to is the most straightforward of the relationships. When you say your model belongs to another model, it just means that only one object will be on the other side of the association. The ID of that association is stored directly in this model. In our example, each cow belongs to just one farmer, so the Cow model would look like the following:

```
class Cow < ActiveRecord::Base
    belongs_to :farmer
end
```

Referring to the cow table, you can see that one cow will only ever belong to one farmer at a time, because the table definition for the cows contains the foreign key of the farmer to whom it belongs. In the world of SQL, the cow table foreign key is the "one" side of a one-to-one or one-to-many relationship. With this association defined, we can fulfill the following real-world requirement: get the farmer who owns a given cow.

Here, we are starting with the cow table, and we know which cow we want. We need to join the farmer table based on farmer_id so that we can see the name of the farmer who owns the cow. This means we want to do a left join (we want all the data from the cow table for this cow *and* we want the farmer's name from the farmer table). With SQL, our join query would look something like the following:

```
# this is the T-SQL version (MS SQL Server uses T-SQL)
cow = Cow.find_by_sql("Select farmer.name as farmername from
  cow inner join farmer on cow.farmer_id = farmer.farmer_id")
puts cow[0].farmername # => "Farmer Fred"
```

The Active Record equivalent should look something like the following (regardless of which version of SQL your database supports!):

```
cow = Cow.find(:first)
cow.farmer.name # => "Farmer Fred"
```

As you can see, with this simple association, you automatically have access to all the attributes of the associated table (farmer).

Note *Inner joins* return only records that have a match in both tables (we would not get results if we tried to find a cow that didn't have an owner). *Left joins* return all the records from the left table, even if there is no matching record in the right table (in this case, we would get the cow information even though it belonged to no farmer). Inner joins are generally denoted by the use of the keyword AND in their plain English representation.

---

has_many

On the other end of belongs_to, there is has_many. It's pretty easy to think of where this can be applied: A farmer owns many cows. A blog has many posts, which may have many comments. A customer has many orders, each of which has many products, and a product has many images. A site has many pages. We could go on all day.

This association, like has_one, does not keep track of its own foreign key (looking at our farmer table, you see that there are no foreign keys defined within that table). This means that any number of other objects can be associated with this one, and the database can still keep a normalized form (that is, without excess duplication of data). This becomes more clear with our example, so let's define our farmer model and show the association in action:

```
class Farmer < ActiveRecord::Base
    has_many :cows
end
```

The has_many association returns an array of objects from the table containing the matching foreign key from the table specified. Again, walking through a plain English version makes this easier to understand, so let's use this association as follows: get a list of the cows a given farmer owns.

Here, we are starting with the farmer table—we know the farmer we want information about, and we want to get a list of cows that this farmer owns. This is really a lot like our belongs_to example, in that we just want to join the two tables together based on farmer_id. However, this time, we are starting in the farmer table with just the farmer ID. With SQL, our inner join would look like the following:

```
# this is the T-SQL version (MS SQL Server uses T-SQL)
cowlist = Farmer.find_by_sql(["Select cows.name as cowname from
  farmer inner join cows on farmer.farmer_id = cows.farmer_id
  where farmer_id = ?",1])
cows.each do |rec|
  print rec.cowname + ", "
end
# => Bessie, Spotty,
```

The Active Record equivalent should look something like the following (again, regardless of which version of SQL your database supports):

```
fred = Farmer.find(1)
fred.cows each do |cow|
  print cow.name + ", "
end
# => Bessie, Spotty,
```

As you can see, with this simple association, you automatically get the collection of associated records from the associated table (cow) and have access to all the attributes of those records (like the cows' names).

has_one

Sometimes, you don't have a collection of items to associate; sometimes, you have just one. In this case, has_one is what you need. Basically, has_one is the same as has_many, but Active Record will return only one object instead of all of them.

To be honest with you, it should be a rare case that you find yourself using the has_one association, because you would more likely just add the fields to one master table rather than split them across two tables and create a one-to-one relationship. Still it does happen, so let's take a look at one possible example. First, here's the migration for the extra table we are going to use for this example:

```
create table :tractors do |t|
  t.column :name, :string
  t.column :farmer_id, :integer
end
```

And we would then update the Farmer model to the following for this example:

```
class Farmer < ActiveRecord::Base
  has_many :cows
  has_one :tractors
end
```

Note This is actually bad table design, in our opinion, because each tractor can be owned by only one farmer, and because of our has_one association, each farmer can own only one tractor. In real life, we would more likely just add the tractor name field to the farmer table or make this a many-to-many relationship so that each farmer could own multiple types tractors, and each type of tractor could be owned by more than one farmer. Still, this example lets us quickly demonstrate the use of has_one.

With the model defined, we can now achieve the following real-world requirement: get the tractor a farmer owns.

Again, we are starting with the farmer table, and we know which farmer we want information about; we just want to get the name of the tractor that this farmer owns. The SQL query for this example would look something like the following:

```
# this is the T-SQL version (MS SQL Server uses T-SQL)
tractor = Farmer.find_by_sql(["Select tractor.name as tractorname from
  farmer inner join tractors on farmer.farmer_id = tractors.farmer_id
  where farmer_id = ?",1])
tractors.each do |rec|
  print rec.cowname
end
# => Big Red
```

The Active Record equivalent should look something like the following (regardless of which version of SQL your database supports):

```
tractor = Farmer.find(1)
tractor.tractors each do |tractor|
  print tractor.name
end
# => Big Red
```

As you can see, the code is identical to the has_many code; it's really only the results that are limited.

Note The difference, basically, between has_many and has_one is the same as the difference between find(:all) and find(:first).

---

has_and_belongs_to_many

Our tractor example showed a serious design flaw in that each tractor type could only be owned by one farmer and each farmer could only own one tractor at a time. That is probably unrealistic. It's more likely that a given farmer would own one or more tractor types and each tractor type would be owned by one or more farmers. That is, this would have been better implemented as a many-to-many relationship.

In theory, a many-to-many relationship is the same thing as two has_many relationships tacked back to back. However, in a normal has_many relationship, one of the tables is supposed to hold the foreign key of the other table. Doing that would only allow one of the tables to be associated to many records in the other (it would only be a many-to-one relationship). In order to keep the database normalized, a has_and_belongs_to_many (habtm) association uses an extra table, generally referred to as a join table, which is nothing more than a pair of foreign keys for each associated model.

Going back to our original example, let's say we wanted our farmer to be able to distribute the milk from his cows. He would need to have resellers. And a reseller should be able to sell the milk of many farmers. Clearly, a farmer has_and_belongs_to_many resellers, and a reseller has_and_belongs_to_many farmers.

As we've mentioned throughout this book, Active Record is part of an opinionated framework. As such, it has some default assumptions about the naming convention for join tables:

1. Take the names of the two tables.

2. Alphabetize them.

3. Join them with an underscore.

With these rules in mind, the table that would be used to join our farmers with their resellers would be named farmers_resellers (refer to our table definitions at the start of this section). Since this is nothing more than a join table storing the association between farmers and resellers, only one column for each side of the association is needed in this table: reseller_id and farmer_id. Our models would be updated to look like the following:

```
class Reseller < ActiveRecord::Base
  has_and_belongs_to_many :farmers
end
class Farmer < ActiveRecord::Base
  has_many :cows
  has_one :tractors
  has_and_belongs_to_many :resellers
end
```

Now that we have our associations defined, let's look at another plain English requirement: get a list of resellers for a given farmer.

With this example, we are starting with the farmer table, we know the specific farmer about whom we want information, and we want to get a list of resellers associated with the given farmer. Our SQL version would look something like the following:

```
# this is the T-SQL version (MS SQL Server uses T-SQL)
resellerlist = Farmer.find_by_sql(["Select resellers.name as resellername from
  farmer, farmer_reseller, reseller where
```

```
    farmer.farmer_id = farmer_reseller.farmer_id and
    farmer_reseller.reseller_id = reseller.reseller_id and farmer.farmer_id = ?",1])
resellerlist.each do |rec|
    print rec.resllername + ", "
end
# => Dairy Barn, McDonalds,
```

The Active Record equivalent should look something like the following (regardless of which version of SQL your database supports):

```
fred = Farmer.find(1)
fred.resellers each do |rec|
    print rec.name + ", "
end
# => Dairy Barn, McDonalds,
```

■**Note** When you're using the has_and_belongs_to_many association, it works just like a has_many association: you can push new records onto it; you can iterate over it with each, and you can do basically anything else you could with a has_many association. The difference is that both sides of the association can do the same things.

---

has_many :through

Many-to-many associations can be very powerful, but sometimes, you need to add more to the many-to-many relationship than just a direct tie between the two tables. Let's say you want to know the price of milk that a given farmer will sell milk to a given reseller for. Ideally, our application should allow each farmer to sell milk to each reseller at a unique price. This design means that we can't store the price of milk in the farmer table (because it differs for each reseller each farmer deals with), and we can't store the price in the reseller table (because resellers buy it at different prices depending on the farmer). What we really want to do is store the price of milk in the join table that associates each farmer to each reseller. By adding attributes like this to the join table, we are molding it into something more than just a join table; we're making it a join model.

In Active Record, we call this type of model and association a has_many :through relationship. As you saw in our has_and_belongs_to_many example, Active Record glosses over the existence of a join table, generally, because from a code point of view, it's not important to know it's there. The join model, on the other hand, is like a join table, in that it has two foreign keys, but because there is a model attached, it allows the intermediate table to have attributes that can more fully describe the relationship than a simple join table.

Let's define our new table and refactor our models so we can use this type of association:

```
class Reseller < ActiveRecord::Base
  has_many :distributions
  has_many :farmers, :through => :distributions
end
class Distributions < ActiveRecord::Base
```

```
  belongs_to :reseller
  belongs_to :farmer
end
class Farmer < ActiveRecord::Base
  has_many :distributions
  has_many :resellers, :through => :distributions
end
```

Going back to our example, let's use this type of association. Here's our question: at what price does a given farmer sell milk to a given reseller?

We know which farmer and which reseller we want information about; we just need to get the price of milk to which these two have agreed. In SQL, this would look something like the following:

```
# this is the T-SQL version (MS SQL Server uses T-SQL)
milkprice = Farmer.find_by_sql(["Select farmers.name as farmer,
  resellers.name as reseller, distributors.milk_price as price from farmer,
  distributors, reseller where farmer.farmer_id = distributors.farmer_id and
  distributors.reseller_id = reseller.reseller_id and farmer.farmer_id = ?",1])
milkprice.each do |rec|
  puts "#{rec.farmer} sells to #{rec.reseller} for $#{rec.price} per gallon"
end
# Fred sells to Mary's Market for $0.50 per gallon
# Fred sells to Sam's Shop for $0.65 per gallon
```

The Active Record equivalent should look something like the following (regardless of which version of SQL your database supports):

```
fred = Farmer.find(:first)
fred.distributions.each do |distribution|
  puts "#{distribution.farmer.name} sells to #{distribution.reseller.name} for
  $#{distribution.price} per gallon"
end
# sells to Mary's Market for $0.50 per gallon
# sells to Sam's Shop for $0.65 per gallon
```

As you can see, the resellers association also works as a has_many association would work. The only difference is in getting the two models association with each other. It is no longer the case that you can add a reseller with fred.resellers << new_reseller. Now, you must create the join model and add that to the association:

```
puts fred.resellers.size # => 2
Distribution.create( :farmer => fred, :reseller => sallys_store )
puts fred.resellers(true).size # => 3
```

Association Modifiers

Now that we've covered all the types of associations that Active Record supports, we can dig even deeper and talk about all the various association modifiers. As you've seen throughout this book, Active Record makes a lot of assumptions about the structure of your database to keep things simple, so you can imagine that associations are no exception. For example, the standard foreign key is the class's table name plus _id (e.g., farmers_id).

But what if your tables weren't designed with Active Record in mind or you just don't want to use the default assumptions for some reason? Do you lose your power to use Active Record associations? Luckily, no. You can set various attributes of all of the Active Record associations at definition to override any of the defaults. Let's take a look at all of these options in detail now.

Finder Options

All of the options that can be applied to finders can also be applied to associations. When used, they scope the results. This means you can use :conditions, :order, :group, :limit, and :offset exactly like you would in a finder.

The following example would limit the association of cows to only farmers with the name of Fred:

```
class Farmer < ActiveRecord::Base
  has_many :cows, :conditions => "farmer.name = 'Fred'"
end
```

:class_name

The class name attribute is for when your association's name doesn't match up with the class's name. For example, let's say we have a class defined as comment, and we also want to refer to the association as comment (not the plural label of comments as the default assumption wants us to). We could specify this as such:

```
class Account < ActiveRecord::Base
  has_many :comment, :class_name => "comment"
End
class Comment < ActiveRecord::Base
end
```

Now, when you reference your association collection, you would use the comment label as well, since that is now our collection name (again instead of comments, which was the default):

```
Temp = Account.find(:all)
Temp.each do |rec|
  Puts rec.comment.collect {|c| c.subject}
  # =>  Note we used comment instead of comments.
end
```

:foreign_key

Sometimes, Active Record will not be able to directly infer the foreign_key name, most often when the class_name option is not enough to specify the relationship in the database. In this case, you can specify the foreign key specifically. Again, this option is also useful if the column is named differently from the normal conventions:

```
class Person < ActiveRecord::Base
  has_many :children, :class_name => "Person", :foreign_key => "parent_id"
end
```

:through

The :through option is used to define through associations as described previously. You'll pass in the name of a has_many or has_one association already defined in the model, and Active Record will use that association as the join model.

:polymorphic and :as

Our examples so far have covered normal associations, which are between two models. In the real world, however, there are times when you will want to have your class implement an association with multiple models using just one key. For example, both our farmers and resellers should have an association to addresses, and since all addresses contain the same basic data types we want this to be just one table. This is called a polymorphic association, and Active Record supports it quite nicely.

Technically, polymorphic associations use a technique similar to single-table inheritance, where a type column is used to specify the associated model. But it's not as hard as it sounds. Let's walk through our farmers example to prove it. First, we need to define the address table via our migration scripts:

```
create table :addresses do |t|
  t.column :street, :string
  t.column :city, :string
  t.column :addressable_id, :integer
  t.column :addressable_type, :string
end
```

Next, since it is on the model that contains the primary key, the polymorphic option is really on the belongs_to method. The name of the relationship is the name that's used for the :as option when specifying the other sides of the relationship. This means our models would look something like the following:

```
class Address < ActiveRecord::Base
  belongs_to :addressable, :polymorphic => true
end
class Farmer < ActiveRecord::Base
  has_one :address, :as => :addressable
end
class Reseller < ActiveRecord::Base
  has_one :address, :as => :addressable
end
```

Now, we have a polymorphic association that allows us to reference address data for both farmers and resellers, all stored in one address table, as the following example demonstrates:

```
Example = Reseller.find(:first)
Puts example.address.city # => Edinboro
Example = Farmer.find(:first)
Puts example.address.city # => Somerville
```

By convention, the fields required by a polymorphic join are the association name plus
_id and _type. For the preceding example, the important fields in the address table were
addressable_id and addressable_type.

:join_table

In a has_and_belongs_to_many relationship, this modifier specifies the name of the join table. It
is required only if you choose to ignore the naming rules outlined earlier, which said to take the
names of the two tables, alphabetize them, and join them with an underscore.

For example, if you wanted to use the distributors table in your has_and_belongs_to_
many relationship, you could do so like the following:

```
class Farmers < ActiveRecord::Base
  has_and_belongs_to_many :resellers, :join_table "distributors"
end
class Resellers < ActiveRecord::Base
  has_and_belongs_to_many :farmers, :join_table "distributors"
end
```

:association_foriegn_key

In a has_and_belongs_to_many relationship, the association_foreign_key is the association on
the other side of the relationship and is only required if you go against the default naming
conventions for your foreign keys (which is tablename_id):

```
class Farmer < AR::Base
    has_and_belongs_to_many :shared_tractors,
    :association_foreign_key => "tractor_id"
end
```

:dependent

The :dependent attribute allows the associated model to depend on the existence of the model
referenced. If you set it to :destroy, all associated objects are instantiated and have their destroy
methods called. In that case, it's semantically equivalent to the before_destroy callback.

```
def before_destroy
    association.each {|each| each.destroy }
end
```

You can also pass :delete_all as an option, which will, as it says, delete all associated
objects from the database, but Active Record won't instantiate them or call the destroy method
on any of them.

Finally, you can also pass :nullify to set the foreign ID of the associated object to NULL in
the database. This lets you keep the associated record without worrying about RecordNotFound
exceptions, because the association is cleared.

Two Core Features Down, One to Go

We don't know about you, but all this talk of cows and milk has gotten us in the mood for a nice cup of milk and a warm chocolate chip cookie! But don't take too long for a snack break, because we've still got a lot more to tell you about Active Record. To be honest, at this point, if you didn't bother to read another page, you should have enough knowledge to build quite powerful and full-featured Active Record programs. But don't put this book down just yet, because we are far from finished. Active Record still has a lot more to offer, including one more core feature—data validations.

Validations

Data validations within Active Record are simply code-based rules applied to data. They ensure that the data is of a certain format, type, length, or value. Some plain English examples of data validation rules would be

- Account usernames must be seven characters long to be saved into the database.

- Promotional codes must be one of our predefined values or reset to "none" before being saved into the database.

- Phone numbers must contain only numbers to be saved into the database.

Active Record validations are actually just specialized callbacks. Within the life cycle of an Active Record object, validations occur on attribute values before your data is saved into the database—that is, before a SQL insert or update clause is actually executed.

From a technical point of view, all Active Record objects have an associated `ActiveRecord::Error` object associated with them. Data is only mapped to the database, via SQL insert or update calls, when this object is empty. So when applying validation code, you simply need to add data to the `ActiveRecord::Error` object when a validation rule fails, and this will prevent the SQL insert or update clause from being executed.

Why Bother with Validations?

Data validation with Active Record is really a pretty simple concept and very easy to implement. Still, there are a few questions you might have, and some quick tips that will hopefully make things even easier for you, so let's address those now.

Why do you need to validate data in the first place? Well, believe it or not, there are a lot times when it comes in handy:

- Data validations are a handy way to ensure that your data is always in a clean and expected format before it gets into your database. From a programmer's point of view, if you know your data is cleaned and scrubbed, you won't need to write as many checks and balances or deal with as many potential error-handling procedures (though you probably should still have that code in place just in case future programs bypass your data validations). From a database administrator's (DBA) point of view, it also means there is less need for database checks and procedures to ensure data integrity. From a user's point of view, it usually means a more intuitive experience where typos and common errors are automatically caught and dealt with.

- Many times, business logic is applied to specific data values or types; validations make for more accurate results and expected execution in these situations.

- Validations make your database more secure; potentially harmful data or scripts can be prevented from getting into your database.

- Validations help save on bandwidth and processing; rejecting data and throwing an error as early as possible within the life cycle of your Active Record object saves on resources. There is no need to involve the expensive call to the database until the data is really ready to be stored.

As you can see, there can be lots of reasons to do data validations, and hopefully, by now, you've decided that data validations really are useful. But how do Active Record validations actually work?

Implementing Validations

What are the options for implementing data validations? As you probably guessed, there are a couple of approaches you can take:

- You can use Active Record validations in your models and Active Record class files. Since this is a book about Active Record, you can probably guess that this is our suggested route. By putting your data validation code into your Active Record models, you get all the benefits outlined in this chapter with very little downside (however, there is a little bit of a downside, and we'll cover the pros and cons in a minute).

- You can use custom code throughout your applications (generally in your controller methods and client-side code such as JavaScript). In some situations, this will meet your needs just fine; for example, perhaps you want to check that a field contains a certain data value only in certain situations within your controller, or you're just developing a quick and dirty unit test. However, outside of the most trivial situations, it makes more sense to centralize the validation code into your model so that any instance of the Active Record object can take advantage of it. This isn't to say that you can't use multiple approaches together, and in fact, it's often a good idea to use some level of validations in your controllers and JavaScript to make a better environment for your users and to double-check that those validations are properly enforced within your models.

- You can use database constraints, triggers, and stored procedures. As a Ruby developer, this option probably doesn't appeal to you, because it means taking the control out of your hands and giving it to your DBA (if you're also the DBA, at a minimum, it still means taking off your Ruby hat and putting on your DBA hat). The other big downside to this approach is that your validations would be database- and schema-specific, which makes migrations or switching to another database backend more difficult down the road. Still, if you've got more than one application accessing your database, especially if they aren't all using Active Record to do so, you'll probably want to move—or at least duplicate— your critical validations directly inside of the database. This way all applications are dealing with the same rules and can reasonably expect the data to be in the same format regardless of its originating source.

This last implementation option really shines a light on the main design decision you have to make when thinking about implementing data validations—do you implement them in Ruby or directly in your database? Before you make your choice, consider these pros and cons of Active Record validations:

- *Pros*: The good news is that because Active Record objects are really just Ruby objects, Active Record validations are database independent. You don't need to know any special syntax or language such as TSQL or PL/SQL; you just write Ruby methods with Ruby code. Additionally, the validations occur on the object before data gets mapped to the database via SQL calls, which means that you save expensive (in terms of bandwidth and processing) database calls for just those times that you really want them.

- *Cons*: The bad news is that Active Record validations are only applied within your Ruby code. If other applications or programs, such as Java programs, access your database, they would need to do their own data validations.

In the end, it's up to you, the developer, to choose where and how to implement your data validations. My personal recommendation is that you centralize your validations within your database via constraints and other database-specific features when more than one application or program will be directly accessing your database—especially if they all won't be written in Ruby. But I also recommend adding Active Record validations to your models in all your Ruby applications. It won't hurt your program and can only help to ensure that at least your Ruby applications and programs are inserting and dealing with clean data.

OK, enough theory and design, let's get into the details of how Active Record validations work and how to implement them within your models. Implementing Active Record data validations is a very simple two-step process:

1. Add a protected `validate` method to your model.

2. Within that `validate` method, simply add items to the `ActiveRecord::Error` object when your validation rules are not met.

Using these steps will ensure that data will be saved to the database only when your validation rules are adhered to. Let's look at a quick example where we only want to save new accounts or update accounts that have a value for the `Account_Name` field and that value must be `"Kevin"`:

```
Class account < ActiveRecord::Base
protected
    def validate
        if self.Account_Name == nil
            errors.add(":Account_Name", "You must supply an account name")
        elsif self.Account_Name != "Kevin"
            errors.add(":Account_Name", "Account name must be Kevin!")
        end
    end
end
```

There are also `validate_on_create` and `validate_on_update` methods, which, as expected, allow you to implement custom validations only on record creation or record updates, respectively. As you can see in the following examples, from a developer's view, everything is the same as in our previous example except the method name:

```
Class account < ActiveRecord::Base
protected
    def validate_on_create
        if self.Account_Name == nil
            errors.add(":Account_Name", "You must supply an account name")
        elsif self.Account_Name != "Kevin"
            errors.add(":Account_Name", "Account name must be Kevin!")
        end
    end
end
Class account < ActiveRecord::Base
protected
    def validate_on_update
        if self.Account_Name == nil
            errors.add(":Account_Name", "You must supply an account name")
        elsif self.Account_Name != "Kevin"
            errors.add(":Account_Name", "Account name must be Kevin!")
        end
    end
end
```

That's basically all you need to know to happily implement data validations in Active Record.

Convenience Functions

Active Record was initially developed to be used with Rails. In typical Rails fashion, there are a number of convenience methods (currently 11 to be exact) built into Active Record that make the common case validations even simpler to implement. Keep in mind that Rails is a web-based framework, so many of these validations are specific to applying validations to data submitted via HTML forms. Let's take a quick look at each one of these convenience methods in a little more detail.

validates_each

The validates_each method evaluates each listed attribute against the associated block. The current record, the attribute to be evaluated, and the current value associated with the attribute are passed as parameters to the block. The following example uses validates_each to ensure that the submitted account_name value is "Kevin":

```
Class Account < ActiveRecord::Base
    validates_each :Account_Name do |rec, attr, val|
        if val != "Kevin"
            rec.errors.add(":Account_Name", "Account name must be Kevin!")
        end
    end
end
```

You can also specify a few options with validates_each, :on, :allow_nil, and :if. The :on option allows you to specify if the validation should occur :on => :save, :on => :create, or on => :update. Here's our example again, but limited to just updates:

```
Class Account < ActiveRecord::Base
    Validates_each :Account_Name, :on => :update do |rec, attr, val|
        If val != "Kevin"
            Rec.errors.add(":Account_Name", "Account name must be Kevin!")
        end
    end
end
```

The :allow_nil option (:allow_nil => true or :allow_nil => false) lets you perform the validation block for those attributes listed that do or do not have nil values. The :if option evaluates a specified method, proc, or string and execute the associated block only if the return value from the call was true (remember that Ruby returns true by default in most situations). Here's our example one more time, now limited to executing only when the associated ID attribute is at a value of 1:

```
Class account < ActiveRecord::Base
    Validates_each :Account_name, :if => :checked do |rec, attr, val|
        If val != "Kevin"
            Rec.errors.add(":Account_Name",
            "Account name must be Kevin for this record!")
        end
    end
private
    def checked
        return false if self.ID != 1
    end
end
```

validates_confirmation_of

The convenience method validates_confirmation_of is designed to simplify the process of confirming two HTML form field values—a common practice for things like password fields. Your table has one field associated with an attribute, and your HTML form has two fields that are similar except that one of them has _confirmation appended to its name. An example explains this best:

1. In your HTML form, you need to have something like this (it's more common to use the Rails helper methods for this, but I'm going to use straight HTML to keep the focus on just Active Record specifics):

   ```
   <input type="password" name="password">
   <input type="password" name="password_confirmation">
   ```

2. Now, when the data is submitted to your model, the validates_confirmation_of method will check that the values in these two fields match as part of the validation process. If they do match, the data from the password field would be mapped to the password field in your account table. The duplicate password_confirmation value would not map to anything in the database and would quietly be ignored beyond the validation steps.

```
Class Account < ActiveRecord::Base
    validates_confirmation_of :password
end
```

Again there are a few options that you can use with this method: :message => "" allows you to specify a custom error message when the values don't match. :on => :create, :on => :save, and :on => :update limit the validation check to just those types of actions, and :if operates just as explained in the validates_each method.

validates_acceptance_of

The convenience method validates_acceptance_of is designed to simplify the process of ensuring that an HTML check box was checked when data was submitted. This HTML field does not map to any field in your database. Again, an example explains this best:

1. In your HTML form, you need to have something like this:

```
<input type="checkbox" name="terms" >
```

2. Now when your data is submitted, the following code will make sure that the user did, in fact, select the check box:

```
Class Account < ActiveRecord::Base
    validates_acceptance_of :terms
end
```

The options you can add to this method are :message, :on, and :if, as explained for the previous methods, as well as an :accept option. The :accept option allows you to define what value the check box needs to pass in order for the value to be accepted. The default value of :accept is 1, which is generally the default value submitted by HTML check boxes. Here is a custom example:

```
<input type="checkbox" name="terms" value="accepted">
class Account < ActiveRecord::Base
    validates_acceptance_of :terms, :accept => "accepted"
end
```

validates_presence_of

The validates_presence_of method ensures that the values of specified attributes are not blank by applying the Ruby Object.blank? method:

```
Class Account < ActiveRecord::Base
    validates_presence_of :Account_Name
end
```

The options for this method are `:message`, `:on`, and `:if`, which all operate as explained in the previous methods.

■Note It's important to remember that the `validates_presence_of` method is for confirming the presence of attributes and their values, not for confirming the presence or value of the associated object. If you attempt to confirm the presence of the object, you'll get errors when both the parent and child objects are new.

---

validates_length_of

The method `validates_length_of` allows you to check that the values of specified attributes are of a certain length or within a certain range of lengths. The following example requires that the submitted `Account_Name` is five characters long:

```
Class Account < ActiveRecord::Base
    validates_length_of :Account_Name, :is => 5
end
```

The options for this method include `:message`, `:on`, `:allow_nil`, and `:if`, as explained in other methods. You can also specify `:minimum` and/or `:maximum`, which allow you to state what the minimum or maximum length of the attribute can be. The `:is` option, like we used in the preceding example, allows you to specify the specific length an attribute must be, while the `:within` and `:in` options allow you to specify a range of values that the attribute's length may fall within (you can use a combination of the `:minimum` and `:maximum` options to achieve the same results). Additionally, you can use the `:too_long`, `:too_short`, or `:wrong_length` options to specify custom error messages for those specific situations.

validates_uniqueness_of

`validates_uniqueness_of` ensures that the value of the specified attribute is unique within the field of the database. Again, an example helps to make this most clear. In the following example, every submitted `account_username` will be checked to ensure that no other records already have the submitted value (on updates, it excludes its own record):

```
Class Account < ActiveRecord::Base
    validates_uniqueness_of :Account_Username
end
```

The `:message` and `:if` options explained in the previous methods are available. Additionally, you can use the `:scope` option, which allows you to limit your uniqueness check to specific groupings of fields. Here's an example that will ensure that a user can answer a question only once:

```
Class Answer < ActiveRecord::Base
    Validates_uniqueness_of :account_id, :scope => [:question_id]
end
```

The `:scope` option can be an array of fields to limit by.

validates_format_of

Use `validates_format_of` to ensure that the value of the specified attribute adheres to a regular expression. The following example ensures that the `account_name` contains only uppercase or only lowercase letters:

```
Class Account < ActiveRecord::Base
    validates_format_of :Account_Name, :with => /[a-zA-z]+/
end
```

The `:with` option is required and must contain a regular expression.

validates_inclusion_of

Use `validates_inclusion_of` to ensure that the value of the specified attribute is within a supplied enumerable object, such as an array. The following example once again checks that the submitted `account_name` is `"Kevin"`:

```
Class Account < ActiveRecord::Base
    validates_inclusion_of :Account_Name, :in => ["Kevin"]
end
```

The `:in` option allows you to specify the enumerable object that is searched and used for the comparison. The other options available to this method are `:message`, `:allow_nil`, and `:if`, which operate as explained in previous methods.

validates_exclusion_of

The `validate_exclusion` method ensures that the value of the specified attribute is not within a supplied enumerable object, such as an array. The following example checks that the submitted `account_name` is not `"Marshall"`:

```
class Account < ActiveRecord::Base
    validates_exclusion_of :Account_Name, :in => ["Marshall"]
end
```

The `:in` option allows you to specify the enumerable object that is searched and used for the comparison. The other options available to this method are `:message`, `:allow_nil`, and `:if`, each of which operates as explained in previous validation methods.

validates_associated

`validates_associated` ensures that the associated objects are all valid themselves. We talk more about associations in their own chapter, but for now, consider the following example, which ensures accounts are associated with `accountrights`:

```
class Account < ActiveRecord::Base
    has_many :accountrights
    validates_associated :accountrights
end
class Accountright < ActiveRecord::Base
    belongs_to :account
end
```

There are two important things to remember when doing this type of validation:

- You should only put the `validates_associated` method on one side of the association. If you place it on both sides, you will create a dreaded infinite loop! Consider this example (*do not do this!*):

```
class Account < ActiveRecord::Base
    has_many :accountrights
    validates_associated :accountrights
end
class Accountright < ActiveRecord::Base
    belongs_to :account
    validates_associated :account
end
```

- The `validates_associated` method only ensures that the association is valid; it does not check that the association is present. To do that, you should also include the `validates_presence_of` method, as in this example:

```
class Account < ActiveRecord::Base
    has_many :accountrights
end
class Accountright < ActiveRecord::Base
    belongs_to :account
    validates_associated :account
    validates_presence_of :account, :on => :update
end
```

Validates_associated also accepts the :on and :if options explained in previous validation methods.

validates_numericality_of

Use `validates_numericality_of` to ensure that the value of the associated attribute is numeric. The following example ensures that the submitted value of account_age can be converted with `Kernal.Float`:

```
class Account < ActiveRecord::Base
    validates_numericality_of :Account_Age
end
```

Like many of the other validation methods, validates_numericality accepts the :message, :on, :allow_nil, and :if options. You can also specify :only_integer => true if you want to ensure that the value is specifically an integer (in this case, the value is tested against the regular expression /^[+\-]?\d+$/). The default :only_integer => false uses the `Kernal.Float` conversion to test if the value is a number.

Your Core Is Strong

You've now been exposed to all three of what we view to be the core features and biggest advantages of Active Record. Hopefully, you feel pretty comfortable with all the concepts, but as we've mentioned before, real-world practice of these concepts and techniques is what will truly make you an expert. So if you haven't already picked an Active Record project of your own to play around with, we suggest you do that now and start getting your feet wet.

In any case, you've completed your initial Active Record training. You've got the basics and core understanding of Active Record concepts and are now ready to move on to all of the really fun stuff. Throughout the rest of this book, we'll focus on various tips, tricks, bonus features, and using Active Record in the real world.

CHAPTER 5

■■■

Bonus Features

"**I**t slices. It dices. It even chops! But wait, there's more..."

Like those great infomercials you find on late night television, Active Record piles on so many nice extras you almost can't resist wanting to become an Active Record developer! These bonus features include observers to allow you to monitor various actions through the life cycle of your objects, aggregations that allow you to group common data sets or attribute groupings into objects themselves, and acts-as packages that allow you to make your Active Record objects mimic other structure types like lists or trees. Each of these features fill their own small niche, and each is very useful within it. Even better (as is common with Active Record) all of these bonus features are pretty simple and straightforward to implement. Let's take a quick look at the details of each.

Active Record Observers

Active Record observers are a great way to include functionality to your model that isn't necessarily a core concept. Everything you define within an Active Record observer can, instead, be defined within callbacks directly in your Active Record classes. However, adding things like transaction logging within your callbacks may clutter up and obfuscate the main role your model fills. Observers are a nice, clean way to keep this functionality without cluttering up the actual data model. If you're coming from a database background, observers are a lot like triggers, except that they are fired on various Active Record callbacks (see Chapter 5 for more on callbacks) rather than by SQL statements or actions.

Implementing observers is a pretty simple procedure, but there is one small catch: you must first configure Active Record to be aware of any observers. You do this with a call to the `ActiveRecord::Base.observers` method to specify either the symbols that correspond to your observer class names, or explicit class names. For example, the following code will make Active Record aware of `AccountObserver`:

```
ActiveRecord::Base.observers = :account_observer
ActiveRecord::Base.observers = AccountObserver
```

Note In Rails applications, you would include your observer configurations in your `config/environment.rb` file.

Within your actual observer class, you simply define the callback methods you want to perform observations on. Probably the most common use of observers is to populate a trans-action log or to send notification alerts on specific actions. So let's take a quick look at an example class that populates a log every time an Account record is saved:

```
class AccountObserver < ActiveRecord::Observer
  def after_save(record)
    @@logger.info "Account ID #{record.ID} was just saved at #{Time.now}!"
  end
end
```

Note Ruby 1.8 and beyond includes the nice Logger library, which is often used with Active Record observers to log various events and actions to a local log file. Rails is configured for Logger support out of the box. For more information on Logger, visit `http://log4r.sourceforge.net`.

By default, observers map to the class they share a name with, so in our example, AccountObserver would be attempting to observe the Account class. Sometimes, you might want to abstract an observer, say to observe more than one class. You can do this by calling the observe method within your observer class. In the following example, our generic observer would send an e-mail whenever a new comment or vote is placed:

```
class GenericObserver < ActiveRecord::Observer
  observe Comment, Vote
  def after_save(record)
    Alerts.deliver_alert(info@falicon.com,"New posting", record)
  end
end
```

Canned Functionality

I wish I had a dollar for every time I found myself saying, "I wish my *X* had a feature like my *Y*," or "I wish my *X* acted more like my *Y*." I sure would be a rich Ruby programmer instead of just "acting as" one! All kidding aside though, many developers have felt this pain before as well, and in response, the acts_as features were built into Active Record.

Basically, the acts_as_* methods add various methods to your Active Record objects so that they act as other types of objects or collections.

Note It's important to keep in mind that acts_as does not actually change the object type. It merely adds functionality to the Active Record object.

By default, Active Record has three primary acts_as methods—acts_as_list, acts_as_tree, and acts_as_nested-set—though others do exist and more are in development. Each acts_as method is really quite useful and comes with its own set of rules and implementation options. Because acts_as features work on collections, each relies on the various data association methods (see Chapter 4) to work properly.

Acting as a List

We've all seen top-ten lists; we've all put together a grocery list, and as programmers, we've certainly all had to deal with to-do lists. So I'm pretty sure we're all familiar with the core traits of a list. As I'm sure we all know, lists can be powerful things. It only makes sense that, at times, you may want to add list-like functionality to some of your Active Record collections, and as luck would have it, Active Record gives you just that ability with an acts_as_list method. Using acts_as_list requires a minimal amount of work to set up. Here are the steps to follow:

1. Make sure that your Active Record associations are correctly set up.

2. Make sure that the table containing records that will essentially be the items in your list contains an Integer column to be used for ordering the list.

3. Add the acts_as_list method to model that relates to the items your list will contain.

Let's break each of these steps down into a little more detail, so we fully understand them.

Step 1: Setting Up Your Associations

Technically, this isn't a required step at all. If you really wanted to, you could add list-like functionality to any Active Record model simply by following the other two steps. However, it's most common to deal with a list that is associated with a parent object. Every item in a top-ten list would be related to the list title; every item on a grocery list is associated with the grocery store you will be shopping at, and every to-do list is associated with a person or entity that is responsible for getting the items on the list done. So in most cases, you'll deal with acts_as_list along with models that have data associations, and when that is the case, the acts_as_list method will generally go in the model that has the belongs_to method, as you can see here:

```
class TopTenTopics < ActiveRecord::Base
  has_many :top_ten_items
end
class TopTenItems < ActiveRecord::Base
  belongs_to :top_ten_topics
  acts_as_list :scope => :top_ten_topic
end
```

Because we cover data associations in detail in Chapter 4, we will not dive into the design issues of the TopTen associations at this time. Just know that a given top-ten topic record would have a number of associated top-ten item records for this example.

Step 2: Defining an Integer Column Used for Sorting the List

Sometimes, like with a grocery list, you won't really care about the order of the list, but that doesn't mean that it doesn't have an order. The list has a beginning and an end, and each item is either before or after other items on the list. In fact, order is a basic and fundamental element of all lists, so it should come as no surprise that, to use `acts_as_list`, within Active Record you need to have an integer field within your database that stores the order of items within your list. By default, `acts_as_list` assumes that this field name is `position`, but you can override that by passing the name of the column with your `acts_as_list` method, as the following example shows (we use the column named `listorder` instead of the default column name of `position`):

```
class TopTenItems < ActiveRecord::Base
  belongs_to :top_ten_topics
  acts_as_list :scope => :top_ten_topic, :column => "list_order"
end
```

Requiring this integer field becomes obvious when you think about how you would actually implement some of the list-like features if you had to write the code yourself. For example, if you want to move an item lower in the list, you would obviously need to know the current position and have some way of adjusting that position as well as the position of all the items on the list that were previously below the item you are moving.

■**Note** Many of the `acts_as_list` methods attempt to directly manipulate the value of integer field sort key within the database even if you never make a call to the `update` or `save` method.

Step 3: Adding the acts_as_list Method

Adding the `acts_as_list` method is what really includes all the list-like functionality to your model. There are two basic parameters that this method accepts, `scope` and `column`. Both parameters are actually optional, but using the `scope` parameter allows you to store multiple lists in the same table. If you omit the `scope` parameter, the entire model will represent a single list.

The `scope` attribute allows you to specify the criteria records must meet to be considered an item for the list. Scope equates to the `where` part of a SQL `SELECT` statement. In fact, you can specify a string that would be the same as your `where` clause to narrow the specific records you want this list-like collection to include. The other option for `scope` is to list a symbol for the parent table of your list-like collection. When you do this, `acts_as_list` will automatically append `"_id"` if it's not already a part of your symbol, and then attempt to find a foreign key field of this name in your table. A quick example will express this idea more clearly:

```
class TopTenItems < ActiveRecord::Base
  # creates a list-like collection with the same top_ten_topic ids
  # and that were posted to the system in the last year
  belongs_to :top_ten_topics
  acts_as_list :scope => "top_ten_topics_id = #{top_ten_topics_id} " +
                         "and posted > (sysdate - 365)"
end
```

```
class TopTenItems < ActiveRecord::Base
  belongs_to :top_ten_topics
  acts_as_list :scope => :top_ten_topics
  # => same as "top_ten_topics_id = #{top_ten_topics_id}"
end
```

The column parameter lets you specify the column in your table that will hold the order the list's items are in. It should be an integer column, and it is usually called position by default. You can name it anything you wish, as long as you specify its name. Typically, the default name is good enough.

What acts_as_list Gives You

Now that you've got your Active Record models set up to act as a list, you're probably thinking, "Now what? What did that work actually get me?" Well, believe it or not, a lot! You now have 13 different list-like methods you can use to examine and manipulate your collection. We'll use our Top Ten example:

```
class TopTenTopic < ActiveRecord::Base
  has_many :top_ten_items
end

class TopTenItems < ActiveRecord::Base
  belongs_to :top_ten_topics
  acts_as_list :scope => :top_ten_topic
end

todayslist = TopTenTopic(1)
listdetails = todayslist.top_ten_items
```

We'll go over the methods we get from acts_as_list in the following sections.

insert_at(value)

This method changes the value of the position column to the value specified and moves the values of the other items as needed to correctly insert an item at this spot. This method immediately saves the change of these position column values to the database.

```
listdetails[0].insert_at(3)
```

This method adjusts the position column to now hold a value of 3, and, if needed, updates other records so that no other item is at the third position.

move_lower

If the collection contains an item with a position column value that is one greater than the current one, this method will swap the values of those position columns. This method immediately saves the change of these position column values to the database. This example would swap the position value for the listdetails[0] and listdetails[1] records:

```
listdetails[0].move_lower
```

move_higher

If the collection contains an item with a position column value that is one less than the current one, this method will swap the values of those position columns. This method immediately saves the change of these position column values to the database. This example would swap the position value for the listdetails[1] and listdetails[0] records:

listdetails[1].move_lower

move_to_bottom

The move_to_bottom method changes the value of the position column to the highest-numbered position column value in the collection (thinking of position as an index) and adjusts the other positions accordingly. This method immediately saves the change of these position column values to the database. This example moves the first record to the end of the list:

listdetails[0].move_to_bottom

move_to_top

This method changes the value of the position column to 1 and adjusts the other positions accordingly. This method immediately saves the change of these position column values to the database. This example moves the fourth item in the list to the top of the list:

listdetails[3].move_to_top

remove_from_list

This method removes the specified item from the list in memory and updates the other items' position columns to reflect the absence of this item from the list. This method immediately saves the change of these position column values to the database. This example removes the first record from the in-memory collection and subtracts one from each of the "lower" items' position column values:

listdetails[0].remove_from_list

Caution The item is only removed from the in-memory list-like collection. The Active Record collection still has the record, and the record remains unchanged in the database. In fact, if you rerun your finder and rebuild your list-like collection, this item would once again be included in the list (assuming you didn't update your code to specifically exclude it) and would have the same position column value it did previously (which would now be the same as the item that had previously been one position value higher).

---

increment_position

This method increments the position column value by one, regardless of the rest of the collection members' position column values. This method immediately saves the change to the database. This example makes the position value one number higher than it previously was. Note that this is not the same as move_lower, as it does not renumber the other records in the list.

```
listdetails[0].increment_position
```

decrement_position

Use this method to decrement the position column value by one, regardless of the rest of the collection members' position column values. This method immediately saves the change to the database. Like increment_position, this does not renumber the other list records, so it does not act like move_higher would. The following example lowers the position column by one:

```
listdetails[3].decrement_position
```

first?

The first? method determines if the item is in the first position of the list and returns either true or false.

```
listdetails[1].first?
```

last?

This method determines if the item is in the last position of the list and returns either true or false.

```
listdata[1].last?
```

higher_item

The higher_item method returns the item with a position column value one number lower or returns nil. Remember, "higher" in the method name refers to the first element of the list (numbered 1) as the top, so the lower the position column's value is, the closer to the top of the list it is, for example:

```
listdetails[2].higher_item #=> listdetails[1]
```

lower_item

The lower_item method returns the item with a position column value one number higher or returns nil.

```
listdetails[0].lower_item # => listdetails[1]
```

Acting as a Tree

Let's face it, lists are great, but they will only let you go so far in defining the relationship among a collection's items. This is because lists lack depth. Say, for example, you want to build a simple comment board application. You want your comment board to have various topics, various threads within each topic, and various posts or replies within those threads. Actually, lists could work for this application, but your code would get awfully messy, awfully fast. Luckily, there's a better structure to deal with this sort of problem—trees. Even better, there's an Active Record `acts_as_tree` method that was designed to help you to deal with collections of just this sort!

Though it usually takes a little bit of work to visualize the concept of a tree structure, once you do, it's quite simple to implement:

1. Define a foreign key column in your table that maps back to the primary key of the same table.

2. Call the `acts_as_tree` method.

Let's break each of these steps down into a little more detail to help you fully understand them.

Step 1: Defining a Foreign Key Column in Your Table

Your first step is to define a foreign key column that maps a recursive relationship back to the primary key of your table. Trees are really a way of describing a parent/child relationship. In our comment board example, we need a way to know when a record in our comments table is a topic, a thread within a topic, or a comment/reply within a thread. We could use an additional field that described the type, but this only gets us halfway there, because we still wouldn't know things like which thread a given comment relates to.

A better solution is to add a foreign key field that simply maps back to the primary key within the same table. This way, our comments can each have a foreign key value that maps to a specific thread's primary key. Our thread records would have a foreign key value that maps to a specific topic's primary key and so on. With this design, we can tell the type of a specific record by its depth in the tree and we can also tell what record a given comment, thread, or topic is a child of (if any). Cool.

■Caution `Acts_as_tree` relies heavily on a `has_parent?` method that, as expected, returns `true` when the foreign key field properly maps to a record with that primary key value. This means that you cannot assign a valid value to the foreign key field of a top-level record. If you were to set the foreign key value to, say, the same value as the record's primary key, calling a method like `ancestors` would actually create an infinite loop!

Step 2: Defining Your acts_as_tree Method

Adding an `acts_as_tree` method is what really includes all the tree-like functionality in your model. There are three basic parameters that the method accepts: `foreign_key`, `order`, and `counter_cache`. All of these parameters are optional. This is the most basic tree you can have:

```
class Comment < ActiveRecord::Base
  acts_as_tree
end
```

As good as the defaults may be, the options to `acts_as_tree` are worth explaining.

foreign_key

By default, the `acts_as_tree` method assumes that the foreign key column in your table has a name of `parent_id`. If you use this column name, you do not need to specify the `foreign_key` attribute, but if you want to use a different name for your foreign key column, you can change it here. This is an example of setting the `foreign_key` to a nondefault value:

```
class Comment < ActiveRecord::Base
  acts_as_tree :foreign_key => "related_id"
end
```

order

The `order` parameter can be added as a SQL snippet to sort siblings. It is the equivalent of the `ORDER BY` clause in a standard SQL statement. Here's an example of setting the `order` parameter:

```
class Comment < ActiveRecord::Base
  acts_as_tree :order => "comments_posted"
end
```

counter_cache

The `counter_cache` attribute can be used to tell your model to store the number of children a record has within the database. Using this attribute helps to improve performance when you want to know how many children a given record has, as it will avoid accessing the database unnecessarily. Your table must contain a `children_count` column of `integer` type for this feature to work. By default, this attribute is set to a value of `false`.

What acts_as_tree Gives You

`acts_as_tree` really only adds three methods—`ancestors`, `root`, and `siblings`—but each is very useful for navigating tree-like structures. To help make the breakdown of each of these methods easier to understand, let's first take a step back and define the generic comment table we referenced previously:

```
Comments table
id, integer (primary key, auto-incremented)
subject, varchar
parent_id, integer (nulls ok)
```

And recall our `Comment` class:

```
class Comment < ActiveRecord::Base
  acts_as_tree
end
```

Now that we're all on the same page for the following examples, let's also assume our database has at least the following three records:

```
id: 1
subject: Post 1
parent_id: null

id: 2
subject: Post 2
parent_id: 1

id: 3
subject: Post 3
parent_id: 1
```

Finally, let's assume that we have a program that eventually executes the following line:

```
temp = Comment.find(2)
```

With all this preliminary stuff out of the way, we should now be ready to explore the three tree-like methods.

ancestors

Use the `ancestors` method to return a collection of ancestors, starting from the parent of the current record and continuing through the root record. If the current record is a top-level record or does not have a valid foreign key value, this method will return an empty collection, for example:

```
temp.ancestors.each do |rec|
  puts rec.subject # => Post 1
end
```

The collection does not include the actual instance from which you are calling the method. This makes sense when you think about the name "ancestors," as you would not include yourself in a list of your ancestors.

root

Invoke the `root` method to return the top-most record in the ancestor tree for the current record. If the current record is a top-level record or does not have a valid foreign key value, the `root` method will return the current record value. We can get the subject of the topmost comment like so:

```
temp.root.subject # => Post 1
```

siblings

Call `siblings` to return a collection of siblings, that is, records that have the same `foreign_key` value as the current record. If the current record is a top-level record or does not have a valid `foreign_key` value, the `siblings` method will return an empty collection. This example will print out the subjects of all the comments that are replying to the same comment as `temp`:

```
temp.siblings.each do |rec|
  puts rec.subject # => Post 3
end
```

The `siblings` collection does not include the actual instance you are calling the `siblings` method from, which makes sense when you think about the name "siblings," as you would not include yourself in a list of your siblings.

Acting as Nested Sets

Though powerful, a tree structure may still have some performance issues. They are especially obvious when you need to select the children of all the descendants of a given branch. With a tree structure, that would require a new query for each child node. Luckily, there is a structure that was specifically created for this type of scenario—nested sets. Actually, in practice, nested sets work a lot like tree structures but involve a little more setup and design work. They can be a little complex to grasp and manage, but as we mentioned, they do come with some added performance benefits.

Since nested set structures are a little hard to conceptualize, we'll dig into some example code to show how it all works. For now though, let's start by covering the steps required to get `acts_as_nested_set` working:

1. Define three foreign key columns in your table that map back to the primary key of the same table.

2. Call the `acts_as_nested_set` method.

Step 1: Defining the Foreign Keys

Nested sets contain information about a parent/child relationship just like a tree structure, but they also contain information about what items each item is next to within the structure. The nested set structure relies on having each record reference the primary key of the record to the right of itself and the primary key to the left of itself. Actually, the left and right values do not have to directly relate to the primary key of the records directly to the right and left the current record but rather need to be small and large enough to include the values of those primary keys (this is because a SQL `between` clause is used to find those left and right records).

By default, the `acts_as_nested_set` method assumes that the three foreign key field names are `parent_id` for the reference to the parent record, `lft` for the reference to the lower sibling boundary, and `rgt` for the upper sibling boundary. Of course, each of these defaults can be overridden, but we'll save the details of that for the next step (since it's really done there).

Step 2: Defining Your acts_as_nested Method

Adding the `acts_as_nested` method is what really includes all the nested set functionality to your model. There are four parameters that this method accepts: `parent_column`, `left_column`, `right_column`, and `scope`. All of these parameters are optional, making the following example the most basic working example possible:

```
class Comment < ActiveRecord::Base
  acts_as_nested_set
end
```

The optional parameters show very clearly how the nested set can work both like a list and like a tree at the same time.

parent_column

Use the parent_column parameter to specify a name for the foreign key column in your table. By default, the acts_as_nested_set method assumes that the foreign key column in your table has a name of parent_id. If you use that column name, you do not need to specify it via the parent_column attribute. But if you want to use a different name for your foreign key column, you do need to specify that name via the parent_column attribute. For example, the following example specifies a foreign key column name of realtedID:

```
class Comment < ActiveRecord::Base
  acts_as_nested_set :parent_column => "related_id"
end
```

Keep in mind that the foreign key column named by the parent_column parameter is intended to reference the parent record of the current record. If the current record is a root record, the column's value should either be nil/null or set to a nonexistent key (probably something like 0).

left_column

Use the left_column parameter to specify an alternative name for the left boundary column. The left boundary column stores the lowest primary key value that the current record shares a level with. By default, this column is assumed to be named lft. If you want to use a different name for your left boundary column, specify that name via the left_column parameter, for example:

```
class Comment < ActiveRecord::Base
  acts_as_nested_set :left_column => "lower_boundary"
end
```

right_column

The right_column parameter is analogous to left_column. The right boundary column stores the highest primary key value plus one that the current record shares a level with. By default, this column is assumed to be labeled rgt. If you want to use a different name, specify that name via right_column. The following example specifies higher_boundary as the right boundary column name:

```
class Comment < ActiveRecord::Base
  acts_as_nested_set :right_column => "higher_boundary"
end
```

scope

The scope parameter allows you to further limit what is considered a part of a given set. If you specify a symbol that does not end in _id, then _id will automatically be appended to the symbol. For example, the following calls to acts_as_nested_set are equivalent:

```
class Comment < ActiveRecord::Base
  acts_as_nested_set :scope => :related  #=> actually uses the column related_id
end
class Comment < ActiveRecord::Base
  acts_as_nested_set :scope => :related_id  #=> actually uses the column related_id
end
```

If you require even more control on the scope for nested sets, you can simply pass an entire string that will be used as the where clause. Here's an example that limits the set to only those records with a related_id equal to zero:

```
class Comment < ActiveRecord::Base
  acts_as_nested_set :scope => "related_id = 0"
end
```

What acts_as_nested_set Gives You

The acts_as_nested_set method provides nine methods. To help make the breakdown of each of these methods easier to understand, let's define our comments table with default acts_as_nested_set columns:

```
Comments table
id, integer (primary key, auto-incremented)
parent_id, integer (nulls ok)
lft, integer (nulls ok)
rgt, integer (nulls ok)
subject, varchar (nulls ok)
```

And recall our Comment model class:

```
class Comment < ActiveRecord::Base
  acts_as_nested_set
end
```

And, so that we're all on the same page for the following examples, let's also assume our database has at least the following records:

```
id, parent_id, left, rgt, subject
1,null,1,16,'root topic'
2,1,2,'node 1'
3,2,3,'node 1 child 1'
4,2,5,'node 1 child 2'
5,1,8,'node 2'
6,5,9,'node 2 child 1'
7,5,11,'node 2 child 2'
8,1,14,'node 3'
```

Finally, let's assume that we have a program that eventually executes the following line:

```
temp = Comment.find(1)
```

With all this preliminary stuff out of the way, we should be ready to explore the nested set's methods.

root?

Since nested set structures are fairly complex, you'll often find yourself wanting to do a quick check just to see where in the structure you are. The root? method simply returns true if the current record is the root of the structure. The following example will print true if the temp record is the root of the tree:

```
puts temp.root? #=> true
```

child?

The child? method returns true if the current record is a child within the current structure. This will print true if the record is *not* the root of the tree and false if it is:

```
puts temp.child? #=> false
```

unknown?

Depending on the depth of your structures, it can become pretty easy to lose track of the depth of the current item. The unknown? method returns true if it can not currently be determined if the current record is the root or a child.

```
puts temp.unknown? #=> false
```

add_child

Use add_child to add a child node to the current object in the tree. All elements of the structure will be updated to shift them one position to the right as needed. If the current object has not been initialized within the structure, it gets set up as the root. The following example first creates a new record and then adds it as a new child node to our nested set example:

```
new_comment = Comment.new(:subject => 'node 4')
new_comment.save
temp.add_child(new_comment)
temp.save
```

children_count

This method returns the number of direct children that the current record has. If the current record is the root, this method will return the total number of items in this structure. This example assumes that the previous add_child example has been run and is still in the database; it shows how to find the number of children for a given node:

```
temp.children_count #=> 8
newexample = Comment.find(2)
puts newexample.children_count #=> 2 (node 1, child 1 and node 1, child 2 )
```

full_set

The `full_set` method returns the entire structure set of data, including the current record this method is being called against. This example prints out all eight titles, including the root's:

```
temp.full_set.each do |rec|
  puts rec.subject
end
```

all_children

This method returns all the children records of the current record. The result is similar to that from the `full_set` method, but `all_children` does not return the current record as an item in the structure. This example will print out all of the children's titles, but not the root's:

```
temp.all_children.each do |rec|
  puts rec.subject
end
```

direct_children

Return just those records that are immediate children of the current record with this method. The result of this example will be the subjects of children 1, 2, and, 3.

```
temp.direct_children.each do |rec|
  puts rec.subject
end
```

before_destroy

`before_destroy` is a callback method that is not intended to be referenced directly. It assures that the structure depth is kept intact when you are destroying objects within the structure. With this following call, we will not only destroy record 2 (which is Node 1), but it will also destroy the child records:

```
comment.destroy(2)
```

   `before_destroy` is actually a standard Active Record callback, not something special for this functionality.

Aggregations

Many times, you'll have multiple fields within a table that are almost always grouped together and treated as a single entity throughout your application—like an address that is made up of a street, city, state, and ZIP code information. Active Record aggregations give you the ability to wrap these fields into a single object—generally referred to as a value object—making the data collection more logical for your application (or rather, for us humans who are programming the application) to deal with.

Implementing Active Record aggregations is actually a pretty simple process:

1. Place the macro-like `composed_of` method call in the table's class, passing the related attribute mappings.

2. Define your value object.

Step 1: Calling the composed_of Method

This is a pretty straightforward and self-explanatory step. There are only three parameters for the method call: the name of your value object, the actual class name of your value object (`class_name`), and the mapping of your attributes (`mapping`). In the example that follows, we are adding the value object of `Songinfo` to our `Song` class. We'll start by defining a simple `Song` table:

```
Song table
id integer (primary key, autoincremented)
artist varchar
songtitle varchar
songlength varchar
```

Next, we'll define our Active Record class to reference this table and include our call to implement our value object:

```
class Song < ActiveRecord::Base
  composed_of :songinfo, :class_name => "Songinfo",
                    :mapping => [%w(artist artist),
                                   %w(songtitle songtitle),
                                   %w(songlength songlength)]
end
```

Now that we have our example code in place, let's quickly talk about each of the options we passed to `composed_of` above in a little more detail before we go on to step two.

The Name of Your Value Object

Since the name of your value object is the name that you will use to reference your aggregated object, that name is a required parameter and can be any nonreserved, standard, Ruby-like variable name.

■**Note** If you choose a value object name that is also the name of a field within your database table, the aggregated object will override the table attribute and its methods. After that, using the aggregated object will be the only way to access the overridden value. What this means is that if your table has a `balance` field and you decide to create an aggregated object referenced by the name of `balance`, you will only be able to get and set the balance value within the database through the implementation of the aggregated object—you will not be able to directly set the balance value like you do with other fields in the table, as in `Account.username = "Kevin"`.

---

class_name

The class_name parameter specifies the name of the value object's class and can be any nonreserved, standard, Ruby-like class name. This parameter is optional and, by default, assumes the class is named the same as the aggregation's name. For example, both of the following examples would reference the class Userinfo:

```
composed_of :userinfo, :mapping => %w(username username)
composed_of :personalstuff, :class_name => "userinfo",
                            :mapping => %w(username username)
```

mapping

The mapping parameter associates table fields with value object attributes. Each association should be an array containing the database field name (the attribute on the model) and the parameter name (the attribute on the value object). To assign multiple attributes, you group them as an array of arrays. The order in which you define your attributes within your value object is the order in which these values will be set.

Some examples should clear things up a little bit. Let's assume we have an accounts table with an account_username and account_password field and a Userinfo value object with username and password attributes. We can use the mapping option to tell Active Record where to look for our data in the aggregated objects. Here, we create an aggregation, first with just the username field, and then with both username and password fields:

```
composed_of :userinfo, :mapping => ["account_username","username"]
composed_of :userinfo, :mapping => [["account_username","username"],
                                    ["account_password", "password"]]
```

Step 2: Defining Your Value Object

For the most part, defining your value object is just like defining any other standard Ruby class. You can include references to any other objects or classes that you want to extend, inherit, or otherwise manipulate, and you can write any methods for which you want this class to provide functionality. However, it's important to remember that you must at least define the attributes you specified in the mapping parameter and an initialize method, or your class really won't know how to collect the database information into an object state.

Once again, an example helps explain the details a little better, so let's create a value object for some basic song information. To make things a little more interesting than just grouping things together, we'll also define a method that lets us automatically get all the songs of the same name as the current record but recorded by other artists. Here's our new value object:

```
class Songinfo
  attr_reader :artist, :songtitle, :songlength
  def initialize(artist, songtitle, songlength)
    @artist, @songtitle, @songlength = artist, songtitle, songlength
  end
  def  by_other_artist
    Song.find(:all, :conditions => ["songtitle = ? and artist != ?",
                                    songtitle, artist])
  end
end
```

Note that this is just a regular Ruby object, not a descendant of `ActiveRecord::Base`. The idea behind the value objects used in aggregation is to encapsulate functionality and keep related data and behavior in a separate place, as it's easier to understand.

Putting It All Together: Using Aggregations

Now that we've set up our code, let's use that code to take a quick look at how a program might actually use aggregations. Let's assume that our simple song table has the following records:

```
id,artist,songtitle,songlength
1, Johnny Cash, Walk the Line, 166
2, Four Tet, Hands, 341
3, Jimi Hendrix, Red House, 223
```

Our example is simply showing the basic idea of aggregations, so we aren't cluttering up our table with additional data. It's important to remember that in the real world it's more likely that your tables would have more fields than just those involved in your aggregations, and that the other fields' data would be handled in traditional, Active Record ways mentioned throughout the rest of this book.

To start our demonstration, let's have our program create a few new records. We'll create one record by using the value object approach and a second record using the traditional Active Record approach. Here's the code for both approaches:

```
temp = Song.new
temp.songinfo = Songinfo.new("The Books","Tokyo",223)
temp.save #= > adds "4, The Books, Tokyo, 223" to our table
temp = Song.new
temp.artist = "Albert King"
temp.songtitle = "Red House"
temp.songlength = 336
temp.save # => adds "5, Albert King, Red House, 336" to our table
```

Finally, let's use the value object with an existing Song record to display some information about that song. The following examples will print out the name and artist of the last song:

```
temp = Song.find(5)
puts "#{temp.songtitle} : #{temp.artist}"
puts "#{temp.songinfo.title} : #{temp.songinfo.artist}"
```

In this example, we can find use the by_other_artist method we defined on the value object to get all songs of the same name by different artists:

```
temp.songinfo.by_other_artist.each do |rec|
    puts rec.artist # => Jimi Hendrix
end
```

■**Caution** Value objects are immutable, that is, their values can't be changed once set. Instead, you should create a new value object. For example, calling `song.songinfo = Songinfo.new("Judas Priest","Exciter","303")` is correct, but calling `song.songinfo.artist = "Prince"` would throw an error. To change the value object associated with this record, you would actually need to once again call `song.songinfo = Songinfo.new("Prince","1999","371")`. This is because value objects are intended to represent a given value strongly dependent on its data, such as a specific song that is a specific instance of a generic `song` object, rather than a reference to just the generic `song` object. The Active Record documentation also suggests you read more about value objects at `http://www.c2.com/cgi/wiki?ValueObject` and the dangers of not keeping value objects immutable at `http://www.c2.com/cgi/wiki?ValueObjectsShouldBeImmutable`.

As you can see, implementing and using Active Record aggregations is pretty simple and is also a good way to keep your code clean, organized, and more object oriented.

Extending Active Record

One of the most wondrous parts of Active Record is the fact that it was built using Ruby. As a result, any part of it can be modified, replaced, tinkered with, and enhanced. Ruby classes are extremely malleable, so it's very easy to change the behavior of classes even while your application is running. Where code writes other code, this practice is called metaprogramming. You can use it to add declarations (the same way `has_many`, `validates_presence_of`, and `acts_as_list` do), or you can use it to modify how pieces of Active Record work.

According to DHH the original code for the plug-in system for Ruby on Rails was written in five lines. It's grown a bit since then, but the basis of it is still grounded around the principle that Ruby classes and objects are always open to modification. Since you can inject your own code wherever you want, the plug-in system doesn't have to worry about making sure there are hooks for you; it can just get on with business.

■**Note** While Rails has the concept of plug-ins, they only work automatically with Rails as a whole. You can still use plug-ins meant for Rails with Active Record apart from Rails, but you'll have to do the work of initializing them yourself, much like you have to worry about setting up your own database connection. In practice, it's about as simple as that as well: just `require` the `init.rb` file in the plug-in and most of the time that should be enough.

Extending Active Record the Easy Way

The easiest way to add functionality to Active Record is to open the `ActiveRecord::Base` class and define some new functions. For example, we can add a method, which will be available to all models, that can greet the user and display its class name and ID:

```
class ActiveRecord::Base
  def hello_world
    "Hello from #{class.name}, World! My ID is #{id}."
  end
end
cow = Cow.find_by_name("Bessie")
cow.hello_world # Hello from Cow, World! My ID is 5.
```

The hello_world method is now available to all Active Record objects. If we added our code into a file called ar_hello_world.rb, all we have to do to make sure it gets included is add the following line to our program:

```
require "ar_hello_world"
```

Yes, modifying Active Record classes really is that simple. But, admittedly, the previous example is a simple case. We're not really messing with the guts of Active Record, and we're also not doing anything terribly useful. But, the course of action is much the same even in more complicated cases.

Writing Code That Writes Code

To make changes to Active Record, we're going to have to metaprogram. This is somewhat of a dark art to some people, and a lot of times when programmers from Java or C# are exposed to it for the first time, they grow fearful because of the power you have over other people's code. The paradigm of other languages has a tendency towards protecting your code, whereas in Ruby, it's often expected that your classes will get tinkered with at some point. The basis behind metaprogramming is the concept of writing code that writes code. While this may sound difficult, it's actually pretty easy to do in Ruby.

Let's say we want to change the way ActiveRecord::Base.find is called. We have the whole power of Ruby at our hands, and ActiveRecord::Base.find isn't a very Ruby-looking function. What if we could pass a block in that we could use it to specify our conditions in a more Ruby-like way? As it turns out, there are a number of plug-ins that will do just this (including one that Jon's written—we know, we know; you're shocked, right?). We can still use the concept as a basis for exploring both metaprogramming and extending Active Record. The example we'll be building lets you specify a query that would normally look like this:

```
Cow.find(:all, :conditions => ["breed = ? AND gallons_per_day >= ?", breed, amount])
```

and turns it into this:

```
Cow.find(:all) do |cow|
  cow.breed == breed
  cow.gallons_per_day >= amount
end
```

The plug-in represents a fairly extensive change to the normal operation, but the change covers a large portion of the information we are able to get out of Active Record. Other versions of this functionality actually do a fair bit more than what we're presenting here, but we can use this as a good basis for example; and since we're trying to make our queries more Ruby-like, we'll call this extension RQuery.

First things first, you need to know how to override `find`. The simplest method is to open up the `ActiveRecord::Base` class like we did at the beginning of the chapter and write a new one. Of course, `find` does a lot of things already, and it's not the best idea to go overwriting existing code. Whenever possible, you should make sure the old functions are still callable. We can use `alias_method` to make sure that the original `find` call is available after we're through poking around:

```ruby
class ActiveRecord::Base
  class << self
    def find_with_rquery(*args, &blk)
      # We'll get to this in a minute. But for now, don't break anything.
      find_without_rquery(*args, &blk)
    end

    alias_method :find_without_rquery, :find
    alias_method :find, :find_with_rquery
  end
end
```

Note In Active Support, there exists a method that will basically do what we just did, but in a more straightforward manner. It's called `alias_method_chain`. You give it the name of the method you want to override and the name of the feature you're adding, and it will handle all of the aliasing itself. That amounts to exactly what we just did, but it looks nicer. However, it's only available when you're using Active Support, so if you're using Active Record on its own, you have to handle the aliasing yourself.

Now we have our two functions: the original find, which has been renamed to `find_without_rquery`, and the new find that will be replacing it, which is called both `find_with_rquery` and `find`, thanks to the `alias_method` call. If you were to call `find` now, you'd be calling our newly defined version (which just so happens to do nothing at all except call the original version). These functions are supposed to appear on the class itself (i.e., we want to be able to call `Cow.find`), and so we need to define them in an eigenclass.

Note Eigenclasses, also called singleton classes, are used to define methods on a specific object. Normally, a `def` or `define_method` call inside a class definition means that instances of that class can call that newly defined method. When you use an eigenclass, which uses the form `class << foo`, you'll be able to define methods that only `foo` can call. You do a similar thing when you define a class method with `def self.foo`. The difference is that the eigenclass lets you work on the class with any class methods that would normally be available, like `include`, `attr_accessor`, and `alias_method`. We'll have more on eigenclasses later in this chapter.

Now we have a method that's in the right place but doesn't actually do anything. This is great, because we have a place to start building our functionality. Something to note is that the new version of find expects to be passed a block, which is what the &blk parameter becomes. This block contains code which will eventually get parsed into a format suitable for ActiveRecord::Base#find. Since the original find doesn't take a block at all, we can use its presence to determine whether or not the user wants to use the extension we're adding with RQuery:

```ruby
class ActiveRecord::Base
  class << self
    def find_with_rquery(*args, &blk)
      if blk
        conditions = RQuery::Conditions.new(&blk)
        amount = args.first
        options = args.last || {}
        find_without_rquery(amount, options.merge(:conditions =>
                                            conditions.to_find_conditions))
      else
        find_without_rquery(*args)
      end
    end

    alias_method :find_without_rquery, :find
    alias_method :find, :find_with_rquery
  end
end
```

Now we know that if there is no block passed in, we obviously don't want to be using our new block syntax, so we forward them to the original version, and everyone is happy. But what's that new RQuery::Conditions object? And what's it doing? You caught me, I jumped forward a bit. We need an object to actually do the work for us, and we do need to call the original find method in the end. Like I said, it does a lot of stuff already, so we shouldn't go messing around with something that's already working if we don't need to.

Meet method_missing

The RQuery::Conditions class is what actually runs the block we've passed into find that contains the comparisons, but it can't run the block as it is; it needs to know a few things beforehand. First, what's the cow object that gets passed in? And how does it turn comparisons into SQL? Well, to answer that, you need to know something about Ruby method calling.

When you call a method, like some_array.size, Ruby looks for the size method in its method tables for the class in question, and if Ruby finds the method, it executes the code that's associated with it. If not, Ruby searches all the superclasses of that object until it finds one that has a method of that name. If it can't find such a method, Ruby calls a special method called method_missing and passes in the name it was trying to find and the arguments it was given.

Here's an example where we've added method_missing to the String class, which will print out a message to the user instead of raising an error:

```ruby
class String
  def method_missing method_name, *args
```

```
      puts "You tried to call #{name} and I don't know what that means!"
    end
end
"Hello".foo_method
# prints "You tried to call foo_method and I don't know what that means!"
```

We can use the behavior of method_missing to our advantage, because we can make an object that will use the method names passed to it through method_missing and build our SQL, for example:

```
module RQuery
  class Conditions
    def initialize(&blk)
      @columns = []
      blk.call(self) unless blk.nil?
    end

    def method_missing(name, *args)
      column = Column.new(name)
      @columns << column
      column
    end
  end
end
```

So we have a skeleton of how the code will get executed. We keep the amount (the :all or :first that's normally in a find call) and the options (like :limit and :offset) stashed away so we can get to them later, and we make an array that we can use to hold the conditions we're building. Then we call the &blk block (finally) and pass in the Conditions object itself as the parameter.

Now we know what cow was in the example when we started, and we know what will get its method_missing called when we use the name of an attribute. What about those pesky comparisons, though? They aren't arguments to the method; they're methods themselves. How will we get that data into a usable form? The answer lies in the Column object being created and returned (which you probably wondered about when you saw it—and I'm only telling you about now).

Like I said, the equality symbols are actually methods on the objects, and they can be overridden. We can define a whole bunch of methods that, instead of returning true or false like a normal comparison, will actually record the whole comparison into the object they were called on. Once we have that, we can turn that object into a format suitable for handing to find_without_rquery.

The only annoying part is that we're basically going to be writing the same method over and over, so we can loop over a list of method names and use define_method to keep our code straightforward. Keep in mind that using define_method is almost exactly like using def, except you use a symbol for the name of the function instead of just typing it. This means our comparison functions will be named according to the symbols :==, :<, :>, :<=, :>=, and :=~. Since the body of each comparison will be the same, we can iterate over an array containing the operators and use define_method, like so:

```ruby
module RQuery
  class Column
    attr_reader :name, :operator, :operand
    def initialize(name)
      @name = name
    end

    [:==, :<, :>, :<=, :>=, :=~].each do |operator|
      define_method(operator) do |operand|
        @operator = operator
        @operand = operand
      end
    end
  end
end
```

After executing our block, we have an array full of `Column` objects for which we know exactly what column was specified and how and what they were compared to. We're well over halfway there now. All we need to do is translate the resulting `Column` objects into a format like `find`'s `:conditions` array. We have the condition operators stored in our objects, but the problem is that SQL doesn't use all the same operators as Ruby. We can use the following mapping to make sure we're using the right SQL syntax:

```ruby
module RQuery
  class Column
    OPERATOR_MAP = {
      :==  => "=",
      :>=  => ">=",
      :<=  => "<=",
      :>   => ">",
      :<   => "<",
      :=~  => "LIKE"
    }

    def to_find_conditions
      [ "#{name} #{OPERATOR_MAP[operator]} ?", operand ]
    end
  end
end
```

There, when we call `to_find_conditions`, we'll get the right SQL syntax. Next, we need to convert and merge the whole array of `Column` objects into one big array we can pass to `find_without_rquery`. Here's the code to do that:

```ruby
module RQuery
  class Conditions
    def to_find_conditions
      sql_strings = []
      arguments   = []
```

```
        columns.each do |column|
          # Get the conditions of each column
          sql_string, *column_arguments = column.to_find_conditions

          # Append them to the rest
          sql_strings << sql_string
          arguments   << column_arguments
        end

        # Build them up into the right format
        full_sql_string = sql_strings.join(" AND ")

        # Return them in one nice, flat array
        [ full_sql_string, arguments ].flatten
      end
    end
end
```

If we try to use our new SQL generator, we should be able to create a new `Conditions` object, give it a block, and be able to see the SQL that comes out, for example:

```
conditions = RQuery::Conditions.new do |cow|
  cow.breed == breed
  cow.gallons_per_day >= amount
end
conditions.to_find_conditions
# => ["breed = ? AND gallons_per_day >= ?", "Holstien", 8]
```

which is exactly how we want the conditions to come out! Next, we can see that when we pass the same block to `find`, we'll get the correct result set back:

```
original_cows = Cow.find(:all, :conditions =>
                                  ["breed = ? AND gallons_per_day >= ?",
                                  breed, amount])
rquery_cows = Cow.find(:all) do |cow|
  cow.breed == breed
  cow.gallons_per_day >= amount
end

original_cows == rquery_cows # => true
```

So now we have an extension to Active Record that will take a block of actual code and convert it—without much hassle—into an array fit for passing as the `:conditions` argument to `ActiveRecord::Base.find`, *and* that process of conversion is completely transparent to `find`'s normal operation. Not bad.

Still, our solution could use some tweaks. There is one big problem with relying on `method_missing` to tell us the name of the column we want: that approach only works if there isn't already a method by that name, like `id`. I admit I glossed over this problem for simplicity, but now that it's out in the open, we can do something about it. We can ask Active Record for the name of the columns and define methods ourselves.

What Column Did You Want, Again?

Defining methods on the fly is an important part of metaprogramming—it's the very heart of code that writes other code. We can use the column_names array that Active Record supplies and define a function for every column. This method will perform the same actions as the method_missing we used before, but instead of being called implicitly (as method_missing does), they will be called explicitly. This will remove any ambiguity and let us be sure our methods refer to columns in the database.

However, we'll need to rearrange our conditions class a little, for example:

```
module RQuery
  class Conditions
    def initialize(active_record, &blk)
      @active_record = active_record
      @columns = []
      define_column_methods
      blk.call(self) unless blk.nil?
    end

    def define_column_methods
      active_record = @active_record
      (class << self; self; end).class_eval do
        active_record.column_names.each do |column|
          define_method(column) do
            column = Column.new(column_name)
            @columns << column
            column
          end
        end
      end
    end

    def method_missing(name, *args)
      raise "The column #{name} was not found on #{@active_record.class.name}"
    end
  end
end
```

The define_column_methods method is where our new work is getting done. Adding a method to a class at runtime is a little trickier than it seems. We need to add the methods at runtime, and we need to make sure they only get added to this particular object. That's where the eigenclass comes in: it holds the methods we're adding, and it's only visible to this instance of the Conditions object. See the eigenclass sidebar for more details.

A NOTE ABOUT EIGENCLASSES

Let's talk more about eigenclasses. The only difference, practically speaking, between classes and objects in Ruby is that classes are objects that are able to have methods.

"But I can call methods on objects!" you say. Well, yes, you can, but when you do that, Ruby actually starts looking for the method definition in the object's class. Under normal circumstances, all instances of an object have the same parent class. If the method you're trying to access isn't defined in the class (e.g., if you called `object_id` on a `String`), Ruby will look in that class's parent class (or `Object` in this case) for the method. It will continue along doing this until it runs out of superclasses. Then, it will start over by calling `method_missing` on the original object (which, as you guessed, means it starts searching in that object's class).

Now, here's why eigenclasses are sometimes called singleton classes. When you define methods using an eigenclass, Ruby actually inserts a fake class object between the real class and your object. So if you define a new `to_s` method for this object, Ruby will find that one before it finds the one defined in the class with `def to_s`. This means there's only ever one instance of that special class object, and it only ever applies to that one object. Similarly, if you use an eigenclass like we did at the beginning of the chapter, you still make the special class, but it's inserted above the class's class. This is where metaprogramming can really tweak some people's brains.

Now that we have our methods, we don't need to worry about `method_missing` picking up any slack. It would be nice, however, to have some better error messages if we do happen to type something wrong, so we can have it raise an error, since it couldn't find a column we were talking about.

Now, we're able to accomplish the following:

```
Cow.find(:all){ id == 2 }
```

If we had done that previously, we would have gotten a list of all of the cows, because `id` would have called the `id` method on `Object` instead of triggering our `method_missing` to add a new `Column` object.

But What About the Farmer?

Not only does Active Record allow you to find the names of the column in your models, but you can also get the names of all the relationships defined in the model as well. We can use this information to let our extension create joins automatically too.

There are a number of ways to get the names of the associations. You can obtain a list of all of them with `ActiveRecord::Base#reflect_on_all_associations`. That method will return an array of `AssociationReflection` objects, which hold all the information you need about a particular relationship including the source and destination classes, the name, the type (e.g., `has_many`, `belongs_to`), and any options that were defined on them. We can iterate over these associations like we did for the column names to create functions with the names of our relationships. In the following code, you can see the new method that will create more methods based on the association names, as well as a method that will return a list of associations generated during the condition block's execution:

```ruby
module RQuery
  class Conditions
    def initialize(active_record, &blk)
      @active_record = active_record
      @columns = []
      @associations = {}

      define_column_methods
      define_association_methods

      blk.call(self) unless blk.nil?
    end

    def define_association_methods
      active_record = @active_record
      (class << self; self; end).class_eval do
        associations = active_record.reflect_on_all_associations

        associations.each do |association|
          define_method(association.name) do
            @associations[association.name] = Conditions.new(association.klass)
          end
        end
      end
    end

    def to_find_includes
      includes = {}
      @associations.each do |name, association|
        includes[name.to_sym] = association.to_find_includes
      end
      includes
    end
  end
end
```

Our new method for defining the association methods looks an awful lot like the method for defining the column methods. The big difference is that we're placing the associations into a hash table, which will make building the :include definition for find that much easier. Remember, you pass :include options to find in a nested hash formation, so building the placeholders in the same format will be advantageous to us. We've also added a method for turning the new Conditions objects into the hash that the :include option expects. If we referenced a relationship like cow.farmer.distributor, this would build a hash of {:farmer => {:distributor => {}}}, which is exactly what you'd pass to :include.

The only thing we're not doing is getting the conditions that are being built by the conditions objects. We can change our to_find_conditions call in the following manner:

```ruby
module RQuery
  class Conditions
    def to_find_conditions
      sql_strings = []
      arguments   = []

      @associations.each do |name, association|
        sql_string, *column_arguments = association.to_find_conditions

        sql_strings << sql_string
        arguments   << column_arguments
      end

      @columns.each do |column|
        sql_string, *column_arguments = column.to_find_conditions

        sql_strings << sql_string
        arguments   << column_arguments
      end

      # Build them up into the right format
      full_sql_string = sql_strings.join(" AND ")

      # Return them in one nice, flat array
      [ full_sql_string, arguments ].flatten
    end
  end
end
```

If we treat the association condition blocks like any others, we can get the conditions it would have generated and append them to the rest. Let's see the new code in action:

```ruby
Cow.find(:all) do |cow|
  cow.farmer.state     == "MA"
  cow.gallons_per_day >= 8
end
```

This generates the exact same query and result as the following:

```ruby
Cow.find(:all, :conditions => ["state = ? AND gallons_per_day >= ?", "MA", 8],
               :include => {:farmer => {}})
```

There are a few more things we can do to make our little plug-in here more robust, but they're outside the scope of this chapter. Suffice it to say that, thanks to Ruby, we were able to do a lot more in modifying the behavior of find than we could ever have done with a more traditional language.

Overriding and wrapping Active Record functions allow for a lot of flexibility in how you can write your code. Even better, often you don't have to worry about doing the heavy lifting (i.e., writing out all the SQL) because you can still call the original Active Record methods, allowing you to change the look without changing the ultimate behavior.

Adding Class Methods

Not all problems are solvable through such gross procedures as overloading a method that everyone uses. Sometimes, you only want things to happen to one or two models or even one or two attributes in a single model. Fortunately, using the same techniques of adding in methods at runtime and overloading existing methods, we can add our own class methods that can alter behavior.

Class methods like has_many, validates_presence_of, and even attr_accessor aren't anything new, but to people who first get involved with Ruby (lately, often through Ruby on Rails), they can look as though they're part of the language. After all, they look like keywords (because you can call them, like all Ruby methods, without parentheses on their arguments), and they're used bare inside a class (which is just plain weird if you're coming from something like Java or C++). We can use them to add functionality to a model the same way Active Record does.

Your plain basic class method is typically defined in a class by prefixing either the class name or self to the name of a method:

```
class ActiveRecord::Base
  def self.print_args(*args)
    p args
  end
end
```

Then, you can execute the following code:

```
class Cow < ActiveRecord::Base
  print_args [1,2,3], { :one => 1 }
end
```

and it will print out this:

```
[[1,2,3], {:one => 1}]
```

For the most basic case, the preceding example shows all you need to do to add a method that can be called inside the class definition to a model. In practice, things should be a little more complicated, because well, hopefully what you want to do is more complicated.

■**Note** There is a subtle difference between the include and extend methods. If you include a module in your class, the methods defined inside that module will act as though they were defined inside the class. Basically, if you include a module, those methods will be accessible to instances of that class. If you extend an object with a module, then the methods defined in the module will be available to that object and that object only. The include method works on classes and will affect every instance of that class; the extend method works on objects themselves and affects only that object.

For the most part, if you want to use a class method, you want the instances of that model to have some particular behavior. That means you'll have to add both class methods and instance methods. Best practice for making sure both class and instance methods get added is to separate them out into modules called ClassMethods, InstanceMethods, and SingletonMethods.

Here's a simple skeleton set of modules that will demonstrate the general concepts, using a module that will allow your models to track and save changes to their fields:

```ruby
module Auditable
  def self.included(base)
    base.extend ClassMethods
  end

  module ClassMethods
    def auditing_columns
      @auditing_columns
    end

    def audits *columns
      include Auditable::InstanceMethods
      extend  Auditable::SingletonMethods

      @columns = columns
    end
  end

  module InstanceMethods
  end

  module SingletonMethods
  end
end
```

The linchpin of this technique is the `self.included` method. It's called on a module when that module is `included` in another class. In this case, when the `Auditable` module is included in a class it gives that class access to all the methods in the `ClassMethods` module. That makes the `audits` method available to your models but doesn't add any other code until you actually want it. For example, we can include our `Auditable` module like so:

```ruby
class ActiveRecord::Base
  include Auditable
end
```

which will add the `audits` method to all models. Once we have done that, we can call it like so:

```ruby
class Cow < ActiveRecord::Base
  audits :name, :gallons_per_day, :farmer_id
end
```

When you call `audits` inside the class, two things happen: your class then has access to the methods in the `SingletonMethods` module (which means, in this case, that the `Cow` class has access to methods that other models don't), and all of your instances have access to the methods in the `InstanceMethods` module (so all of your individual `Cow` objects have extra functionality). Now that you know where everything goes, we can start implementing our methods.

The next thing we need is a way to know if a column has changed, since we can't record the change if we don't know it's changed. We can keep track of column changes by overriding the attribute setter methods in the model instance. Since we're given the columns we want to audit in the call to the `audits` class method, we can use those names to create new attribute setters, like so:

```ruby
module InstanceMethods
  def self.included(base)
    base.class_eval do
      auditing_columns.each do |column|
        define_method :"#{column}=" do |new_val|
          @previous_attribute_values[column] ||= {}
          @previous_attribute_values[column][:old] ||= base.send(column)
          @previous_attribute_values[column][:new] = new_val
          write_attribute(column, new_val)
        end
      end
    end
  end
end
```

This code creates a setter method for every symbol specified in the call to `audits`. In this case, `base` is whatever model we were in when we called the `audits` method. Using `class_eval` means we're working exactly as though we were inside the class, which lets us access the `auditing_columns` method and call `define_method` to make the setters.

At this point, we have a command that will let us be able to tell when columns were overwritten but doesn't let us keep a record of all the changes that have been made along the way. We need to tinker with `ActiveRecord::Base#save` so we can record the audits the same time the record gets saved. We can add the following code to the `self.included` function inside the `InstanceMethods` module, which will wrap the `save` function:

```ruby
  def save_with_auditing(validations = true)
    if save_without_auditing(validations)
      @previous_attribute_values.each do |column, values|
        Audit.create(:model => self, :column => column, :record_id => self.id,
                     :changed_from => values[:old], :changed_to => values[:new])
      end
      @previous_attribute_values = {}
    end
  end

  alias_method :save_without_auditing, :save
  alias_method :save, :save_with_auditing
```

With this code in place, we will have a number of `Audit` records created every time we save a record: one for each column that we are watching and that we changed. For reference, here is the migration I am using for the `Audit` class:

```ruby
create_table :audits do |t|
  t.column :model, :string
```

```
    t.column :column, :string
    t.column :record_id, :integer
    t.column :changed_from, :string
    t.column :changed_to, :string
    t.column :created_on, :datetime
end
```

Since we'll be leaving such a trail of Audit objects (every change to a Cow object, for example, can create up to three Audit objects), we should have a way of getting relevant ones. We can use the SingletonMethods module for this. Here is a method that can query the Audit model for us, in a nice, neat package:

```
module SingletonMethods
  def revisions_for object
    id = object.is_a?(ActiveRecord::Base) ? object.id : object
    Audit.find(:all, :conditions => ["class_name = ? AND record_id = ?",
                                         self.name, id])
  end
end
```

We can pass in the id of the record we wish to query or the object itself, and we will receive an array of Audit objects. Because the methods in the SingletonMethods module are (not surprisingly) singleton methods, they are applied only to the class we originally called audits on. Therefore, we should call the revisions_for method through that class. In this case, we should call the following:

```
Cow.revisions_for 1
```

which will give us all of the changes we've ever made to the Cow with an id of 1.

These are the basic building blocks for extending, not just Active Record, but any Ruby class. Metaprogramming is a powerful tool that Ruby provides eagerly to everyone, and it can create some very clean and easy to read code. Likewise, Active Record gives you a lot of information about your database and its contents. You can use these two features together to create nearly anything, from simple helper methods to automatic, transparent database connection pooling.

Don't Shoot Yourself in the Foot

Active Record hands you a lot of power in manipulating your data. While it gives you methods like acts_as_tree out of the box, the fact that it is written in Ruby means you can write your own methods that can grant a wide array of functionality with very little code.

While being able to modify Active Record is powerful, it's also potentially problematic. Being able to open classes and redefine methods is very useful, but you can easily overwrite necessary functionality by accident. Metaprogramming can be difficult and sometimes confusing, and using it inside a library as large as Active Record even more so. Fortunately, there are a wealth of testing and debugging aids at your disposal, so you can be sure your code is correct.

## CHAPTER 6

Active Record Testing and Debugging

As you've seen throughout this book, a number of features and intentional design decisions went into Active Record to make it quite unique in the world of database communication libraries. Testing and debugging are two more areas in which Active Record was designed to be both easy and useful to implement.

To be honest, Active Record doesn't really have testing built in so much as it was designed to take full advantage of Ruby's preexisting Unit Testing library. An in-depth look at unit testing is outside the scope of this book, but we do need to cover a large portion of the concepts and options so that we can write some Active Record tests.

We'll start this chapter by covering the details of Ruby unit testing as they relate to Active Record tests. And because testing is really all about preparing for and dealing with problems and exceptions, we'll also spend a little time talking about the specific Active Record exception types—what each means and how to gracefully handle them all. We'll wrap up this chapter by providing a number of tips and examples on debugging your Active Record programs in the real world. So let's dive right in with unit testing.

Unit Testing

Let's face it; if you're like us (and most programmers), you were probably thinking about skipping this chapter, because you hate testing, and writing tests seems like it would be a waste of time (you could be writing real code instead of wasting time writing tests, right?). However, there really are some big advantages to writing unit tests when you're building database-reliant applications, so before we get into the details of writing unit tests, let's take a minute to outline those advantages.

Why Write Unit Tests?

In our opinion (and experience) formal testing doesn't really become an important part of your programming tool set until you start to work on large applications over a lengthy period of time. When a project is small, or you are just doing something quick, it's easy to write quick ad hoc code to ensure things are working; you can always refer to the full code base to determine what the application is really doing.

The problem is that once you start working on larger projects, you'll quickly find that reading through the full source code trailing a logic path to locate a bug can be quite time consuming. Having to do it six months or more after having last worked on the application will make it even harder! So with that in mind, here's a list of our top five reasons to bother with unit testing:

1. *Assures you that your code works as you expect it to*: This is a pretty obvious reason, since it's the whole point of any test. If you've been a programmer for any length of time, you've noticed that sometimes features don't always work as advertised (yes, even in Ruby). Sometimes, your logic is just off. The only way to know if the code you wrote works the way you intended is to actually execute it. If you let the first time that happens be in front of your user, you'll deserve the lack of faith they put in you and your work *when* it doesn't work as expected.

2. *Helps document how you expect your code to work*: Unit tests have an interesting side result in that, by defining your tests, you essentially end up saying, "This is how I expect and want my code to work." Down the road, if other programmers (or yourself) need to address a certain section of your code, they can refer to the tests to see just what you expected the code to be able to handle (and they can add to the tests to determine what they need to do for new updates). Believe it or not, reading through the source code (and even code comments, if you are lucky enough to have them in the source) does not always reveal the true intention of the programmer; the source and comments just state what the code actually does. However, reading through the unit testing logic does give you the developer's intentions, and therefore, allows you to build from there without having to worry about breaking anything the original developer expected to work.

3. *Helps you to distinguish among data, communication, and logic problems*: This is especially important in database applications, because there are a lot of layers of complexity going into the final application. When a program starts going awry, how do you know just where the problem is? Is it a specific type of data or data value that is causing a problem? Is it just a problem connecting or communicating with the database? Or is it really a problem in the programming logic that needs to be addressed? If you have done proper unit testing, you'll be able to quickly remove the question of it being your programming logic (the real time killer in debugging) and oftentimes even remove questions of it being data related. At a minimum, you'll be able to work in some quick additional tests to test a new and unique data value set. This gives you more time to focus on working through the other layers of potential problems.

4. *Simplifies the process of finding trouble areas in code*: Without solid unit testing, debugging becomes a time-consuming process of reading through your application line by line, tracing the process flow until the trouble spot is located—and you'll have to do this every time for each bug! With unit testing, you build your application flow into your testing, making it easier to access and execute a specific function or chunk of code for testing. So when trouble pops up, you can start at any number of key points within your application to narrow down the real issue (rather than starting from scratch each time).

5. *Helps document feature sets and how various parts of your code are related to (or rely on) one another*: One of the nice things that Ruby unit testing does is allow you to roll each unique test case into a group of tests, referred to as a test suite. Test suites can also be rolled into larger test suites and so on. This design gives you the power to test down to a specific line or section of code in a test case, up to the entire program flow from start to finish, and anywhere in between.

In the end, as a programmer, you are only as good as your programs, and your programs are only good if they work as expected. Writing good unit tests helps ensure your reputation as a quality programmer (and saves you a lot of headaches down the road).

Hopefully, we've done a good enough job selling you on the importance of unit testing. So let's get down to business and talk about how to actually write good unit tests for your Active Record applications.

How to Write Good Unit Tests

Unit testing in Ruby, as most Ruby tasks are, is actually very simple. It relies on the Unit::Test library maintained by Nathaniel Talbott and comes as a part of the core Ruby installation, so it should always be available for all your Ruby applications.

As its documentation states, "The general idea behind unit testing is that you write a test method that makes certain assertions about your code, working against a test fixture." So it only make sense that the key methods in your unit tests will be assertions, and the data that generally is used within your tests is defined in data sets called fixtures.

Before we go into detail about each of these, though, it's probably easiest to show a basic example, so we have something to work from throughout the rest of this chapter. Obviously, in order to write tests, we first need some code that we want to test against. Let's start with the following generic example, which does very little but return a few vanity messages and do some basic calculations:

```
# artest.rb ActiveRecord example code to test against
class Artest

  # set up our account class (ties to account table in DB)
  class Account < ActiveRecord::Base
  end

  # make our connection to the MS SQL Server database
  ActiveRecord::Base.establish_connection(:adapter => "sqlserver",
: host => "localhost",:database => "myapp", :username => "sa", :password => "",
 :port => "1433")
```

```
  def appreciate(account_id)
    # return a message of appreciation
    return Account.find(account_id.to_i).account_name + " is great!"
  rescue
    return nil
  end

  def insult(account_id)
    # return a mean message
    return Account.find(account_id.to_i).account_name + " is lame!"
  end

  def earnedmoney(account_id)
    # return the money this account has earned
    return Account.find(account_id.to_i).account_earned.to_f
  rescue
    return nil
  end
end
```

The really important thing to note about our test program is that we put in very generic exception handling. Basically, in the event of any type of error, our various methods are simply going to return a nil value. This means that the program will not halt within a given method even if we pass an invalid account_id or if some type of database communication error occurs.

■Note Without proper testing, handling exceptions by passing a nil value makes debugging very difficult, because it's very quietly handling potentially fatal errors. If, for example, a record was not found, the program would continue on and fail only when a future part of the program expected to deal with the results of a method and instead found a nil value. Most programmers who are believers in unit testing would not be very happy to see this type of exception handling in your code, but we use it here to help illustrate the benefits of good testing in identifying issues that your code may otherwise unintentionally mask.

Now that we have a very simple program, we can write our first test against it. Here, we will just do the most basic of tests—checking to see if the right message is returned for the account ID we pass in (this, of course, assumes we know the data that should be associated to the given ID, but we'll talk about that more in a minute).

```
# test_artest.rb Unit Test example
require 'artest'
require 'test/unit'

class TestArtest < Test::Unit::TestCase
  def test_simple
    temp = Artest.new
```

```
    assert_equal("Kevin Marshall is great!", temp.appreciate(1).to_s)
  end
end
```

Running this test will produce one of two results. If the first record in your account table does, in fact, have an `account_name` value of `"Kevin Marshall"`, you will have a successful test looking something like the following:

```
Loaded suite test_artest
Started
.
Finished in 0.765 seconds.

1 tests, 1 assertions, 0 failures, 0 errors
```

Otherwise, you should get an error message like the following one (here, the name `"Catherine Marshall"` was associated with the ID we passed instead of `"Kevin Marshall"`, as our test expected):

```
Loaded test suite test_artest
Started
F
Finished in 0.906 seconds.
1) Failure:
Test_simple(TestArtest) [test_artest.rb 6]:
<"Kevin Marshall is great!"> expected but was
<"Catherine Marshall is great!">.

1 tests, 1 assertions, 1 failures, 0 errors
```

This is a pretty generic example, which makes just one assertion, and it is unrealistic, because it relies heavily on the specific data found in our database for a given ID (something that is likely to change given its dynamic nature). Still, it should help you to see the basic concepts of unit testing with assertion methods, and we can build from here.

Before we dive into more realistic examples, though, let's take a minute to cover the various assertion methods we have available to us.

Assertions

As we mentioned, the basic concept of unit testing is to attempt various assertions against our code. These assertions should either pass or fail, that is, they will be either true or false, and as such, provide us with details about how our code is actually executing in real-world situations.

There are currently 18 assertion methods to choose from when writing our tests. The functionality of most is fairly obvious thanks to logical naming. Still, we'll show an example of each in an effort to be complete (and to show just how easy and painless unit testing is).

assert

The most basic of all assertion methods is simply the `assert` method, which evaluates a Boolean value. It will pass all cases except for Boolean values that are `false` or result in `nil`.

Note It's important to remember that all values in Ruby other than the specific `false` and `nil` values resolve to be Boolean values of `true`. This means that if you attempt to assert a string, it would always pass, because strings are `true` values in Ruby.

The `assert` method accepts two parameters, the Boolean value (or expression that returns a Boolean value) and an optional message you would like to display in the event that the assertion fails. In the following example, we rewrite our test case using just the `assert` method. The important thing to note is our use of the `==` operator, which makes our expression return a Boolean value:

```
# test_artest.rb Unit Test example
require 'artest'
require 'test/unit'

class TestArtest < Test::Unit::TestCase
  def test_simple
    temp = Artest.new
    assert ("Kevin Marshall is great!" == temp.appreciate(1).to_s)
  end
end
```

assert_nil

As the name implies, this assertion method checks if the given expression or value is equal to `nil`. This method also accepts two parameters, the expression (or value) to be evaluated and an optional message you would like display in the event that the assertion fails.

The important thing to remember with the `assert_nil` method is that your expressions or values are only being checked to see if they are `nil`—anything other than the value of `nil` will fail. In this example, we check the value returned for an account that is not currently in our database (this case does happen to return `nil`, and therefore passes, because the generic exception handling within our code is triggered when a record cannot be found).

```
# test_artest.rb Unit Test example
require 'artest'
require 'test/unit'

class TestArtest < Test::Unit::TestCase
  def test_simple
    temp = Artest.new
    assert_nil(temp.appreciate(100).to_s)
  end
end
```

assert_not_nil

The `assert_not_nil` method is simply the inverse to the `assert_nil` method; it checks that value is anything but `nil`.

Please note that anything that is not `nil` will pass the test, including an expression testing against the value of nil (because that would be a Boolean expression returning a value of `true` or `false`). In our example, we check that the return value is equal to `nil`.

As we mentioned, this specific example will always pass the test regardless of the value returned by the appreciate method call, because it's a Boolean value from the expression that is actually evaluated and therefore is either `true` or `false` (never `nil`).

```
# test_artest.rb Unit Test example
require 'artest'
require 'test/unit'

class TestArtest < Test::Unit::TestCase
  def test_simple
    temp = Artest.new
    assert_not_nil(temp.appreciate(1) == nil)
  end
end
```

assert_equal

This method simply checks the equality of the first two parameters passed. A third parameter can be optionally provided to display a specific message in the event that the assertion fails. This is probably one of the most common types of assertions you will make, "Is *X* really equal to *Y*?"

The key here is that the default failure message reports what both the expected *and* actual values were, based on the order in which you provide the parameter values (the order is expected first, actual second).

■**Note** It's also important to note that, like Ruby itself, case does matter when comparing strings. `"Kevin"` is not equal to `"kevin"`. When you want to ignore case in your tests, you should `upcase` or `downcase` both strings first.

We already showed an example of this method at the start of this section, but since it's so commonly used, we'll provide another quick one:

```
# test_artest.rb Unit Test example
require 'artest'
require 'test/unit'

class TestArtest < Test::Unit::TestCase
  def test_simple
    temp = Artest.new
```

```
      assert_equal(temp.appreciate(1).to_s, nil)
    end
end
```

assert_in_delta

Computers have always had a little bit of trouble accurately dealing with floating point values. This method allows you to test that a given floating point value is within a given range of another floating point value. It's up to you, as the application developer, to determine an acceptable range for floating point accuracy.

This method accepts four parameters: The first is the expected floating point value you want to test against. The second parameter is the actual floating point value you want to test. The third parameter is the floating point value that is the range for which the actual value may vary in relation to the expected value. Finally, the fourth parameter is an optional message to display in the event that the assertion fails.

Just remember, you are comparing numbers within a given range, so it's not strictly a comparison of two values (hence the word "delta" in the method name).

Our example checks if a given user is within five cents of the expected balance of $6.50:

```
# test_artest.rb Unit Test example
require 'artest'
require 'test/unit'

class TestArtest < Test::Unit::TestCase
  def test_simple
    temp = Artest.new
    assert_in_delta(6.50, temp.earnedmoney(1), 0.05)
  end
end
```

assert_raise

The assert_raise method is executed in block form and expects an exception of given type to be thrown during execution. It accepts any type of exception, or a list of exceptions, as its parameters to be passed into the block.

The important thing to remember with this method is that it only passes when the correct exceptions are thrown. That is, if the expected exception does not occur, this test will fail. Having your tests pass only when an exception is thrown is a little confusing at first, so hopefully, an example will clear up the concept.

Here, we expect our insult method to throw an ActiveRecord::RecordNotFound error, because we are using an account ID that is not in our data at this time (and we did not use any exception handling on the insult method within our application):

```
# test_artest.rb Unit Test example
require 'artest'
require 'test/unit'
```

```
class TestArtest < Test::Unit::TestCase
  def test_simple
    temp = Artest.new
    assert_raise ActiveRecord::RecordNotFound do
      temp.insult(1000)
    end
  end
end
```

Again, because a record for this account does not currently exist in our database, an ActiveRecord::RecordNotFound error is thrown. This, in turn, allows our test to actually complete successfully, that is, everything happened as we expected it to. We'll cover the various Active Record exception types later in this chapter.

assert_nothing_raised

This is simply the inverse to the assert_raised method; it checks that no exceptions are raised within the block.

The interesting thing here is that this assertion acts much like a transaction wrapper, where any exception within the block will cause the entire method to fail.

In our example, we take multiple steps, most of which will evaluate correctly, but because we include a call to a method with an ID that is not in our database, an ActiveRecord::RecordNotFound exception is thrown and, therefore, causes our entire assertion block to fail.

```
# test_artest.rb Unit Test example
require 'artest'
require 'test/unit'

class TestArtest < Test::Unit::TestCase
  def test_simple
    assert_nothing_raised do
      t = 100.0
      a = t * 50.0
      temp = Artest.new
      assert_in_delta(6.50, temp.earnedmoney(1000), 0.05)
    end
  end
end
```

assert_instance_of

This method just checks if a given object is an instance of a given class. Calling the assert_instance_of method is really the equivalent of calling the instance_of? Ruby method.

This method accepts three parameters: the class to which you want to assert an object belongs and instance of the object, and an optional message to display in the event that the assertion fails.

```
# test_artest.rb Unit Test example
require 'artest'
require 'test/unit'

class TestArtest < Test::Unit::TestCase
  def test_simple
    temp = Artest.new
    assert_instance_of String, temp.insult(1)
  end
end
```

assert_kind_of

This method checks if a given object is a kind of a given class. Invoking the assert_kind_of method is really the equivalent of calling the kind_of? Ruby method.

This method accepts three parameters: the class of which you want to assert an object is a kind, the object, and an optional message to display the in the event that the assertion fails.

```
# test_artest.rb Unit Test example
require 'artest'
require 'test/unit'

class TestArtest < Test::Unit::TestCase
  def test_simple
    temp = Artest.new
    assert_kind_of String, temp.insult(1)
  end
end
```

assert_respond_to

This method checks if a given object responds to a given method call. The assert_respond_to method accepts three parameters: the object, the method to which you want to assert that this object responds, and an optional message to display in the event that the assertion fails.

Please note that you can check that your object responds to user-defined methods as well as Ruby methods. In our example, we check that our result responds to the upcase method (which is a part of the String class) and that our object itself responds to our appreciate method.

```
# test_artest.rb Unit Test example
require 'artest'
require 'test/unit'

class TestArtest < Test::Unit::TestCase
  def test_simple
    temp = Artest.new
    assert_respond_to temp, :appreciate
    response = temp.appreciate(1)
    assert_responds_to response, :upcase
  end
end
```

assert_match

The asset_match method checks that a given regular expression has a match within a given string value. The method accepts three parameters: the regular expression, the string to apply the regular expression to, and an optional message to display in the event that the assertion fails.

The key thing to keep in mind is that this test simply checks that the regular expression has at least one match in the given string. In our example, we check that the username we expect is a part of the return value of our method call.

```
# test_artest.rb Unit Test example
require 'artest'
require 'test/unit'

class TestArtest < Test::Unit::TestCase
  def test_simple
    temp = Artest.new
    assert_match /Kevin/, temp.appreciate(1)
  end
end
```

assert_no_match

This method is simply the inverse of the assert_match method, the big difference being that the test will pass so long as the given regular expression cannot be found within the given string. Therefore, even though the regular expression match technically fails, the assertion passes.

In our example, we use a regular expression looking for digits; if any are found in our response, our test will fail.

```
# test_artest.rb Unit Test example
require 'artest'
require 'test/unit'

class TestArtest < Test::Unit::TestCase
  def test_simple
    temp = Artest.new
    assert_no_match /\d+/, temp.appreciate(1)
  end
end
```

assert_same

This method checks that two objects are actually equal and of the same instance. The method accepts three parameters: the expected instance, the actual instance, and an optional message to display in the event that the assertion fails.

Of special interest is that when comparing instances of objects, you are really comparing object_id values. When you create a new object, you generally assign it a new object_id, but when you use an operator such as the equal operator, you are simply assigning a reference to the existing object_id. Using the equal operator makes them the same.

In our example, our first assertion should pass, because both objects are associated to the same object_id. However, our second assertion will fail even though the actual value of the two objects is the same, because when we created our third object, it was associated to a new object_id by default.

```
# test_artest.rb Unit Test example
require 'artest'
require 'test/unit'

class TestArtest < Test::Unit::TestCase
  def test_simple
    obj1 = Artest.new
    obj2 = obj1
    obj3 = Artest.new
    assert_same obj1, obj2
    assert_same obj1, obj3
  end
end
```

assert_not_same

This method is simply the inverse of the assert_same method.

Again, the important thing to remember with this method is that you are really comparing object_id values. It's also important to remember that in this case, you are checking that the objects do not have the same object_id value—only when the IDs are different does the test actually pass.

In our example, our first assertion should pass, because our first and third objects are, in fact, associated to different object_id values. However, our second assertion will fail, because our first and second objects are associated to the same object_id value.

```
# test_artest.rb Unit Test example
require 'artest'
require 'test/unit'

class TestArtest < Test::Unit::TestCase
  def test_simple
    obj1 = Artest.new
    obj2 = obj1
    obj3 = Artest.new
    assert_same obj1, obj3
    assert_same obj1, obj2
  end
end
```

assert_operator

The assert_operator method compares two given objects using the given operator. It accomplishes that comparison via the Ruby send method. The method accepts four parameters: the first object you want to compare, the operator as a symbol that you want to use to compare the objects, the second object you want to compare, and an optional message to display in the event that the assertion fails.

The important thing to remember with this method is that you should pass the operator as a symbol (otherwise, you will get a syntax error). It's also important to remember that this method is the equivalent of running object1.send(operator, object2) and treating the Boolean response value as the assertion result.

In our example, we create two distinct objects and use assert_operator to check that the values of the objects are equal.

```
# test_artest.rb Unit Test example
require 'artest'
require 'test/unit'

class TestArtest < Test::Unit::TestCase
  def test_simple
    obj1 = Artest.new
    obj3 = Artest.new
     assert_operator obj1, :==, obj2
  end
end
```

assert_throws

This method checks that a given symbol is thrown during the execution of the block. The method accepts three parameters: the expected symbol, an optional message to display in the event that the assertion fails, and an optional proc to execute against.

Note We have not covered Ruby proc statements in this book, but they make up a very powerful feature set that is worth knowing about. If you are not familiar with them, you should refer to your Ruby documentation or one of the many good Ruby tutorial books available.

Pay close attention to the fact that the assertion will pass only if the expected symbol is thrown within the execution of the block. The throw can occur directly within your test (as it does in our generic example that follows) or anywhere within your code so long as that code is executed at some point within this assertion block.

In our example, we check for the instance of a specific string in our result and throw the :awesome symbol if it's found. In this example, if the string is anything but "Kevin is great!", the assertion will fail.

```
# test_artest.rb Unit Test example
require 'artest'
require 'test/unit'

class TestArtest < Test::Unit::TestCase
  def test_simple
    temp = Artest.new
```

```
      assert_throws :awesome do
        throw :awesome if temp.appreciate(1) == "Kevin is great!"
      end
   end
end
```

assert_send

The assert_send method checks that a send command executed with the given values returns a value of true. The method accepts two parameters: an array that contains the details of the send method and an optional message to display in the event that the assertion fails.

The important thing to remember is that the details of the send method are sent as an array. The array should contain the object that will receive the send call, the method you intend to execute for the object, and the arguments you are going to pass to the method.

In our example, we test that our temp object has a method called appreciate, which responds properly when passed a valid ID from our database (because we are returning nil when an ID is not found and nil equates to false in a Boolean comparison, if we pass an invalid ID via our send command our assertion will fail).

```
# test_artest.rb Unit Test example
require 'artest'
require 'test/unit'

class TestArtest < Test::Unit::TestCase
  def test_simple
    temp = Artest.new
    assert_send [temp, :appreciate, 1]
  end
end
```

flunk

The flunk method will always cause a failure within your test. The method accepts one optional parameter, which is a message to display at the point of failure.

The important thing to remember with the flunk method is that your test will stop execution at the first flunk method it encounters (unless you handle the exceptions within your tests). So you can use flunk as a break point for your tests and even assign a custom error message to help you narrow down especially tricky problems.

In our example, we use two different messages to help us quickly determine which bit of our test is really being executed:

```
# test_artest.rb Unit Test example
require 'artest'
require 'test/unit'

class TestArtest < Test::Unit::TestCase
  def test_simple
    temp = Artest.new
    if temp.appreciate(1).include?("Kevin")
```

```
      flunk "Kevin was found in our text!"
    else
      flunk "Kevin was not found in our text!"
    end
  end
end
```

So far, we've just been focusing on showing examples of each of the unit test assertion methods. While they are real tests that involve Active Record and our database and are great for helping you to understand each method, they aren't the best examples of the proper way to test against your Active Record programs.

The problem is that many of this chapter's previous examples rely heavily on the tester knowing what values are in the database at the time of testing and on those values remaining unchanged over time (or else our tests would have to be updated to match the data changes). While there are definitely situations where you want to do this type of testing, on another level, it defeats the whole idea of a database, that is, that your data should be somewhat dynamic. It's just unrealistic to think that your data values will not change as you develop, test, and mold your application, even if you have a dedicated test database, as is recommended for proper testing.

But here's the dilemma: you often need to know specific data values to be able to ensure your application logic is correct, but you also need a way to test various data values to see just what sort of data will cause your application to break down (which they all do eventually). So you don't want to spend time writing and rewriting tests with hard-coded values to test against, and you also don't want to continuously update your database test records manually just to test various situations. So what do you do?

The way Active Record approaches this common testing problem is to provide support for something called fixtures, and as it turns out, they solve this dilemma quite nicely.

Fixtures

Fixtures are basically a way of organizing and serving up data that you want to test against. It's sort of like hard-coding your database for testing situations, but doing it in a way that allows for quick and dynamic changes to your data set by simply switching out files or moving around lines within a file. On a basic level, fixtures take care of inserting records into our test database prior to executing our test code and removing these records from the database when our tests are finished. Fixtures also load the test data into memory in the form of a hash, giving us two ways to test and play with our data sets (either through the database or via the in-memory hash).

Fixtures come in three basic formats for our testing use: YAML, CSV, and single file. Before we break each of these formats down, though, let's look at just how fixtures can help us.

Benefits of Fixtures

Since fixtures are used in testing, we need to start with an example test case:

```
# test_artest.rb Unit Test example
require 'artest'
require 'test/unit'
```

```
class TestArtest < Test::Unit::TestCase
  def test_simple
    temp = Artest.new
    assert_equal("Kevin is great!", temp.appreciate(1))
  end
end
```

As we mentioned in our discussion on assertions, in this example, if our database does not contain an account record with an ID of 1 and a username of Kevin, our test will fail. So we need to set up a fixture that matches the data we expect and to tell our test case to use the fixture.

Telling our test case to use fixtures is actually a very simple two-step process:

1. Require the `active_record/fixtures` code. This step is not required when working within a Rails environment, but it won't hurt in any case and is essentially what one of the steps in the Rails environment setup is.

2. Call the `Fixtures.create_fixtures` method. This method accepts three parameters: the directory where your fixture files are located, the table names the fixtures relate to within your database, and the class names to associate with your tables (the class names parameter is optional). Additionally, if you want to create fixtures for more than one table at a time, you can pass in the table names as an array.

In the following example, we update our test case to use a fixture for our account data. Here, we are running our tests on a Windows client directly from the Ruby root (in this case `C:\ruby`) primarily to show that tests with fixtures can be run anywhere using this approach:

```
# test_artest.rb Unit Test example
require 'artest'
require 'test/unit'
require 'active_record/fixtures'
Fixtures.create_fixtures("c:\\ruby\\", :accounts)

class TestArtest < Test::Unit::TestCase
  def test_simple
    temp = Artest.new
    assert_equal("Kevin is great!", temp.appreciate(1))
  end
end
```

Before we can actually run this test (with any success), we need to make sure we create the fixture file that we are referring to. Our `create_fixtures` method call told our code to look for an `accounts.yml` file in our `C:\ruby` directory, so let's create that file now (we'll talk more about the YAML format in just a minute).

```
# Test data set in YAML format saved as account.yml
Kevin:
  id: 1
  username: Kevin
```

Now, we should be able to run our test successfully against our fixture data. To confirm that the tests really are using the data from your fixtures, go ahead and change the username value in your `account.yml` file and rerun the test. Your test should now fail, confirming that you are using fixtures.

Transaction Support with Fixtures

Fixtures also have support for transactions so that your test cases use the begin/rollback approach instead of the default insert/delete. Using transactions is, of course, a pretty simple task—you just set the `use_transactional_fixtures` method to a value of `true`, as shown in the following example:

```
# test_artest.rb Unit Test example
require 'artest'
require 'test/unit'
require 'active_record/fixtures'
Fixtures.create_fixtures("c:\\ruby\\", :accounts)

class TestArtest < Test::Unit::TestCase
  use_transactional_fixtures = true
  def test_simple
    temp = Artest.new
    assert_equal("Kevin is great!", temp.appreciate(1))
  end
end
```

However, there are two key situations in which you should avoid using transactions with your fixtures:

- Don't use transactions with fixtures if you are testing that a transaction is working within your application. This is because nested transactions do not commit until all parent transactions commit. Within tests, transactions are started in the `setup` method and committed in the `teardown` method.

- You can't use transactions if your database doesn't support transactions itself. All of the databases we've mentioned throughout this book, that is, all of the ones that Active Record currently has adaptors for, support transactions *except* MySQL ISAM. We recommended that, if you can, you switch from MySQL ISAM to MySQL InnoDB.

The last thing we need to mention is that with YAML and CSV fixture formats, you can actually use embedded Ruby (ERb). This is especially useful when you need to do testing against the volume of data you expect in your system.

In the following example, we create a fixture file that will result in 1,000 records being added for us to test with:

```
# Test data set in YAML format saved as account.yml
<% 1000.times do |i| %>Kevin<%= i %>:
  id: <%= i %>
  username: Kevin<%= i %>
<% end %>
```

Rails views, and most of the other Ruby web frameworks, also use ERb, so you are likely familiar with the syntax. If you want more information on ERb you should refer to http://www.ruby-doc.org/stdlib/libdoc/erb/rdoc.

Fixture Formats

Now that you know pretty much all there is to know about unit testing assertion methods and the basics of how to actually use fixtures, the last bit we need to cover is the specific details of formatting your fixture files. As we mentioned, there are three basic formats that you can use for defining fixtures: YAML, CSV, or single file. Let's take a look at each of these now.

YAML

According to http://www.yaml.org, YAML is a "machine parsable data serialization format designed for human readability and interaction with scripting languages." It's the preferred default for fixtures with frameworks like Ruby on Rails and is also the format that most Active Record developers use.

YAML fixtures are all stored in one file per model (or rather, one file per database table). Each file should be located in the directory set by the TestCase.fixture_path method (or in the create_fixtures method, as we described previously). Each file should also have the .yml extension. Within the file, each record you want in your data should have a unique name, and each field you for which want to represent data should be indented and represented in the key: value format.

Our previous example fixture files were all in YAML format, but we'll show one more in the next example, with two records this time, to be thorough:

```
# Test data set in YAML format saved as account.yml
Kevin:
  id: 1
  username: Kevin
Catherine:
  id: 2
  username: Catherine
```

The important thing to note with this format is that the records are really unordered (though the use of IDs in the preceding example helps to make this irrelevant in our examples). If order will matter in your testing, you should use the Ordered Mapping Language-Independent (omap) Type for YAML. You can learn more about the omap type and the entire YAML syntax at http://www.yaml.org.

CSV

CSV stands for "comma separated value" and is one of the oldest and historically most commonly used data exchange formats. So it's probably no surprise that you can use that format with Active Record fixtures as well.

Like YAML fixtures, CSV fixtures are all stored in one file per model (or rather, one file per database table). Each file should be located in the directory set by the TestCase.fixture_path method (or in the create_fixtures method, as we described previously). Each file should also have the .csv extension. Within the file, the first line should be a comma separated list of field names, and each additional line should be the actual data, with one record per line.

Since the comma is a special character in the CSV format, you must wrap any data that contains a comma inside of double quotes. Additionally, since the double quotes are used to wrap fields that contain commas, you must also escape any instances of double quotes in your data with another double quote.

In our example, we show three records in our CSV format applying these various rules:

```
# Test data set in CSV format saved as account.csv
id, username
1,Kevin
2,"Marshall, Catherine"
3,"Married ""with children"""
```

The most important thing to remember when working with CSV fixtures is that they will be loaded only if a YAML format cannot first be found. The other thing to note is that, within the CSV format, you have no way of naming each record. Fixture names are, instead, automatically generated from the class name of the fixture file with an incrementing number appended. In our preceding example, we would have accounts_1, accounts_2, and accounts_3 (which only match the record IDs by coincidence).

While YAML is the recommended format because of human readability, many programs such as Microsoft Excel (and all databases that I know of) provide tools to export data in the CSV format. This might save you quite a bit of time and energy if you already have your test data stored in one of these types of applications.

Single File

Single-file fixtures are stored in a directory named after the model (or rather, in a directory named after the database table). The directory should be located in the directory set by the TestCase.fixture_path method (or in the create_fixtures method, as we described previously). Each record is a separate file, and data within the file is presented in key => value format. The files do not require an extension, but you may use the .txt extension if you like.

■Note The single-file format has officially been deprecated in favor of the YAML and CSV formats, so we don't recommend using it. Still, we'll cover the basic idea just in case you run into it while working with legacy applications.

In the following example, we show two files that will equate to two records in our database. The files in this example are located in C:\ruby\accounts:

```
# Test data record in Single File format saved as kevin.txt
id => 1
username => Kevin
```

```
# Test data record in Single File format saved as catherine.txt
id => 2
username => Marshall, Catherine
```

Again, we don't recommend using the single-file format, because it can quickly become a time-consuming task just managing the files involved (and really, with this format, you aren't saving much time as compared to directly doing the work in your database). I think you can see that the YAML or CSV formats are much more friendly choices.

Wrapping It All Up

Believe it or not we have covered only the basics of unit testing. There are a lot more details and scenarios we could go into, as they relate to doing proper testing for your applications (it could probably fill a book in and of itself), but again, that is outside of the scope of this book. Instead, it's our hope that we've given you enough information to get your feet wet and feel comfortable actually writing and using Ruby unit tests with your Active Record programs.

Of course, writing and running unit tests is really only part of the whole testing process. You still need to actually evaluate the results of the tests you run, and to do that, you need to have a thorough understanding of Active Record exceptions. So let's turn our focus to those now.

Active Record Errors and Exceptions

Working with a database means adding at least one additional layer of application complexity, and each layer of complexity, of course, means more potential for errors and exceptions to occur. Sadly, when it comes to having to deal with errors and exceptions Active Record is, uh, no exception (sorry about the horrible pun).

Since Ruby is a pure object-based language, the approach that Active Record wisely took with exception handling was to simply use inheritance, so all of the default error classes that Active Record defines inherit from the general `ActiveRecordError` class. The `ActiveRecordError` class itself inherits from Ruby's `StandardError` class. All of this basically means that Active Record errors and exceptions are simply handled in the same way any other Ruby error is; that is, they can be raised by a `raise` clause and caught by a `rescue` clause.

Perhaps, rather than focusing on how straightforwardly Active Record handles errors, a more important thing to consider is how to prevent errors from occurring altogether. To do that, we need to decipher each error Active Record can throw, what it means when it does throw an error, and what really causes each to occur. Once we know the answers to these questions, perhaps we can update our applications to avoid the exceptions altogether, or at least eliminate them in as many cases as reasonably possible (rather than simply handling them).

Active Record Error Methods

By default, the Active Record `Base` class defines 17 Active Record error types. You can override each of these error types as needed within your application, and each can be caught and dealt with via the Ruby `rescue` clause. As we take a look at the details of each class, we'll attempt to explain when each is raised, why it is raised, and what you can do to try to avoid the error in the future.

ActiveRecordError

This is the generic Active Record error class and the superclass of all other errors that might be raised by ActiveRecord. It's actually very rare that your code would directly raise this error without you explicitly defining the situation and raising the error yourself. The reason is that within the Active Record source code, the ActiveRecordError is raised only in a unique situation of hierarchy traversal where a class for which you are attempting to find the base does not inherit from ActiveRecord itself. Because of Ruby's single-class inheritance rules, this situation is almost impossible to produce and, therefore, very uncommon.

In the following example, to easily show the details of the exception, we raise the exception ourselves when the record with an ID of 1 has the username of "Kevin".

```
# program that throws a general ActiveRecordError
require 'rubygems'
require_gem 'activerecord'

ActiveRecord::Base.establish_connection(:adapter => "sqlserver",
:host => "mydbhost.com", :database => "test", :username => "sa", :password => "")

class Account < ActiveRecord::Base
end

begin
  raise ActiveRecord::ActiveRecordError if Account.find(1).username == "Kevin"
rescue ActiveRecordError => e
  puts "ActiveRecordError thrown: #{e}"
end
```

SubclassNotFound

This error is related to single-table inheritance and improper reference to a subclass from within your data.

Within ActiveRecord, you can define a subclass that inherits from an ActiveRecord::Base class. This class association is stored, within the database in the inherited Active Record superclass table, in a field called type by default (the field you defined with the Base.inheritance_column method overrides this). If, for some reason, you have data in this field that does not relate to a defined subclass within your program, you will generate the SubclassNotFound error.

In the following example, we assume that we have the following data within our database:

```
# data stored in our database (represented here in CSV format to save space)
id,username,type
1,Kevin,Husband
2,Catherine,Wife
```

And now, when we attempt to work with the second record in our data within our ActiveRecord application, we will actually raise a SubclassNotFound error, because we have no defined Wife subclass of Account:

```
# program that throws SubclassNotFound
require 'rubygems'
require_gem 'activerecord'

ActiveRecord::Base.establish_connection(:adapter => "sqlserver",
:host => "mydbhost.com", :database => "test", :username => "sa", :password => "")

class Account < ActiveRecord::Base
end

class Husband < Account
end

begin
  temp = Account.find(2)
  puts temp.inspect
rescue  ActiveRecord::SubclassNotFound => e
  puts "SubclassNotFound: #{e}"
end
```

Also, it should be pointed out that when you do correctly associate the subclass within your data, an instance of the subclass (and not the superclass) is returned. For example, if we changed the preceding code to find the data associated with ID 1, we would see that a Husband object was correctly returned, even though we did the find using the Account class.

For more information about single-table inheritance, you should investigate Martin Fowler's work at http://www.martinfowler.com/eaaCatalog/singleTableInheritance.html.

AssociationTypeMismatch

As you probably expect, this error has to do with improperly associating Active Record objects—if you attempt to assign an object to an association that is not inferred by Active Record (or specifically set with the class_name attribute of the association methods), you will generate an AssociationTypeMismatch error.

In the following example, we raise an AssociationTypeMismatch error when we attempt to add a dog object to our pet collection, because our pet collection only has_many cats; that is, there is no association to the Dog class:

```
# program to raise an AssociationTypeMismatch error
require 'rubygems'
require 'activerecord'

ActiveRecord::Base.establish_connection(:adapter => "sqlserver",
:host => "mydbhost.com", :database => "test", :username => "sa", :password => "")

class Pet < ActiveRecord::Base
  has_many :cats
end
```

```
class Cat < ActiveRecord::Base
  belongs_to :pet
end

class Dog
  attr_accessor :name
end

temp = Pet.find(1)
p1 = Dog.new
p1.name = "Abby"
temp << p1 # => raises the AssociationTypeMismatch error
```

SerializationTypeMismatch

This error is raised when you attempt to assign an object of the wrong type into a field that is to be serialized within the database.

The following example generates a SerializationTypeMismatch error, because we state that data in our yamldata field should be of Array type, but within our actual program, we attempt to assign a Hash instead.

```
# program that raises a SerializationTypeMismatch error
require 'rubygems'
reuiqre 'activerecord'

ActiveRecord::Base.establish_connection(:adapter => "sqlserver",
:host => "mydbhost.com", :database => "test", :username => "sa", :password => "")

class Account < ActiveRecord::Base
  serialize :yamldata, Array
end

temp = Account.find(1)
temp.yamldata = {:problem => "expecting Array, not Hash"}
```

AdapterNotSpecified

This error is raised when you omit the :adapter parameter in your database connection statement (or YAML file).

In the following example, we forget to include the :adapter => "sqlserver" bit, causing the AdapterNotSpecified error to be raised:

```
# program that raises a AdapterNotSpecified error
require 'rubygems'
reuiqre 'activerecord'

ActiveRecord::Base.establish_connection(:host => "mydbhost.com",
:database => "test", :username => "sa", :password => "")
```

AdapterNotFound

Similar to the AdapterNotSpecified, this error is raised when you incorrectly specify an adapter value; that is, you either misspell your adapter or list one that your Active Record library does not currently support.

In the following example, we raise the AdapterNotFound error by misspelling the sqlserver value (as slqserver):

```
# program that raises a AdapterNotFound error
require 'rubygems'
reuiqre 'activerecord'

ActiveRecord::Base.establish_connection(:adapter => "slqserver",
:host => "mydbhost.com", :database => "test", :username => "sa", :password => "")
```

ConnectionNotEstablished

This error is raised when you attempt to perform Active Record actions, like executing a find statement, before you have actually made a connection to your database (via the establish_ connection method).

In the following example, we raise the ConnectionNotEstablished error when we attempt to find the first account, because we have not yet made the actual connection to the database:

```
# program that raises a ConnectionNotEstablished error
require 'rubygems'
reuiqre 'activerecord'

class Account < ActiveRecord::Base
end

temp = Account.find(1)
```

Of special note is that the error does not actually get raised until you attempt to execute a CRUD operation against the database; defining your classes and associations does not cause a problem. This makes sense when you consider the fact that Ruby does not really create an object from a class until the class is actually referenced during the execution of the program.

ConnectionFailed

This error is generally raised when there are problems between the communication of the machine from which you are running your code and the machine that your database is running on (assuming they are different).

This type of error is raised because of issues outside of your code, so we cannot show you an example that creates this error. In our experience, this error is most common when the connection between your application machine and your database machine is lost while your application is running. Generally, after repairing the connection between the machines, you can simply restart your application, and things will once again be fine.

RecordNotFound

This error is raised when a find method cannot find any results within the database.

It's important to note that this error is raised only when doing find operations in association with ID values, that is, only the simple find method. Using find_by_sql or a version of dynamic finders like find_by_username will not raise this error but instead simply return a nil object. Additionally, if you pass a list of IDs to your find method and any one of those IDs does not exist in the database, a RecordNotFound error will be raised.

In the following example, we raise RecordNotFound, because our find method call includes an ID that does not exist within our dataset (we have no record with an ID of 0):

```ruby
# program that raises a RecordNotFound error
require 'rubygems'
reuiqre 'activerecord'

ActiveRecord::Base.establish_connection(:adapter => "sqlserver",
:host => "mydbhost.com", :database => "test", :username => "sa", :password => "")

class Account < ActiveRecord::Base
end

temp = Account.find(1,0)
```

RecordNotSaved

This error is raised if a record could not be saved into the database.

A RecordNotSaved error is generally related to table-locking issues and is, in fact, only called when you are using the save! or update_attributes! methods. The regular save and update_attributes methods will not raise this error if they fail, they will simply not save the data within the database!

What's important to keep in mind is that, even if this error is raised, your Ruby object itself (the object that is tied to your database) was likely updated, so now, your object attributes potentially differ from those of your database values. We covered this situation in more detail within our discussion of data validations previously.

Since this error is primarily raised because of locking issues, it's a bit difficult to show a reliable example you can duplicate. The basic idea would be if you were attempting to do an update to something like a page-count field without using transactions but were at least using the proper save! method. In the event that two or more users hit the update code at the exact same time, one would likely get the RecordNotSaved error rather than both getting the wrong number.

StatementInvalid

This error is raised when the SQL statement that is eventually passed to your database engine by Active Record is incorrect or has syntax errors. The error generally provides specific details about what part of the SQL statement is thought to be invalid for your database.

In the following example, we raise a StatementInvalid error with our find_by_sql method, because our account table has no field named Kevin (our SQL query has the field name and value swapped in the where clause).

```
# program that raises a StatementInvalid error
require 'rubygems'
reuiqre 'activerecord'

ActiveRecord::Base.establish_connection(:adapter => "sqlserver",
:host => "mydbhost.com", :database => "test", :username => "sa", :password => "")

class Account < ActiveRecord::Base
end

temp = Account.find_by_sql("select * from accounts where kevin = 'username'")
```

This should raise an error that looks something like the following (note the first line that tells us `Invalid column name 'kevin'`):

```
/usr/lib/ruby/gems/1.8/gems/activerecord-1.15.3/lib/active_record/
connection_adapters/abstract_adapter.rb:128:in `log':
DBI::DatabaseError: S0022 (207)
[Actual][SQL Server] Invalid column name 'kevin'.: select * from accounts where
kevin = 'username' (ActiveRecord::StatementInvalid)

from /usr/lib/ruby/gems/1.8/
gems/activerecord-1.15.3/lib/active_record/
connection_adapters/sqlserver_adapter.rb:318:in `execute'

from /usr/lib/ruby/gems/1.8/
gems/activerecord-1.15.3/lib/active_record/
connection_adapters/sqlserver_adapter.rb:502:in `select'

from
/usr/lib/ruby/gems/1.8/
gems/activerecord-1.15.3/lib/active_record/
connection_adapters/abstract/database_statements.rb:7:in
`select_all'

from /usr/lib/ruby/gems/1.8/
gems/activerecord-1.15.3/lib/active_record/base.rb:427:in
`find_by_sql' from artest.rb:10
```

PreparedStatementInvalid

This error is raised when you have not provided the correct bind variables for a prepared statement. Prepared statements are often used as a defense against SQL injection attacks (we talk about SQL injection attacks in Chapter 2 and again in Chapter 8) as well as for improving performance with certain compiled languages, such as Java. The most common problem is forgetting to supply the correct number of values for your prepared statement. In the following example, our prepared statement expects a username and password to be supplied, but we only provide a username ("Kevin"), thereby raising a `PreparedStatementInvalid` error.

```
# program that raises a PreparedStatementInvalid error
require 'rubygems'
reuiqre 'activerecord'

ActiveRecord::Base.establish_connection(:adapter => "sqlserver",
:host => "mydbhost.com", :database => "test", :username => "sa", :password => "")

class Account < ActiveRecord::Base
end

temp = Account.find(:first,
  :conditions => ["username = ? and password = ?", "kevin"])
```

StaleObjectError

If you are using optimistic locking (we cover locking in detail in Chapter 2) and you create
more than one object from a given database record, when you save changes to one of the
in-memory objects to the database, the second object will be considered stale. If you then
attempt to save changes to the second object, you will raise a StaleObjectError. An example
helps to make this much clearer.

In our example, we first create two objects from the same record within our database.
Next, we make and save changes to one of the objects (t1) without problems. Finally, when we
attempt to save changes made to the second object (t2), we raise a StaleObjectError.

```
# program that raises a StaleObjectError error
require 'rubygems'
reuiqre 'activerecord'

ActiveRecord::Base.establish_connection(:adapter => "sqlserver",
:host => "mydbhost.com", :database => "test", :username => "sa", :password => "")

class Account < ActiveRecord::Base
end

t1 = Account.find(1)
t2 = Account.find(1)

t1.username = 'Kevin Marshall'
t1.save

t2.username = 'Kevin Nelson Marshall'
t2.save
```

Generally, this type of error results from general programming logic errors, and to handle
them, you will most likely need to rethink the solution to the problem you are really attempting to solve. In our example, we probably don't want to create two objects and instead just
update the first object twice, making it incremental as we expected.

It's also important to remember that optimistic locking relies on the existence of a lock_
version field within your database with a default zero integer value. When you encounter this
type of error, it will be up to you to rework your solution, roll back your code, or otherwise
solve the stale state issue.

ConfigurationError

This error is raised when you attempt to access an association that was either not defined or
does not support the combination of parameters you are attempting to use (for example, you
cannot call a join using both the limit and offset parameters).

In the following example, we attempt to have our find method include the friend association.
However, we have defined that association within our class, so we raise a ConfigurationError.

```
# program that raises a ConfigurationError error
require 'rubygems'
reuiqre 'activerecord'

ActiveRecord::Base.establish_connection(:adapter => "sqlserver",
:host => "mydbhost.com", :database => "test", :username => "sa", :password => "")

class Account < ActiveRecord::Base
end

temp = Account.find(1, :include => :friends)
```

ReadOnlyRecord

This error is raised when you attempt to create or save a record to the database that you have
only read access to. If you encounter this error, you will most likely need to update your account
rights within your database (or update your connection values to use an account with proper
privileges).

AttributeAssignmentError

The AttributeAssignmentError error is raised while doing assignments en masse through the
attributes method.

The most common cause of this error is related to attempting to assign date values in
a Ruby on Rails application using something like the ActionView::Helpers::DateHelper#date_
select helper method. Here's what really happens in a situation like that: if a user has provided
an invalid date (like June 31, 2007), the helper method attempts to use the values to create a date
object (from within ActiveRecord). The Ruby Date.new method throws an error, and that bubbles
up to the Active Record error level, eventually raising an AttributeAssignmentError.

The fix for these type of errors is generally not ActiveRecord-code-based, but rather something that should be dealt with in your business logic (controller code) or at a specific data-value
level (i.e., scrub the data within your database).

MultiparameterAssignmentErrors

This error is raised in the same way as the `AttributeAssignmentError` and is really just a collection of those errors.

Preparing for Problems

Handling exceptions is really about preparing for potential problems. We've now covered the details of the 17 basic error classes that Active Record defines. We've shown examples of how and why each type of error is raised, and hopefully, we've given you enough information to help you avoid most of them in your applications.

In the end, dealing with errors and exceptions is just something every database application has to be prepared to do. Ruby's raise and rescue structure makes it easy to do this, but it's still up to you to implement the proper rescue actions for each of the errors. In many cases, using good unit tests, as shown in the first section of this chapter, should help you to identify the majority of these errors and help you to correct them so that they are very unlikely to occur in your production applications.

Still, there are times when even the best of unit tests and elegant exception handling aren't enough. In those cases, you've got to turn to a few additional tricks.

Debugging Tips and Tricks

Outside of the communication and log issues we've attempted to prepare ourselves to debug and handle in the preceding sections, there is one other large area of concern for most database applications—that is the issue of scale. How well will your code scale as its user base increases and your application becomes more and more popular? Do you know when it will be time to add more hardware or focus on rewriting some business logic to improve performance? What and where are the bottlenecks in your current code?

These are all issues that you should be testing for sooner rather than later (if you intend to keep your sanity throughout your career). But these are also issues that the tests we've previously talked about don't handle very well. They are not issues that reveal themselves easily; these issues can't be pinpointed with "yes, I work" statements, or even "I don't work this way" statements, as unit tests and exceptions can. No, these problems are going to require a little more manual effort, and few more tricks that we'll talk about now.

Active Record and Logging

When it comes to scaling, probably the most important thing to keep an eye on is how much activity is really going on. In other words, "What's really happening when people use my application?" And logging key parts of your application is the simplest way to help answer that question.

The great thing about logging is that you have complete control over what information you want to see. You can pick the critical spots in your code to log activity, and you can define just what information you want to log at those points.

If you are using Active Record through Rails, logging will already be set up and quietly running in the background for key events. The logs themselves will be stored in your `railsroot/log` directory. But even if you are just writing stand-alone Active Record programs (like we have been throughout this book), you can still take advantage of the power of logging. You just need to do a few simple configuration steps:

1. *Define a* Logger *object.* Log4r is a Ruby logging library that comes standard with Ruby and is, therefore, available to all Ruby applications. Creating an instance of a logger is as simple as adding the following line of code:

```
mylog = Logger.new('mylog.txt')
```

In the preceding example, we told the logger to record details to a file called mylog.txt, but we could just as easily have it dump output to STDOUT. Doing that would cause the log details to be reported to the console, as we ran our programs from a command line.

2. *Associate your* Logger *object to your Active Record* Base *class.* Now that we have an instance of a Logger object, we just need to tell the Active Record Base class to use that for logging all activity. We do that with a simple assignment statement like the following:

```
ActiveRecord::Base.logger = mylog
```

3. *Set the logging level, and start logging your key events.* The last step to proper logging is to set the logging level you want your application to use and then, of course, to actually denote what special situations to log.

Breaking down a simple example is probably the best way to show just how powerful and helpful logging can be in your debugging (and code improvement) process. The following example is a complete Active Record program that will manually log a couple of small events we define as well as some background things that we may not have even realized were going on (until we looked at the logs):

```
# Program to show ActiveRecord Logging in Action. (artest.rb)
require 'rubygems'
require_gem 'activerecord'

class Account < ActiveRecord::Base
  set_table_name "accounts"
  has_many :comments
end

class Comment < ActiveRecord::Base
  set_table_name "comments"
  belongs_to :account
end

ActiveRecord::Base.establish_connection(:adapter => "sqlserver",
:host => "mydbhost.com", :database => "test", :username => "sa", :password => "")

mylog = Logger.new('mylog.txt')
ActiveRecord::Base.logger = mylog

temp = Account.find(1)
mylog.info("found a record with username: #{temp.username}")
```

```
mylog.info("About to show comments")
temp.comments.each do |rec|
  puts "#{temp.username} said #{rec.subject}"
end
mylog.info("Done showing comments")
```

Assuming we have some comments in our database for the given user, the following is an example of the output displayed at the command line when we run this program:

```
FaliconMobileMac:~ falicon$ ruby artest.rb
Kevin said Hi.
Kevin said Good Bye
```

While that's nothing too exciting, it had an interesting side affect. Within the directory where you ran the code, you should now see a mylog.txt file. Upon examining that file, you should see something like the following:

```
[4;36;1mAccount Columns (0.069632) [0m     [0;1m
 SELECT
 cols.COLUMN_NAME as ColName,
 cols.COLUMN_DEFAULT as DefaultValue,
 cols.NUMERIC_SCALE as numeric_scale,
 cols.NUMERIC_PRECISION as numeric_precision,
 cols.DATA_TYPE as ColType,
 cols.IS_NULLABLE As IsNullable,
 COL_LENGTH(cols.TABLE_NAME, cols.COLUMN_NAME) as Length,
 COLUMNPROPERTY(OBJECT_ID(cols.TABLE_NAME),
 cols.COLUMN_NAME, 'IsIdentity') as IsIdentity,
 cols.NUMERIC_SCALE as Scale
 FROM INFORMATION_SCHEMA.COLUMNS cols
 WHERE cols.TABLE_NAME = 'accounts'
  [0m
   [4;35;1mSQL (0.079272) [0m     [0m
 SELECT
 cols.COLUMN_NAME as ColName,
 cols.COLUMN_DEFAULT as DefaultValue,
 cols.NUMERIC_SCALE as numeric_scale,
 cols.NUMERIC_PRECISION as numeric_precision,
 cols.DATA_TYPE as ColType,
 cols.IS_NULLABLE As IsNullable,
 COL_LENGTH(cols.TABLE_NAME, cols.COLUMN_NAME) as Length,
 COLUMNPROPERTY(OBJECT_ID(cols.TABLE_NAME),
 cols.COLUMN_NAME, 'IsIdentity') as IsIdentity,
 cols.NUMERIC_SCALE as Scale
 FROM INFORMATION_SCHEMA.COLUMNS cols
 WHERE cols.TABLE_NAME = 'accounts'
  [0m
   [4;36;1mSQL (0.071729) [0m     [0;1m
SELECT * FROM accounts WHERE (accounts.[id] = 1)  [0m
```

```
found a record with username: Kevin
About to show comments
   [4;35;1mSQL (0.193857) [0m    [0m
SELECT
cols.COLUMN_NAME as ColName,
cols.COLUMN_DEFAULT as DefaultValue,
cols.NUMERIC_SCALE as numeric_scale,
cols.NUMERIC_PRECISION as numeric_precision,
cols.DATA_TYPE as ColType,
cols.IS_NULLABLE As IsNullable,
COL_LENGTH(cols.TABLE_NAME, cols.COLUMN_NAME) as Length,
COLUMNPROPERTY(OBJECT_ID(cols.TABLE_NAME),
cols.COLUMN_NAME, 'IsIdentity') as IsIdentity,
cols.NUMERIC_SCALE as Scale
FROM INFORMATION_SCHEMA.COLUMNS cols
WHERE cols.TABLE_NAME = 'comments'
 [0m
   [4;36;1mSQL (0.066720) [0m    [0;1m
SELECT * FROM comments WHERE (comments.account_id = 1)  [0m
   [4;35;1mComment Columns (0.063691) [0m    [0m
SELECT
cols.COLUMN_NAME as ColName,
cols.COLUMN_DEFAULT as DefaultValue,
cols.NUMERIC_SCALE as numeric_scale,
cols.NUMERIC_PRECISION as numeric_precision,
cols.DATA_TYPE as ColType,
cols.IS_NULLABLE As IsNullable,
COL_LENGTH(cols.TABLE_NAME, cols.COLUMN_NAME) as Length,
COLUMNPROPERTY(OBJECT_ID(cols.TABLE_NAME),
cols.COLUMN_NAME, 'IsIdentity') as IsIdentity,
cols.NUMERIC_SCALE as Scale
FROM INFORMATION_SCHEMA.COLUMNS cols
WHERE cols.TABLE_NAME = 'comments'
 [0m
Done showing comments
```

Wow, that's a lot of data for just the simple little program we built and ran! Let's take a minute to dissect what's really in there.

■**Note** The example we walk through in this section is connecting to a SQL Server database and therefore uses the SQL Server adapter. Each adapter has a somewhat unique set of instructions that it performs based on the various things the database engine supports. Many of these instructions or actions are then logged in the log file for review. If you are using a different database engine to run these examples, the queries in your log may look slightly different. However, the overall concepts we show here should be the same across all implementations and, therefore, still useful.

We started our actual program by calling the Account.find method, which our log reveals to in turn to have caused Active Record to execute a number of queries to the database—three in this example, to be exact. The first two appear to be gathering information about the columns available within the table we are querying:

```
SELECT
 cols.COLUMN_NAME as ColName,
 cols.COLUMN_DEFAULT as DefaultValue,
 cols.NUMERIC_SCALE as numeric_scale,
 cols.NUMERIC_PRECISION as numeric_precision,
 cols.DATA_TYPE as ColType,
 cols.IS_NULLABLE As IsNullable,
 COL_LENGTH(cols.TABLE_NAME, cols.COLUMN_NAME) as Length,
 COLUMNPROPERTY(OBJECT_ID(cols.TABLE_NAME),
 cols.COLUMN_NAME, 'IsIdentity') as IsIdentity,
 cols.NUMERIC_SCALE as Scale
FROM INFORMATION_SCHEMA.COLUMNS cols
WHERE cols.TABLE_NAME = 'accounts'
 [0m
   [4;35;1mSQL (0.079272) [0m    [0m
SELECT
 cols.COLUMN_NAME as ColName,
 cols.COLUMN_DEFAULT as DefaultValue,
 cols.NUMERIC_SCALE as numeric_scale,
 cols.NUMERIC_PRECISION as numeric_precision,
 cols.DATA_TYPE as ColType,
 cols.IS_NULLABLE As IsNullable,
 COL_LENGTH(cols.TABLE_NAME, cols.COLUMN_NAME) as Length,
 COLUMNPROPERTY(OBJECT_ID(cols.TABLE_NAME),
cols.COLUMN_NAME, 'IsIdentity') as IsIdentity,
 cols.NUMERIC_SCALE as Scale
 FROM INFORMATION_SCHEMA.COLUMNS cols
 WHERE cols.TABLE_NAME = 'accounts'
```

If we search through the Active Record source code, we find that this query is, in fact, unique to the SQL Server adapter (though each adaptor does have its own query to gather column information and that would be executed here in your log as well).

Active Record uses this information to populate the various instance and class variables, such as the columns collection. It also uses the information from these queries to determine what attributes a given object should have.

The next thing we see in our log is the execution of the actual query the find method built, as well as the details we said to manually log:

```
[4;36;1mSQL (0.071729)[0m   [0;1mSELECT * FROM accounts WHERE (accounts.[id] = 1)
[0m
found a record with username: Kevin
```

The interesting thing about the preceding result is that it shows you both the exact query that was executed and the time required to execute that SQL statement. As your application grows and performance becomes a concern, you may want to use this as a way to compare performance between using the default find methods and executing the SQL directly via find_by_sql methods or other less friendly ways.

■**Note** It's important to note that much of Active Record was designed to make life easier on developers trying to do standard or normal things. The more you adhere to the standard, the more you can benefit from Active Record features. However, one of the things that you are agreeing to give up a little of to gain some of these time-saving development features is performance. As your application grows and performance becomes more and more important, you will likely find yourself having to take back some of those trade-offs and work a little harder to get slighter better performance. Still, using things like logs allows us to make this process much easier, as we use the generated SQL within our logs as a guide or starting point to rewriting our own, hopefully faster, custom SQL statements.

The other thing to note in the preceding SQL query section of our file is the line we manually inserted stating that a record was, indeed, found. More important than the fact that a record was found (since we knew it would be from our unit testing earlier) is the location of line within the file. Using manual logging like this turns out to be a great way to narrow down just when and where various database operations and programming logic is occurring. As you get more comfortable with logging as whole, you can start to add your own timers as well, so that you will not only know when and where but also how long various sections of code take to execute.

The final section of our log shows us the results of accessing data through our Comments association. We bookended this information with manual comments so that we could see what really happens when we access an association though a has_many relationship.

Once again, you see the columns queries being executed (because it's the first time we accessed the comments table), and of special interest is the query that Active Record built and executed to access our children records.

```
[4;36;1mSQL (0.066720) [0m    [0;1mSELECT * FROM comments WHERE
(comments.account_id = 1)  [0m
```

When performance becomes an issue within our application, we can use all of this information to determine what SQL code could be improved, updated, or simply replaced. We will, however, leave those decisions and the details of that work for you to investigate as you see fit.

Our logging example is admittedly very simplistic. There is a lot more you can, and probably should, do with logging when it comes to debugging and tuning your Active Record applications. The logging features inherited from Ruby's Logger class provide a number of additional settings and methods that are outside of the scope of this book.

For example, we simply used the Active Record default logging level of Logger::DEBUG for our examples, which shows you lots of useful information about your queries and other activities. There are a number of other log levels that you can work through as you hit different stages and focus on different parts of your overall testing process.

For more information on Ruby logging, you should visit http://www.ruby-doc.org/core/classes/Logger.html.

Active Record Benchmarking

The final tip we need to mention when debugging and tuning your Active Record applications is the idea of benchmarking. Benchmarking is basically the process of grouping some actions or statements together (like transactions) and timing how long it takes to execute the set.

Active Record provides benchmarking through a method aptly named benchmark, which, in association with a Logger object, makes benchmarking very simple for us. Let's take a quick look at the details of the benchmark method.

The benchmark method accepts three parameters: the message to output in the log along with the benchmark result time, the log level to record benchmarks at, and whether or not to use silence mode.

If you set the log level to something other than that of the current Logger log level, the benchmark will not be logged. This makes it easy to include benchmarking in production code without taking the performance hit of actually executing benchmarks all the time.

Additionally, if you set the use_silence parameter to false, the benchmark will log all of the statements within the benchmark.

The follow example shows our basic program using a benchmark and logging data to our command line terminal:

```ruby
# test program to show benchmark in action
require 'rubygems'
require_gem 'activerecord'

class Account < ActiveRecord::Base
  set_table_name "accounts"
  has_many :comments
end

class Comment < ActiveRecord::Base
  set_table_name "comments"
  belongs_to :account
end

ActiveRecord::Base.establish_connection(:adapter => "sqlserver",
:host => "mydbhost.com", :database => "test", :username => "sa", :password => "")

mylog = Logger.new(STDOUT)
ActiveRecord::Base.logger = mylog

Account.benchmark("Testing benchmark") do
  temp = Account.find(1)
  temp.comments.each do |rec|
    puts "#{temp.username} said #{rec.subject}"
  end
end
```

When we execute the preceding program from a command line, we should get results that look something like the following (assuming we have the data in our database):

```
FaliconMobileMac:~ falicon$ ruby artest.rb
Kevin said Hi.
Kevin said Good Bye
Testing benchmark (1.11170)
```

As you can see, benchmarking is a great way to quickly see how long various blocks of code are really taking to execute.

Testing Is Fun!

OK, so maybe "fun" is a bit of a stretch, but I think you'll agree that Active Record does, in fact, make testing a lot less painful than many other libraries and languages. Hopefully, you've seen the light and no longer have a reason to skip testing your applications. Even if you use only a small percentage of the tips, tricks, and tools we showed you throughout this chapter, we believe your applications will be a lot stronger, more stable, and loved by more people than ever before. Don't believe us? Test it out and see!

CHAPTER 7

Working with Legacy Schema

Kevin lives in New York, NY. He rides a motorcycle. He has jumped out of a perfectly good airplane at 13,000 feet for fun—with his wife no less! Kevin and his wife decided to have two kids. Heck, he even asked Apress to let us write this book! Our point is Kevin seems to have a taste for doing crazy things.

Still, we don't think most people would classify him as insane. Yet within the Ruby world (and especially within the Rails community), "insane" is exactly how you'll be tagged if you intend to work with a legacy database schema!

While Kevin admits he sort of likes the idea of being labeled insane by his peers, we do think it's a bit of an extreme label. He runs a number of Rails sites that use legacy schema behind the scenes, and we do a lot of ad hoc Active Record scripting for various legacy database schema in our day-to-day consulting work. So we speak from a wealth of experience when we say it's really not all that insane. In fact, it's not even all that hard! It just requires a little bit of inside knowledge, a willingness to type a little bit more, and making some key decisions up front.

Throughout this chapter, we'll outline the key decisions you'll have to make. We'll cover the details of what you really need to know to use Active Record with legacy database schema. We'll show you how to do some of the tricky database-specific things like executing stored procedures and triggers. And finally, just in case you decide you really don't want to deal with that legacy schema after all, we'll cover how to move your data to other systems via importing and exporting.

Before we get into any details, though, we should take a second to define just what we consider a legacy database schema so we all start on the same page. For the purpose of this chapter, we are considering a legacy schema to be

> *Any database schema that was not primarily designed to adhere to the Active Record schema recommendations.*

Admittedly, this is a very general definition, but it allows us to think of any schema, whether new or old, as a legacy schema that we can use Active Record to work with. Our general definition also helps us to cover a very wide range of schema designs that stretch from simply choosing to ignore one Active Record recommendation, like how you name your primary key fields, to more complex designs that ignore just about every Active Record recommendation there is.

In any case, now that we have a common understanding of what a legacy schema is for our purposes, we need to cover some of the key decisions that a developer needs to make when they are deciding to use Active Record with legacy database schema.

Give and Take

As with most important decisions in life, working with a legacy schema is always a give and take situation. You have to decide just how much you want to accomplish in Active Record versus how much you want to accomplish within your database. Who's going to be responsible for each development part of your application? How will they want to do what they most frequently need to do? Is there an easier way, or at least a more efficient way, to accomplish everyday chores?

The answers to these questions will help you to design a better application as well as determine just how much you can and should do in Active Record. That means these are all important questions that you should be asking yourself before you even begin to write your first bits of code.

Let's examine some of the finer points about each of these questions now, so we can make more informed design decisions about our applications.

How Much Do You Want to Do in Active Record?

Traditional database applications are considered N-tier applications precisely because they involve multiple tiers of complexity. That is, multiple applications run independently from each other but are connected in some fashion so as to run a unique and complete process together, handing data back and forth between the tiers of complexity as needed. Usually, each tier would be responsible for processing the data in some way before handing the resulting data off to the next tier.

This meant that for a simple database application you could potentially need both an application developer and a database developer (or database administrator depending on how your company views the various roles). Among the people involved, knowledge of the following was a bare minimum to get an application working:

- Application programming syntax and concepts

- How your language of choice communicates with your database of choice

- The SQL syntax your specific database requires

- How your database of choice handles various SQL statements and requests

That's a lot of knowledge required to build even the most basic application. Worse, in many small companies (like the ones we have most often worked in), you are often the only person available, so you have to fill all the roles. That means you've got to have all that knowledge, by yourself! Better start reading all those manuals and tech books fast.

If you're like us, you've longed for solutions that allow you to spend more time in the realms you truly enjoy (in our case, programming) and outside of those that are the necessary evils (in our case, database administration). Active Record goes a long way in addressing just this situation, allowing you to stay within Ruby code for just about everything you need to do. With the help of things like migrations, validations, and callbacks, you barely have to know that there's another tier involved at all.

Still, when it comes to legacy systems, and especially when you are working with a legacy system that has other applications using it, it becomes clear that there are advantages to moving some of the processing into other tiers. For example, your Ruby validations are not going to help prevent bad data from seeping into your database from Java programs hitting it. And how many data scrubbing procedures do you want to write to ensure the data you read in is really as clean as you need it to be when those Java programs continue to let in new variations on bad data? In that sort of situation, it's clear that the database itself should be the gatekeeper, allowing in and sending out only good data.

So, the decision comes down to you, as an Active Record programmer; how much should you deal with directly in your Active Record program, and how much should your database directly handle? In the end, it's a personal decision that each developer will need to make. However, our advice to you is to move central issues, such as data validations, into your database tier but leave custom details, like figuring out the proper tax for your application via a callback, directly in your code.

This way, you maintain as much control (and simplicity) as possible while at the same time only spending time and effort outside of your realm when it really makes sense to do so.

Who's Responsible?

When you are trying to decide just where to place various parts of your application processing, another important issue to consider is who's ultimately responsible for that part of the processing. Who's going to have to fix the problems when they appear (and trust me they will)?

If, ultimately, you are going to be the one responsible for maintaining the application and all its related parts, and you're most comfortable within the Ruby realm, it probably makes sense to keep as much as you can within that realm. On the other hand, if you need to share responsibility, it might make more sense to move more of your application logic inside of the database application and let someone else deal with all the related issues as they occur.

How Do Things Get Done?

Along the same lines of deciding where things get done and who should do them is to determine just how things actually get done. Again, if you are the one who will need to actually maintain the application, resolve issues, and apply updates, it might make sense to keep as much as you can inside of the Active Record realm. If you have another person who feels more comfortable in the database realm or you have other reasons that require you do more in the database realm, it probably makes sense to give up some of the clean and simple Active Record features.

Is There an Easier or More Efficient Way?

Active Record was created to make working with databases simple for Ruby developers. Over time, it's evolved into a pretty complete realm allowing those of us who prefer to keep as much as possible in code to actually stick to our world almost 100 percent of the time. We can do just about everything from defining and setting up our schema with Active Record migrations, to populating massive amounts of data with fixtures, to incorporating complex business logic through data validations and callbacks, and we can even move from one database backend to another with very little effort. And we can do almost all of this without even having to know all that much about the SQL! This means we can spend more time focusing on our business logic and on becoming better Ruby programmers as a whole.

Still, there are times when sticking to just one realm may cause you more trouble than it's worth. For example, many of us have already spent a large amount of our time and energy learning the details of various SQL syntax and database management systems. So sometimes, it's just easier for us to write a quick SQL statement than to define all of our models, specify our associations, and then write the proper finder method.

It really depends on what your current needs are and how long you are going to need to support your scripts (we often just use `find_by_sql` with raw SQL statements for ad hoc stuff but go the proper Active Record route for scripts that are going to exist longer). Only you know what you're really good at, and only you know what realm really makes the best sense for spending the majority of your time. So in the end, it's really about what's most efficient for you.

Configuration Options for Active Record

You've decided that the trade-offs are worth it, and you want to go ahead and use Active Record with your legacy schema, moving most of your work into the Active Record realm. Now, what do you do? How do you get everything to actually work?

As it turns out, the real key to using Active Record with a legacy schema is primarily in the configuration work that you have to do. That is, you have to tell Active Record which of its default assumptions it should not make for your schema, or put another way, what assumptions your schema doesn't adhere to.

It sounds like things could get messy, but it's not so bad. In fact, most database libraries available today do not come with any assumptions built in and instead, require you, the developer, to define all the details of how to interpret your schema for each of your programs. Many times, they ask you to abstract those details into an external XML configuration file.

In our case, though, we don't have to spend hours writing XML configuration files. We can just specify most of our configuration options as simple assignments directly in our applications, which many of our examples throughout this chapter will outline.

Best of all, after you work through the various options listed as follows, you'll probably find your designs are not that far off from the design decisions Active Record assumes, which often means that you only need to make a few small configuration settings to get your legacy schema realizing the full power of Active Record!

Remember that one of the primary design goals of Active Record is to cut down on configurations required to get our programs to work. Active Record achieves that goal by making assumptions about the way most Active Record developers would want or expect something to work.

However, DHH was wise enough to realize that there may be cases where someone needs or wants to override these assumptions, so he made sure that Active Record allows us to override each of these assumptions as we see fit. Thanks to that design decision, we are able to work with just about any schema by doing just a little more configuration than you might see in your average Active Record program.

Each of the settings in the following sections can be combined in numerous ways to accomplish a variety of goals. For example, you can use the `primary_key_prefix_type` setting along with the `set_primary_key` method to fine-tune just how and what Active Record uses as the primary key for a given table.

primary_key_prefix_type

This is an attribute that you set directly on the `ActiveRecord::Base` class that allows you to define the type of prefix that should be used when accessing your tables throughout all of your Active Record instances. If you do not set this attribute, Active Record will assume each table has a primary key of the string ID (except for those models that override this setting via the set_primary_key method). The value options for primary_key_prefix_type are :table_name or :table_name_with_underscore.

If you use a setting of :table_name, Active Record will append the model's class name directly to the string ID (unless you define a different primary key with the set_primary_key method) when it attempts to access the primary key. The following example shows this in action:

```
# Setting the primary_key_prefix_type
ActiveRecord::Base.primary_key_prefix_type = :table_name
class Account < ActiveRecord::Base
end
a = Account.find(1)
#=> executes SQL equal to "Select * from accounts where accountid = 1"
```

If you use a setting of :table_name_with_underscore, Active Record will append the model's class name and an underscore to the string ID (unless you define a different primary key with the set_primary_key method) when it attempts to access the primary key. The following example shows this in action:

```
# Setting the primary_key_prefix_type
ActiveRecord::Base.primary_key_prefix_type = :table_name_with_underscore
class Account < ActiveRecord::Base
end
a = Account.find(1)
#=> executes SQL equal to "Select * from accounts where account_id = 1"
```

■**Note** It's important to notice that the class name is used without the help of the Active Support Inflector class for this prefix. That is, we define our model as an Account model that maps to an accounts table (the Active Support Inflector class helps us to figure out the proper table name that our code should look for), but within that table, we expect to have a primary key of account_id rather than accounts_id. If you think about a record and how it relates to a single instance of a class, this should seem like a reasonable deduction for our code to make. If our primary key does not follow this design, we would need to use the set_primary_ key method within each model rather than just setting this attribute.

It's quite common to see primary keys defined as the table name and the string ID (sometimes with an underscore, sometimes without). So this attribute is a great way to work with that convention without having to override the primary key setting in every model (via the set_primary_key method).

table_name_prefix

This is an attribute that you set directly on the ActiveRecord::Base class that allows you to define the prefix to be used with all tables throughout all of your Active Record instances. The default prefix used when you do not set this attribute is an empty string (which equates to no prefix being used).

The following example states that all of our tables should have the string "draftwizard_" attached as a prefix:

```
# Setting the table_name_prefix
ActiveRecord::Base.table_name_prefix = "draftwizard_"
class Account < ActiveRecord::Base
end
a = Account.find(1)
#=> executes SQL equal to "Select * from draftwizard_accounts where id = 1"
```

This attribute is very handy when you are working within a shared database that has tables for a number of virtual schema. Prefixing all your tables with their project names makes them easier to manage within your database management system (DBMS); by using this attribute, you can quickly and easily utilize the Active Record library with your schema as well.

table_name_suffix

This attribute is also set directly on the ActiveRecord::Base class; it allows you to define the suffix to be used with all tables throughout your Active Record instances. When you do not set this attribute, the default suffix used is an empty string (which equates to no suffix being used).

The following example states that all of our tables should have the string "draftwizard_" attached as a suffix:

```
# Setting the table_name_suffix
ActiveRecord::Base.table_name_suffix = "_draftwizard"
class Account < ActiveRecord::Base
end
a = Account.find(1)
#=> executes SQL equal to "Select * from accounts_draftwizard where id = 1"
```

Much like the table_name_prefix attribute, this attribute is very handy when you are working within a shared database that has tables for a number of virtual schema. By adding the project name as a suffix to all your tables, they can be more easily managed within your DBMS, and by using this attribute, you can also quickly and easily utilize the Active Record library with your schema.

pluralize_table_names

This attribute, which you also set directly on the ActiveRecord::Base class, allows you to tell Active Record whether or not it should use the Active Support Inflector class to determine table names. The default setting is true.

The following example shows how to make Active Record ignore the pluralization assumptions and instead just use the class name as the table name:

```
# Setting the pluralize_table_names
ActiveRecord::Base.pluralize_table_names = false
class Account < ActiveRecord::Base
end
a = Account.find(1) #=> executes SQL equal to "Select * from account where id = 1"
```

Many legacy systems we have worked with do not use a mixed sense of pluralization like Active Record assumes. That is, it has been our experience that a schema would likely have an `Account` table rather than an `Accounts` table (even though technically the table is holding data about a variety of accounts). So we find ourselves setting this attribute to `false` in most of our legacy schema work.

It also helps us to avoid the confusion that our brains seem to add with pluralization. That is, when pluralization is turned on, we often find ourselves having to talk (out loud, to the dismay of those around us) through the relationship a bit more. We have to say things like, "We want to get the `account_id` of the `accounts` table through an instance of my `Account` object." Then we can type out the actual code to accomplish it. Therefore, we also find ourselves setting this attribute to `false` in many of the Active Record systems we start from scratch and avoiding pluralization confusion all together!

colorize_logging

This is an attribute, which you set directly on the `ActiveRecord::Base` class, that tells your logger whether or not to use ANSI codes to colorize your log. Colorizing your log can often help you quickly find things as you review them, but not all programs you use to review your logs may display these colors. When the colors cannot be properly displayed, the extra ANSI color code tends to make the log much harder to read. In those situations, you can use this attribute to turn off the use of those codes. The default value for this attribute is `true`.

The following example shows how to turn log colorization off:

```
# Specify colorize_logging
ActiveRecord::Base.colorize_logging = false
```

Colorizing your log really has nothing to do with working with legacy systems, but we list the attribute here because it is, in fact, one of the configuration options you can specify. We suppose you could make an argument that working with legacy systems can require more involved testing and therefore more involved reviewing of your log files. In which case, colorization would help to ease that process.

default_timezone

This is an attribute, which you set directly on the `ActiveRecord::Base` class, that allows you to have Active Record use either your local system time or coordinated universal time (UTC) when dealing with date and time field types in your database. The default setting is `:local`; the other option is `:utc`.

The following example tells Active Record to use UTC time values when dealing with dates:

```
# Specify the default_timezone
ActiveRecord::Base.default_timezone = :utc
a = Account.find(1)
puts a.created_on #=> Tue Jun 05 22:09:44 UTC 2007
```

A complete discussion on date and time issues is outside of the scope of this book, but I will say that it's worth spending a little time thinking about. The applications of today are becoming more and more global, which, in turn, is causing us to make more and more global decisions about how or why something should work the way it does. Many older systems logged dates and times as local dates and times, because the applications that used the data were expected to also run in that local time zone. Often, that is no longer the case, making standards such as UTC a much more interesting option.

allow_concurrency

The allow_concurrency attribute, again set directly on the ActiveRecord::Base class, lets you tell Active Record if it should use a connection for each thread or if it should simply use a single shared connection for all threads. The default is false, which states that Active Record should use a single shared connection for all threads.

The following example shows a threaded example (each time you run this, the results are likely to be displayed in a different order, as the threads end at various and slightly random times):

```
# Threaded example using concurrency
require 'rubygems'
require_gem 'activerecord'

ActiveRecord::Base.establish_connection(:adapter => "mysql",
:database => "testdb", :username => "root", :password => "", :host => "localhost")
ActiveRecord::Base.allow_concurrency = true

class Direct < ActiveRecord::Base
end

threads = []
20.times do |i|
  t = Thread.new do
    data = Direct.find(i + 1)
    puts "Thread: #{i} #{data.contact_email}"
  end
  threads.push(t)
end
threads.each {|t| t.join }
```

The preceding example assumes, of course, that you have a table called directs with at least the 20 records we reference (ids with values from 1 to 20). It's also important to note that the preceding example is just a generic example of a threaded application where one process manages the single database connection intelligently for a concurrent process.

■**Note** Each Active Record adaptor handles threads in its own way, and that way often depends on how the underlying relational DBMS itself handles threads. You should refer to your specific adapter code and your database documentation for more details.

Threads are a powerful, yet complex, realm to explore. If you intend to do any applications of any serious size, it would probably be worth your time to learn as much as you can about how to best implement and manage them.

generate_read_methods

This is an attribute that you, again, set directly on the `ActiveRecord::Base` class; it tells Active Record whether or not to dynamically generate reader methods. That is, it tells Active Record if it should access an attribute directly and perform a type cast once the presence of a reader method is established for that attribute or if it should always perform the task through the `method_missing` method. The default value for this attribute is `true`.

The following example shows this setting in action with a simple benchmark to show the time processing takes. If you toggle the value for `generate_read_methods`, you should see there is a significant processing hit:

```
# Setting the generate_read_methods
require 'rubygems'
require_gem 'activerecord'
require 'benchmark'

ActiveRecord::Base.establish_connection(:adapter => "mysql",
:database => "testdb", :username => "root", :password => "", :host => "localhost")
ActiveRecord::Base.generate_read_methods = false

class Account < ActiveRecord::Base
end

2.times do |x|
  Account.benchmark("starting benchmark") do
    temp = Account.find_by_username("Kevin")
    puts temp.created_at
  end
end
```

This setting primarily has to do with performance issues, because when you choose not to generate read methods, Active Record is forced to call the `method_missing` method each time you attempt to access an attribute—and calling the `method_missing` method is resource intensive.

Again, this attribute has little to do directly with legacy schema, but we include it here, because it is a configuration option you can set.

schema_format

This is also an attribute that you set directly on the `ActiveRecord::Base` class; it tells Active Record what format to use when dumping the database schema to flat files. The default value is `:ruby`, and `:sql` is the other available option.

If you set the attribute to the `:ruby` value, the schema is dumped as an `ActiveRecord::Schema` format (discussed in Chapter 3), which can then be used to load the schema into any database that supports Active Record migrations. If you set the attribute to `:sql`, according to the

Active Record documentation, the schema is dumped as SQL statements that are likely database specific (since each database uses its own variation of ANSI SQL).

■**Note** At the time of this writing, a search through all of the Active Record source code revealed no real implementation of the `schema_format` attribute. Regardless of the value you set, it appears as though Active Record just acts as though the `:ruby` value was provided; that is, it always dumps the schema in the `ActiveRecord::Schema` format.

This attribute is designed primarily for use with the Ruby on Rails task `rake db:schema:dump`. However, as we outlined in Chapter 3, you can dump the schema from a standard Active Record program as well.

set_table_name

This is a method that you can use within a model to override the table naming assumptions built into Active Record. You may also provide a block rather than a table name, and the result of the block will be the value Active Record attempts to use to locate the table within the database.

In the following example, we override the Active Record assumptions for two models. In the first model, Active Record would normally have attempted to locate an `accounts` table, but we tell it to look for a table called `members` instead. In the second model, we use a block to tell Active Record to use a table name of `feedback` instead of the default of `comments`:

```
# Using the set_table_name method
require 'rubygems'
require_gem 'activerecord'
ActiveRecord::Base.establish_connection(:adapter => "sqlserver",
:host => "localhost", :username => "sa", :password => "" , :database => "testdb")

class Account < ActiveRecord::Base
  set_table_name "members"
end

puts Account.find(1).inspect

class Comment < ActiveRecord::Base
  set_table_name {
    d = ["feed","back"]
    d.join
  }
end

puts Comment.find(1).inspect
```

This method is quite useful when you have tables within your database that would be more logical within your application if they were referred to by different names (our Account versus Member override is a good example of this). This method is also handy for helping you to avoid the pluralization confusion I mentioned in the pluralize_table_name attribute section.

This method will override any Active Record table naming assumptions as well as the pluralize_table_name attribute setting.

set_primary_key

This is a method that you can use within a model to override the Active Record assumption that each table has a primary key labeled id. You may also provide a block rather than a primary key label, and the result of the block will be the value Active Record attempts to use as the primary key.

In the following example, we override the Active Record assumptions for two models. In both models, Active Record would normally assume each table has a primary key in a field labeled id. However, in the first model, we say to use account_id as the primary key, and in the second model, we use a block to assign a primary key of comments_id:

```
# Using the set_table_name method
require 'rubygems'
require_gem 'activerecord'
ActiveRecord::Base.establish_connection(:adapter => "sqlserver",
:host => "localhost", :username => "sa", :password => "", :database => "testdb")

class Account < ActiveRecord::Base
  set_primary_key "account_id"
end

puts Account.find(1).inspect

class Comment < ActiveRecord::Base
  set_primary_key {
    d = ["comm","ents","_id"]
    d.join
  }
end

puts Comment.find(1).inspect
```

set_Inheritance_column

You can use this method within a model to override the Active Record assumption that inheritance is stored in a field labeled type. You may also provide a block rather than a specific inheritance field label, and the result of the block will be the value Active Record attempts to use as the field to store inheritance.

In the following example, we override the Active Record assumptions for two models (Account and Comment). In both models, Active Record would normally assume each table has a field labeled type, which stores the inheritance information. However, in the first model, we say to use account_type as the inheritance column, and in the second model, we use a block to assign the name of the inheritance column:

```
# Using the set_table_name method
require 'rubygems'
require_gem 'activerecord'
ActiveRecord::Base.establish_connection(:adapter => "sqlserver",
:host => "localhost", :username => "sa", :password => "", :database => "testdb")

class Account < ActiveRecord::Base
  set_inheritance_column "account_type"
end

class Reader < Account
end

puts Reader.find(1).inspect

class Comment < ActiveRecord::Base
  set_primary_key {
    d = ["comm","ents","_category"]
    d.join
  }
end

class Storycomment < Comment
end

puts Storycomment.find(1).inspect
```

set_sequence_name

This is a method that you can use within a model to specify the name of the sequence Active Record should use to generate id values for primary keys. You may also provide a block rather than a specific sequence name, and the result of the block will be the value Active Record attempts to use as the sequence name.

Each database may handle sequences in its own way, so there is some variation in what is required from Active Record's point of view. If you are using Oracle or Firebird, Active Record assumes that sequences exist for each of your tables and are in the format of tablename_seq. If you are using Firebird, Active Record will discover the proper sequence for you by default.

■Note Because there is variation here on the Active Record assumptions, I recommend that you review your specific adapter code just to be sure how sequences are handled.

In the following example, we assign an Oracle sequence called `aid_seq` to our `Account` model:

```
# Setting sequence name with Oracle
require 'rubygems'
require_gem 'activerecord'

ActiveRecord::Base.establish_connection(:adapter => 'oci',
:host => 'test, :username => 'tester', :password => 'tester')

class Account < ActiveRecord::Base
  set_sequence_name "aid_seq"
end

acc = Account.new # => this should trigger the execution of the sequence aid_seq
acc.username = 'Kevin'
acc.save

puts acc.id #=> this should display the value of the sequence we executed.
```

Making the Complex Easier

We've got the basic configuration concepts under control, and we think we can at least get Active Record talking to our database in a fairly standard Active Record way using those options. Now, it's time to shift our focus a little bit from setting things up to actually dealing with the more complex issue of working with the things we've set up.

To do that, we need to have an example we can work with. The first thing we should probably do is to define some tables for our legacy schema to use in the examples throughout the rest of this chapter, so we are all on the same page as we work through various issues.

To start, let's pretend that we are going to be writing some Active Record scripts to work with a legacy schema that also has some historical Java applications accessing it. Because the Java applications are distributed to a number of clients (which are not entirely under our control anymore), and we want those Java programs to continue to work, we cannot remove any existing tables or change the existing column names in our database. However, we can probably add columns to tables without causing too much backlash, and we can certainly add data as needed.

Our development and production database systems are SQL Server systems and have hundreds of tables already, but for our interests, we are concerned with only a couple of them right now.

■Note Our examples are using SQL Server data stores for our own simplicity during our writing and testing process, but the theory and details listed should work across all systems unless otherwise noted. If you are comfortable with migrations as discussed in Chapter 3, you may even want to do your development in one DBMS, such as MySQL, and release to another DBMS, such as Oracle, for your production system.

Our first example table is a members table. The members table is where we store all the basic member information like username, password, name, and e-mail address (though we will probably want to refer to it as an account table for our needs). The table is defined with the following basic properties:

```
# members table, basic plain-English definition of fields
Members_ID, int, auto-incremented, primary key
Members_Name, varchar
Members_Email, varchar
Members_Username, varchar
Members_Password, varchar
```

We also are interested in a comments table that stores user comments. The table is defined with the following basic properties:

```
# comments table, basic plain-English definition of fields
Comments_ID, int, auto-incremented, primary key
Comments_Subject, varchar
Comments_Message, text
Comments_Name, varchar
Comments_RealtedID, int
Comments_BoardID, int
Members_ID, int
Comments_DatePosted, datetime
```

Finally, we are also interested in a table called direct that contains a list of our member's direct friends. The table is defined with the following basic properties:

```
# direct table, basic plain-English definition of fields
Direct_ID, int, auto-incremented, primary key
Direct_Name, varchar
Direct_Email, varchar
Members_ID, id
Direct_Added, datetime
```

Now that we have some sample tables to work with, we can talk about what's required to use this schema with Active Record. Believe it or not, our legacy system is not too far off from most of the Active Record assumptions. In fact, we only need to use the set_table_name and set_primary_key model methods to accomplish most of what we want.

The initial setup work we need to do follows:

```
# Example working with Legacy schema
require 'rubygems'
require_gem 'activerecord'

ActiveRecord::Base.establish_connection(:adapter => "sqlserver",
:host => "mydbserver", :database => "testdb", :username => "sa", :password => "")

class Account < ActiveRecord::Base
  set_table_name "members"
```

```
    set_primary_key "Members_ID"
end

class Comments < ActiveRecord::Base
  set_table_name "comments"
  set_primary_key "Comments_ID"
end

class Direct < ActiveRecord::Base
  set_table_name "direct"
  set_primary_key "Direct_ID"
end
```

At this point, you might be wondering why we chose to use the set_primary_key method instead of just setting the class attribute primary_key_prefix_type to :table_name_with_underscore, since it appears that in all of our cases, our primary key is the table name plus an underscore and the string ID. The answer lies in the fact that our column labels are of mixed case. This is an important thing to note, because Active Record will force all column or field names to be lowercase with a call to the Ruby downcase method unless you specifically tell it in which cases not to do so.

■**Note** Active Record is case sensitive. This means that a field name of account_id is not the same as a field name of Account_ID even if your database system itself does not recognize a difference. From within your application, the attributes would be considered two different objects.

We'll spend a little more time on the importance of case in the next section when we cover using the various find methods. For now though, just keep in mind that case does matter, and since our legacy schema uses mixed case for field names, we were required to use the set_primary_key method within each model rather than set the global attribute on the ActiveRecord::Base class.

The other interesting thing to note about our initial setup here is that even though within our database we store member data in the member table, within our application we defined the model as an Account model. This means that our code will reference it as an Account object. It's a subtle thing, but it should help to clear up the meaning of our model as we use it within our code when other humans (if you can consider your developers and testers human) need to read through our code.

Now that we have our models set up, we can finally start doing our CRUD operations.

CRUD Operations and Complex SQL Statements

We covered the basics of the various CRUD operations back in Chapter 2. And so long as you use the various configuration options listed previously, you should be able to accomplish all of the normal CRUD actions and take advantage of things like validations, callbacks, and associations.

Still, there are many times when dealing with legacy systems that you may want to bypass some of the advantages that Active Record gives you in exchange for better performance (obviously, there is some processing overhead that goes into providing all those nice features). And sometimes, it's easier to port your application from another language into Ruby by just using the existing SQL statements, especially if you're comfortable with the SQL syntax your chosen database supports. Depending on your background, you may find working with SQL joins a little less confusing than dealing with model associations.

In any case, if you want to work more with SQL and less with Active Record syntax, your answer is the find_by_sql method. The find_by_sql method simply takes a raw SQL statement and uses the ActiveRecord::Base.connection.select_all statement to execute the provided SQL (we talk about the select_all statement in more detail in the next section).

An example helps us to explore this option a bit more—getting back to our example application, let's pretend that we need to generate a quick report that shows us only what comments a given user has posted. If we had set up our models with proper associations, we could simply use that information to access the subset of data. However, we did not set up our models with proper associations for this section, and since we just want this to be an ad hoc report, we'll use raw SQL and the find_by_sql method to achieve the desired results.

The following example shows our solution using the find_by_sql method:

```
# Code snippet showing use of find_by_sql method in action
acid = 1 #=> this is the id of the account we are going to generate the report for

pc = Account.find_by_sql(["Select * from members, comments where
members.members_id = ? and members.members_id = comments.members_id", accid])

pc.each do |rec|
  puts "#{rec.Members_Name} posted #{rec.Comments_Subject}"
end
```

A few really important things are happening in the preceding example, so we'll take a minute to point out each one:

- We called the find_by_sql method on the Account model. Really, we could have executed the same code against any of our defined models though, since we were passing in a complete SQL string. The find_by_sql method uses only the connection information of the model it's called with.

- The SQL statements we use with the find_by_sql method must adhere to the specific SQL syntax that our backend database supports (in this example, we are using SQL Server so that means we need to use T-SQL syntax). This means, in our example, that we may need to update our SQL statements if we develop against a SQL Server backend but later decide to release to production in Oracle, since each implements a different version of SQL (T-SQL for SQLServer and PL/SQL for Oracle).

- We referenced the members table by its true database label (members) even though we defined the model as Account. This is once again required, because the find_by_sql method directly passes the raw SQL string to the database for execution, meaning that we must refer to tables and columns as the database knows them rather than as our Active Record application would.

- The `find_by_sql` method returns an array of Active Record objects, even if only one Active Record object is in that array. This differs slightly from the regular `find` methods, which return an Active Record object if only one result is found or an array of Active Record objects if more than one result is found.

  In the following example, we use `find_by_sql` to get the number of records in our Direct table. Though we expect only one result, we are still required to use the array to access that data.

  ```
  # Code snippet showing find_by_sql as Array of ActiveRecord objects
  thecount = Direct.find_by_sql("select count(0) mycount from direct")
  puts thecount[0].mycount
  ```

- Finally, since we did a `select *` type of SQL statement, we reference the field values with mixed case, because that is how they are truly defined within the database. If we had, instead, used an SQL statement like select `members_name, comments_subject from . . .` we would have been required to reference the field values in our example as `rec.media_name` and `rec.comments_subject` (lowercase). This is because, in this situation, our SQL statement specifically defined them as lowercase, and Ruby and Active Record result sets are case sensitive. When in doubt, it's probably safer to define your select fields in lowercase so that you can reference them that way in your code. Otherwise, it may become difficult to debug your programs, because it will not always be clear if you are talking about a model attribute, method, or constant.

■Note When working with legacy schema, case is very important to note for table and field labels. If you use a `select *` type of statement with `find_by_sql` and then attempt to reference a value with the wrong case, you will get a `method_missing` error. If you do get a `method_missing` error, you should always check that you are using the correct case for all of your attribute references.

As long as you keep these key issues in mind, the `find_by_sql` method can be a very powerful tool when working with legacy databases. It allows you to quickly execute `select` statements of any level complexity (as long as you can correctly write the complex SQL you need).

Improving Performance and Cutting Out the Middle Man

As powerful and helpful as `find_by_sql` can be when working with legacy systems, there are still times when it's just not enough. Perhaps you have a large data set you need for a number of statements, or perhaps speed is critical to your application and you want to cut out as many of the unnecessary steps as possible.

In these situations, you can bypass just about all of Active Record, except for the connection, and simply call the raw statements themselves. Each Active Record CRUD operation eventually boils down to either a `connection.insert`, `connection.update`, `connection.select_all`, or `connection.delete` statement, so as you can guess, you can directly use any of these as you need.

The following example shows each of these low-level operations in use (in a real-world situation, you would want to include exception handling, because you are opening yourself up to a large number of potential errors when you work with low-level operations):

```
# Code snippet showing use of low level connection statements
ins = ActiveRecord::Base.connection.insert("insert into
  members(members_name, members_username, members_password)
  values('Kevin', 'Falicon', 'CAKNTOBA')")
puts ins #=> should return the id of the record that was inserted

upd = ActiveRecord::Base.connection.update("update members set
members_password = 'CAKNTOBA1' where members_id = #{ins}")
puts upd #=> returns 0 regardless of if the update really ran or not!

sel = ActiveRecord::Base.connection.select_all("select * from members
where members_id = #{ins}")
sel.each do |rec|
  puts "Name: #{rec["Members_Name"]}  Username: #{rec["Members_Username"]"
end

del = ActiveRecord::Base.connection.delete("delete members
where members_id = #{ins}")
puts del #=> returns 0 regardless of if the delete really ran or not!
```

Again there are a few key things we should point out about the previous example.

- Each of these low-level statements requires a full SQL statement that is compatible with your backend database. In the example of SQL Server, that means your SQL statements must be T-SQL compliant, and with Oracle, they must be PL/SQL compliant. Each database uses a variation of ANSI SQL, and when you work directly with these low-level statements, you must know and maintain the details of this on your own.

- Both the update and delete statements return a zero value regardless of their execution. This means that you have no real information saying whether or not the statement executed properly, so checking for proper execution is left up to you.

- When you use these low-level statements, you are bypassing everything Active Record brings to the table, except for the ability to connect to the database. Essentially, you are using Active Record to easily connect to your database, but otherwise, you are writing custom SQL for all of your communication with that database.

- The select_all statement returns an array of hash objects rather than an array of Active Record objects. So rather than access values as if they are attributes, you must access them as you would a hash value (e.g., rec["Members_Name"] instead of the Active Record version of rec.Members_Name).

Again, as long as you keep the preceding points in mind, working with the low-level statements can provide you with significant performance boosts—especially when you are running scripts that move a lot of data around and require a large number of database calls.

Stored Procedures, Custom Functions, and Sequences

There's actually one last low-level statement that we have left to discuss, `connection.execute`. With this statement, we can add support for database-specific features like stored procedures, custom functions, and sequences.

Actually, many of these features can be executed in simple ways that we already know about. For example, most custom functions can be executed as part of normal SQL statements, and many times you can access a sequence in this way as well.

The following example shows how to call custom functions and sequences with Active Record and Oracle:

```
# Script showing use of custom function and sequences
require 'rubygems'
require_gem 'activerecord'

ActiveRecord::Base.establish_connection(:adapter => "oci",
:host => "test", :username => "tester", :password => "tester")

class Direct < ActiveRecord::Base
end

seqval = Direct.find_by_sql("select test_seq.nextval from dual")
puts seqval[0].nextval
#=> will display the next available value from the test_seq sequence

cf = Direct.find_by_sql("select custfunc(123) myres from members where
members_id = 1")
puts ef[0].myres
#=> will display the value that was returned from the custom
# function custfunc when the value 123 was passed to the function.
```

Again, it's worth noting that, because you are using a method like `find_by_sql` for these features, you are relying on SQL statements and features that must be compatible with your specific database situation. It should also be noted that each database may implement (or not support at all) each of these type of features in different ways, so you should always refer to your database documentation before attempting to work with these type of features.

As with our previous examples, you can also choose to go to the lower level and use the `connection.select_all` statement to access sequence or custom function values via SQL statements.

One of the common database features that we haven't talked about yet is stored procedures. Stored procedures are basically encapsulated code or logic stored intended to help apply business logic to your data from directly within your database, and each database has a varying level of support for them (some have no support for stored procedures).

Since one of the primary goals of Active Record is to decentralize your business logic from within your database and instead move that to your application and your models, it's probably no surprise that there is no direct support for stored procedures within Active Record. But that doesn't mean you can't use them, it just means you'll have to do a little more work on your own again.

The secret to executing stored procedures is the final low-level statement we have yet to mention, `connection.execute`. The `connection.execute` method is similar to the other low-level statements we've been talking about in that it accepts a raw SQL statement. However, it varies slightly in that it's more generic than the other statements and, therefore, can execute any type of SQL statement including `insert`, `update`, `delete`, and `select` statements.

It can also execute a series of SQL statements, and this turns out to be the key for accessing stored procedures with certain database systems, such as Oracle. Some examples will probably help make this easier to understand.

In the following example, we make a call to an Oracle stored procedure that resets a sequence within our database (the stored procedure takes the name of the sequence to reset as its lone parameter):

```
# Running an Oracle stored procedure
require 'rubygems'
require_gem 'activerecord'

ActiveRecord::Base.establish_connection(:adapter => "oci",
:host => "test", :username => "tester", :password => "tester")

res = ActiveRecord::Base.conection.execute("begin reset_sequence('test_seq'); end;")
puts res.inspect
#=> because our stored procedure does not return a value we get back an empty Array
```

As this example shows, we execute a begin/end block calling the stored procedure (reset_sequence in this example). As we mentioned though, each database implements stored procedures in its own way, so this example is specific to Oracle stored procedures. To show you what we mean, let's look at one more example with a different database.

The following example executes a built-in SQL Server stored procedure (`sp_helprole`) and displays the results from this stored procedure:

```
# Running a SQL Server stored procedure
require 'rubygems'
require_gem 'activerecord'

ActiveRecord::Base.establish_connection(:adapter => "sqlserver",
:host => "mydbserver.com", :database => "test", :username => "sa",
:password => "", :autocommit => false)

roles = ActiveRecord::Base.connection.select_all("exec sp_helprole")
roles.each do |rec|
  puts rec["RoleName"]
end
```

This example shows a number of interesting differences between Oracle and SQL Server in how they execute stored procedures. First, SQL Server requires that we set the connection parameter of `:autocommit` to `false`. Second, to execute a SQL Server stored procedure, you use the `connection.select_all` statement, instead of `connection.execute` like you do with Oracle (calling the execute statement for SQL Server will not return results). Finally, you can see that the select_all statement returned an Array of Hash values, so we are required to access the data via this array and hash structure instead of as Active Record objects.

These differences alone should highlight the fact that working with stored procedures from within your Active Record programs is a bit of headache and requires some research on your part into how specifically your adapter can support them (as well as how your SQL syntax can execute them).

Because of these various issues and the work required to ensure stable results, we recommend that, where possible, you stay away from accessing stored procedures in your Active Record applications. Still, the previous two examples should at least show that it is possible when you absolutely must deal with a stored procedure within your Active Record code.

Data Types

Now that we've covered all the configuration options, the tips and tricks for CRUD operations, and how to deal with various database-specific features like stored procedures, we have just one more important area worth addressing when dealing with legacy systems—data types, specifically, unique data types and how Active Record handles each.

Ruby itself has only a handful of data types, and for the most part, they can be reasonably mapped to standard database types. For example, String can be mapped to varchar or char types. Integer can be mapped to integer. Float can be mapped to fixnum or float types.

But like most things, there are a few exceptions.

Our first data type exception is the Boolean type. Ruby has a fairly simple definition of Boolean values. Everything is true except for the value false and the value nil. However, many databases also allow values like 0, "false", or null to also evaluate as false Boolean values. To address this, each Active Record database adapter is expected to also accept and properly convert the values of "false" and "0" to Boolean false values.

The next data type of interest to us is the large text object (often referred to as Text or CLOB data types). Each database has a varying level of support for large text objects, but most do implement or support them in one way or another. Throughout our testing, each of the adapters correctly converted data to and from Ruby string types for this type.

Finally, closely related to large text objects are large binary objects (often referred to as BLOB data types). This data type also has varying support from within each database system and relies on each Active Record adaptor to properly map data to and from this type. The equivalent Ruby type is generally :binary, :string, or an I/O stream.

As you can see, data types and their mappings are often unique to each database system and, therefore, are implemented in each Active Record adapter. We recommend you spend a little time in your specific adapter's source code getting familiar with how it handles data type conversions.

Importing and Exporting

While the primary storage mechanism for Active Record objects is a relational database, there are several reasons why you might export the data stored in Active Record objects to other formats. Whether for integration with other systems, reporting, or testing purposes, converting Active Record objects into other formats is, thankfully, easy.

Exporting XML

XML has emerged as a standard data interchange format, and Active Record includes, on every object, a to_xml method that allows you to get an XML representation of the Active Record object.

■**Note** While the to_xml method does take a hash of configuration options, it is generally recommended that for more complex XML generation you should use Active Support's Builder class and either override to_xml or provide a custom method with a different name.

The default generated XML will include all attributes for the object, a type attribute for attributes that are not of type String, and processing instructions. In addition, associations are not expanded by default. An example of the XML for an object of our Account class would be

```
<?xml version="1.0" encoding="UTF-8"?>
<account>
  <id type="integer">1</id>
  <last-name>Pytel</last-name>
  <first-name>Chad</first-name>
  <site-id tyle="integer">1</site-id>
</account>
```

The default name for the root element is the class name of the Active Record object we are formatting. The :root option should be a string and provides you a way to override the name of the root element:

```
account.to_xml(:root => "myaccount")
# => <myaccount>
  <id type="integer">1</id>
  <last-name>Pytel</last-name>
  <first-name>Chad</first-name>
  <site-id>1</site-id>
  <created-at type="datetime">2006-11-10T10:22:56-05:00</created-at>
</myaccount>
```

You can use the :only and :except options to explicitly include or exclude attributes from the resulting XML:

```
account.to_xml(:only => [ :last_name ])
# => <account>
  <last-name>Pytel</last-name>
</account>
account.to_xml(:except => [ :last_name ])
# => <account>
  <id type="integer">1</id>
  <first-name>Chad</first-name>
  <site-id>1</site-id>
  <created-at type="datetime">2006-11-10T10:22:56-05:00</created-at>
</account>
```

As previously mentioned, associations are not expanded in the XML by default. To cause certain associations to also be included in the XML, use the :include option:

```
account.to_xml(:include => [ :site ])
# => <?xml version="1.0" encoding="UTF-8"?>
<account>
  <id type="integer">1</id>
  <last-name>Pytel</last-name>
  <first-name>Chad</first-name>
  <site>
    <id type="integer">1</id>
    <name>Account Site</name>
  </site>
  <site-id type="integer">1</site-id>
  <created-at type="datetime">2006-11-10T10:22:56-05:00</created-at>
</account>
```

Importing XML

While Active Record contains a to_xml method for writing XML, it does not contain a from_xml method for reading it. Thankfully, Active Support extends the hash object with a create_from_xml method. Because Active Record objects can be created by passing in a hash, you can utilize this method to create Active Record objects from XML.

The create_from_xml method expects the same types of XML attributes that are output when using the to_xml method. It uses these attributes, which indicate type, to typecast the values in XML to the correct values in the hash.

Given the following XML markup

```
<?xml version="1.0" encoding="UTF-8"?>
<account>
  <id type="integer">1</id>
  <last-name>Pytel</last-name>
  <first-name>Chad</first-name>
  <site>
    <id type="integer">1</id>
    <name>Account Site</name>
  </site>
  <site-id type="integer">1</site-id>
  <created-at type="datetime">2006-11-10T10:22:56-05:00</created-at>
</account>
```

the create_from_xml method would return the following hash:

```
{"account"=>{"site_id"=>1, "id"=>1, "site"=>{"name"=>"Account Site", "id"=>1},
"first_name"=>"Chad", "last_name"=>"Pytel",
"created_at"=>Fri Nov 10 15:22:56 UTC 2006}}
```

You can then pass the generated hash into the model's new, create, or update_attributes method. The create_from_xml method can also be used to read in XML that contains markup for more than one model record. The following code is a simple script that reads in an XML file that contains data for multiple accounts. In our data, it assumed that some records do not yet have a primary key, while others do. Therefore, if the primary key in the XML is not nil, the script will attempt to find the corresponding record and update it. If the record is not found, or if the primary key was nil, then the record will be created.

```
accounts_xml_string = File.read("accounts.xml")
accounts = Hash.create_from_xml(accounts_xml_string)
accounts.each do |account|
  if account["id"].nil? || !Account.exists?(account["id"])
    Accounts.create(account)
  else
    Accounts.find(account["id"]).update_attributes(account)
  end
end
```

While, the preceding code may not be considered production ready (it does not include any error checking or reporting), you can see that in a few simple lines, we can import an entire XML file of accounts into our database, updating records that already exist. If, for instance, you know that none of the records exist, you can even eliminate that part of the program.

Exporting YAML

YAML, which stands for "YAML Ain't Markup Language," is a data serialization format first proposed in 2001 by Clark Evans, who designed it together with Ingy döt Net and Oren Ben-Kiki. In Active Record, YAML can be used as Active Record fixture data for testing purposes. As YAML continues to grow in popularity, it can be useful as a lightweight markup language.

Regardless of your specific use of YAML, you get the benefit that a YAML parser and generator are included in the Ruby standard libraries and are fully supported by Active Record. Each Active Record object contains a to_yaml method, which returns a String, which is the YAML representation of the object. Collections also support the to_yaml method, and therefore, the code to export your entire accounts table in YAML is straightforward:

```
Account.find(:all).to_yaml
```

The configuration options are minimal and are used to configure the output format of YAML. In addition, model associations are not included in the default YAML output.

Because of the minimal configuration options, if you need to customize the actual data output from to_yaml, it may be best write your own custom YAML output methods.

Importing YAML

The Ruby YAML parser has a transform method that converts the parsed YAML into Ruby objects. This method can be used to convert the YAML generated by the to_yaml method back into Active Record objects.

Given a file named accounts.yml, the contents of which are the YAML output by the command Account.find(:all).to_yaml, we can create a simple program to read in the file and save the objects to the database. The relevant code follows:

```
accounts_yaml_string = File.read("accounts.yml")
accounts = YAML::parse(accounts_yaml_string).transform
accounts.each { |account| account.save }
```

Exporting CSV

Like YAML, CSV is a data type that is supported by Active Record fixtures, which are used for unit, functional, and integration tests. In addition, CSV is a popular file type for importing or exporting from legacy systems or providing information to users for importing into their spreadsheet or other programs. Because the Ruby standard libraries contain CSV reading and writing capabilities, output of Active Record objects as CSV data is straightforward.

In the following example code, we export all of our accounts to a CSV file. We utilize the Account model's content_columns method to give us just the content of the class; this excludes the primary key, all columns ending in _id or _count, and the column used for single-table inheritance. If, for instance, you do not wish to export only the content columns and you actually want all of the columns, you can replace the calls to content_columns with columns.

```
headers = Account.content_columns.collect { |column| column.human_name }
only_columns = Account.content_columns.collect { |column| column.name }
accounts = Account.find(:all)
outfile = File.open('csvoutput.csv', 'wb')
CSV::Writer.generate(outfile, ',') do |csv|
  csv << headers
  accounts.each do |account|
    csv << account..attributes(:only => only_columns).values
  end
end
```

■**Tip** While writing out your Active Record objects as CSV data is relatively straightforward, there is a useful Active Record plug-in that augments your Active Record objects with a to_csv method. This plug-in makes it even easier to export your model data as CSV and allows you to easily customize the output. You can find out more about this plug-in, called Convertible to CSV at its web site: http://rubygreenblue.com/project/convertible_to_csv.

Importing CSV

The CSV format is a very common format that is used in countless situations. These situations may vary from initial or repeated batch imports of large data sets to providing a user with a way to upload a small data set. Therefore, the method you might use to import data from CSV may depend heavily on the nature and purpose of the CSV data.

Frankly, if you need to do a very large import of well formatted data into your database, the best solution may not be to use Active Record at all. Rather, your database software may have a mechanism to import CSV data directly. This will result in a much faster import, and if you know the data is well formed, the benefits of using Active Record as an intermediary may not be necessary.

Using your database mechanism for CSV importing aside, there are several benefits to writing a program using Active Record to import your CSV data. You can use Active Record validations to verify the validity of your CSV data, and either address the issues in your program or exclude those records. In addition, if you know you need to do data manipulations, such as concatenating and modifying fields in the CSV, it can be very effective to write a Ruby program to do this import.

In the following code snippet, we read in a CSV file to import into our accounts data that contains a first name and a last name column:

```
CSV::Reader.parse(File.open('accounts.csv', 'rb')) do |row|
  Account.create(:last_name => row[0], :first_name => row[1])
end
```

If any one of the records that are being imported fail validations, it will not be created. Our program could attempt to fix these errors and try again or just log these errors.

You're on Your Way to Becoming a Legend

Throughout this chapter, we've tried to lay the groundwork for you on dealing with legacy schema in your Active Record programs. Still, the real learning will come when you get into your applications and start getting your hands dirty with the actual issues and problems associated with your legacy systems.

When it comes down to it, working with legacy systems in Active Record is more about making sound design decisions and choosing what to implement in Active Record (instead of another language or application) than it is about learning specific syntax or configuration options. Like many things in life, the more you do it, the better you will become at making the right decisions. Before you know it, you'll be a legendary Active Record developer, able to take even the most insane of legacy schema and bend it to your will with nothing more than Ruby code and your Active Record know-how and experience!

First, though, you've got to get out there in the real world and start playing around with Active Record. With that in mind, in the next—and final—chapter, we will try to get you started by giving you some final tips, hints, and tricks that we've learned in our Active Record experiences out in the real world.

■ ■ ■

## CHAPTER 8

Active Record and the Real World

Throughout the previous chapters, we've covered just about everything Active Record has to offer. We've talked about all the theory and design issues, walked you through as many examples as we could reasonably fit into a book of this size, and tried to show you all the tips and tricks we know and use ourselves.

Still, as any experienced developer knows, what you find in a book is often quite different than what you find in the real world of coding and problem solving. With that in mind, we put together this last chapter as a starting point for you to address those unknown questions or issues as you go out into the real world and move forward as an Active Record developer.

Exploring Active Record Source Code

When Kevin was a kid, he once got an OmniBot robot as a gift. The OmniBot was basically a remote-controlled programmable robot with a built-in tape recorder; it was the size of a small office trash can (it sort of looked like one too, in retrospect). The remote control could be used to steer it and as a walkie-talkie system you could speak through. You could also program steps and words for it to replay at any time (so it seemed like it had artificial intelligence, though it really didn't). In any case, OmniBots cost about $300—a small fortune in his world at that time and more than his family spent in an entire week—so you can imagine that it was quite a special gift! You can also probably guess that Kevin, being a young geek in training, had a blast with that thing and spent hours mapping out commands for it.

Even though it was a very expensive gift and Kevin knew he shouldn't, he just couldn't resist tearing it apart to see how it really worked, what it was built from, and of course, if he could get it back together and working after he had explored its guts! He fought and fought with his urge to rip apart his precious OmniBot, but alas, the urge was too strong. Within about two weeks of getting it, Kevin had removed every single screw, bolt, and nut he could. He explored all the circuits and wires. But best of all, he somehow managed to successfully rebuild it using *almost* all of the parts he had taken out (there were a few leftover screws and parts that it clearly didn't need).

Looking back, Kevin was always doing stuff like that. Regardless of the cost or the consequences, he just has to know how things work. We're guessing that, as a fellow programmer, you do, too. So while it's not really a requirement to developing great Active Record programs, knowing just where the Active Record source code is and how it really works is something we think we should spend a little time on. This way you can rip the guts out and take a look whenever you want—just remember to put it all back together before your mom gets home!

Finding the Code

At the start of this book, we mentioned that Active Record is really nothing more than Ruby code. This turns out to be a great fact for those of us who want to dive into the source code, because all we need to know is where the files are and, of course, how to follow a Ruby program.

Active Record is distributed as a Ruby gem, so hopefully, it seems pretty obvious that its source code is stored within your Ruby gems' folder structure. The exact location of this folder depends on where you have installed Ruby and, to a lesser extent, on what version of Ruby Gem you are running. In most cases, though, once you've located your root Ruby directory (we'll refer to that location as YourRubyRoot in this chapter), the Active Record source files are found in the following location:

YourRubyRoot\lib\ruby\gems\1.8\gems\activerecord-1.15.3\lib

■**Note** The 1.8 in the path refers to the specific version of Ruby gems we are running, and activerecord-1.15.3 refers to the specific version of Active Record we have installed. These values may vary slightly depending on the version you are running. Browsing the directory at the locations specified in the path should make the correct values obvious for your specific situation.

Following the Code Trail

Now that you know where all the Active Record source code is physically located, we can start working our way through it. Since there's only one Ruby file located in the lib directory, called active_record.rb, that seems like a good place to start. Load active_record.rb into your favorite editor, and let's walk through some of the most interesting tidbits of code.

Walking Through active_record.rb

The first thing you should notice in active_record.rb is that Active Record requires the Active Support library. Active Support was primarily built, as was Active Record, for use with the Ruby on Rails framework, and according to its documentation, it "is a collection of various utility classes and standard library extensions that were found useful for Rails."

Probably the most important thing Active Support adds to Active Record is the inflection support for pluralization of table names. There are, of course, a number of other things Active Support adds, but going into detail about each is outside of the scope of this book. However, we do recommend that you take some time to browse the Active Resource documentation or source code. It can only help to improve your overall knowledge about how things work within your Ruby and Active Record programs.

Beyond the Active Support requirement, the active_record.rb file really just loads the various source files that make up the whole of the Active Record library. Many of these files are self-explanatory, and the details of methods they contain are covered throughout various parts of this book, so we won't repeat that information here. However, there are a few key files like base.rb, abstract_adapter.rb, and connection_specification.rb that do warrant a little bit more detailed explanation, so let's walk through those now.

Walking Through base.rb

You've probably noticed by now that we've been directly referencing the base.rb file in almost all of our examples throughout this book with a line like the following:

```
class Account < ActiveRecord::Base
```

We use the preceding syntax to define an Active Record model that directly maps to a table within our database. That line basically says that our new class inherits from the Active Record module's base class. Before we break down that base class, though, let's open the source file and see what we find.

When you open the base.rb file, the first things you should notice are the dependencies or requirements. Surprisingly, there are only four dependencies listed here: base64, yaml, set, and active_record/deprecated_finders. Let's briefly look at what each of these gives us.

base64: This library contains methods that are designed to handle base64 encoding and decoding of binary data; base64 is the default representation most databases use for handling binary data.

yaml: YAML stands for "yet another markup language" and is often used in configuration files throughout Ruby. Active Record also allows you to set configuration values via YAML files. Serialization and the to_yaml method also rely on the YAML library. We cover YAML in more detail in Chapters 6 and 7.

set: The set library adds functionality to manage collections of unordered, unique values. Its documentation bills it as "a hybrid of Array's intuitive inter-operation facilities and Hash's fast lookup."

active_record/deprecated_finders: This simply provides backward compatibility for older, and now deprecated, Active Record finder methods. The current list of deprecated finders follows:

- find_on_conditions: You should now use find(ids, :conditions => "").

- find_first: You should now use find(:first, . . .).

- find_all: You should now use find(:all, . . .).

Immediately following the requirements, a number of Active Record error and exception classes are defined. We covered the details of these exceptions in Chapter 6, so we won't go into them again here. The most important thing to note about this section of the code is that all the Active Record errors inherit from Ruby's standard StandardError class, which itself inherits from the Exception class.

Past the exception definitions, we find the Rdoc documentation that briefly outlines the details of the ActiveRecord class. This information provides the base for the official Active Record documentation and for much of this book. Of course, most things are only briefly explained in the Rdoc (or there would be no need for this book). Still, reading through the documentation there is *always* a good idea.

Moving on, we finally get to the definition of the Base class itself—this is where all the action really starts to happen. We've covered many of the details of the methods listed here throughout various parts of this book, so we won't go into fine-grained detail again for these either. Instead, we'll just point out of the most interesting tidbits about the details and methods in this class and leave it to you to do additional exploration as you see fit. Here's our high-level view of important features the Base class provides to all Active Record objects:

Event logging: Active Record supports detailed event logging and, by default, uses the Log4r class. The specific logger to use is set through the cattr_accessor method. We covered logging in detail in Chapter 6.

Configuration settings: One of the first things defined in the Base class are the various class variables that store the Active Record configuration settings. Here, you can see all the Active Record default assumptions and get a brief explanation of what each means. We covered the details of overriding each of the configuration settings in Chapter 7.

Finder methods: Finder methods are probably the most used methods in Active Record programs, so exploring these methods is highly recommended and educational. Of particular interest is the use of connection.select_all for the find_by_sql method (we'll come back to this point later when we review the private and protected methods of this file). We covered the details of the find methods in numerous places throughout this book.

Other CRUD methods: The create, update, and delete methods have also been covered in numerous spots throughout this book. Again, the interesting thing to note about the update and delete methods is the fact that they all eventually boil down to connection.update or connection.delete methods.

Guessing table names and keys: Here, you see just how Active Record attempts to guess your table names and primary and foreign keys based on your Active Record class names. This guessing relies heavily on the Active Support Inflector class. We covered the details of picking proper table and key names and overriding the preferred defaults in Chapter 7.

Various methods: Just below the methods for guessing table and key names are a variety of simple methods that add a lot of nice little features, such as the abilities to get a list of columns from a table, check if a given table exists in the database, and sanitize SQL statements (which, interestingly, just defers the sanitization to the connection.quote method).

Benchmarking: Benchmarking is important to any database application that expects to have a significant number of statements executed throughout its life cycle. Here, you can see that benchmarking really only occurs when the log level of the logger matches the application's log level. We cover benchmarking in detail in Chapter 6.

Scope: Handling scope is an interesting logic problem from a programming point of view, so it's well worth examining the source code to see just how Active Record implements support for scoping. We cover the details of Active Record scope in Chapter 2.

Private and protected methods: Most of the public methods throughout the Base class really just pass their values to the various private methods listed here, so this is where a lot of the real Active Record code occurs. These methods include functionality that builds the actual raw SQL that gets executed against your database. You can also see the details of the method_missing method that is ultimately the true secret behind the magic of Active Record. Here, you can also see that all finder methods are eventually molded into find_by_sql calls (and, therefore, eventually execute a connection.select_all statement).

Public methods: We've covered all of these methods throughout the course of this book, so there shouldn't be any big surprises here. Some of the methods worth looking into here include the destroy method (because of its direct use of the database connection), the update_attribute method (because it's overwritten by the validation module), and the reload method (because it clears cache values for aggregations and associations before reloading).

Walking Through abstract_adapter.rb

In the end, Active Record programs are all about communicating with a database, and to do that, you need to start by establishing a connection to your database. Active Record accomplishes this connection through each unique database-specific connection adapter, and each of those adapters follows the interface laid down in the ConnectionAdaptors module defined in this abstract_adapter.rb file.

Probably the most important thing to note about this file is the requirement of connection_specification, because that is where the real database connection is set up (we talk a little more about this in the next file walk-through). Of course, each adapter has its own special set of methods, rules, and logic that it adds to this outline, and for those details, you should refer to the source code of your specific adapter choice (also located in the connection_adapters folder).

Other things to note about the methods in this file include the support of methods to determine the state of the connection as well as methods to tell your Active Record programs what features the specific database supports (such as require_reloading? and prefetch_primary_key?).

Walking Through connection_specification.rb

Active Record connections are ultimately achieved through calling the Base.establish_connection method that is defined in this module. Each connection requires a set of configuration values either passed as a Ruby hash variable or loaded through a YAML file in your Rails environment (assuming you are using Active Record with the Ruby on Rails framework). We covered the details of each adaptor's configuration values in detail in Chapter 1.

Putting It All Back Together

By now, you should be an expert in everything Active Record, or at least have a very solid understanding of how it all works and where to look in the source code for more details as you need them. We started this book attempting to make the point that the Active Record library is really nothing more than Ruby code, and our exploration of the source has just reiterated that statement. What's more important to note, though, is that since it really is nothing more than Ruby code, you can change and mold it as you see fit. You can play with it as much as you want until you feel like you have a full grasp of how it all works.

If, in your coding or in playing around, you find that the library is not handling something the way you would like it to, you can change it. And if you think others can benefit from that change as well, you can submit it to the official distribution for inclusion and be a central part of the future of Active Record. Incidentally, this leads us nicely to our next topic.

The Future of Active Record

While it may seem like Active Record (and the related Ruby libraries) have appeared overnight on the developer's landscape, it's actually taken years of thought and work by a variety of contributors just to get where we are today. Still, it's true; in the big picture, Active Record is just a baby. It has a lot of room to evolve and luckily, being open source software, it has a lot of interested parties working on it, so the future should be a bright one.

At the time of this writing, there are only a few new additions in the edge version of Active Record slated to be a part of the next release of Active Record. We'll talk about each of these in just a minute.

Note The latest Ruby on Rails–related libraries, such as Active Record, are referred to as "edge," because they are considered to be on the cutting edge of development. You can obtain edge versions of various libraries with a Subversion client directly from `rubyforge.org`.

To be completely honest, though, Active Record does not necessarily have a roadmap of new features that are slated to be included from one release to another. Active Record development is more organic than that. It's hand pruned by a small group of core developers and contributed to by hundreds (if not thousands) of others from around the world who use it for their day-to-day work. As such, like many open source applications, the future of Active Record truly will be determined by the needs of its users like you.

The Keys to the Enterprise

As Active Record, Ruby, and the Ruby on Rails framework see more adoption in the marketplace, it is clear that the direction of Active Record will tend toward more enterprise-level functionality. However, the core team is committed to the very simple "getting real" methodology that made Active Record everything it is today and have decided to tackle the big enterprise challenges in, hopefully, simple ways that solve the main problems for 80 percent of all uses.

One such modification is database caching. Because instantiating objects from rows in the database can be expensive, many ORM frameworks implement some method of caching the results return by the database. The ORM framework then watches whether any of the objects it has cached have been modified, and if so, invalidates the cache.

Until now, Active Record has had no method of caching database results. Unfortunately, the problem of caching is a tricky one, and in this case, the Rails core team decided to knock some low-hanging fruit off the tree first, rather than implement a more complex object caching methodology.

In the latest version of Active Record slated for release with Ruby on Rails 2.0, they've implemented a simple cache that caches the results of each SQL query. If the exact query is called, and there have been no updates or inserts since the results were cached, then the cached results are returned. However, if there have been *any* updates or inserts (with no attention paid to the actual records updated or inserted) the cache is invalidated, and the query is performed again. While it's not a sophisticated caching strategy for queries such as you might find in an enterprise database management system like Oracle, it's better than nothing. And it is one example of the enterprise features being added to Active Record, as well as an excellent example of the mindset of the core team implementing those features. Finally, this example shows that some Active Record solutions are still being actively sought out.

Little by Little, Big Things Will Happen

While no one is ruling out the possibility of major changes to Active Record, the authors of Rails and Active Record have said that many of the upcoming changes to the framework will be minor changes intended to make working with Active Record easier and more enjoyable.

One such upcoming change is the integration of the ideas contained in plug-in that was called Sexy Migrations. Sexy migrations are a new shorthand form of migration.

Note We covered migrations in detail in Chapter 3.

Previously, to create a table called `products` with several fields, you might do something like the following:

```
create_table "products" do |t|
  t.column "shop_id",    :integer
  t.column "creator_id", :integer
  t.column "name",       :string,   :default => "Untitled"
  t.column "value",      :string,   :default => "Untitled"
  t.column "created_at", :datetime
  t.column "updated_at", :datetime
end
```

With the new migrations shorthand, the preceding table-creation code can now be expressed as follows:

```
create_table :products do |t|
  t.integer :shop_id, :creator_id
  t.string  :name, :value, :default => "Untitled"
  t.timestamps
end
```

Two Steps Forward, One Step Back

In addition to taking ideas that originally appeared in plug-ins to Active Record and integrating them into it, the core team has also indicated that some features will be removed from the core of Active Record and instead be available only as plug-ins. The reasons for this are being explained as a result of various features being deemed outside the scope of the primary intention of Active Record or of features not working well enough to be included in the core at this time.

Pagination, which is basically the process of displaying or working through a data result set in small chunks (rather than all at once), is one example of a feature expected to be removed and made available only via a plug-in. Actually, pagination isn't really a part of Active Record even right now; it's a part of the Action Controller library that only appears to be a part of the Active Record feature set. This is possibly part of the issue with the current pagination implementation that many developers have. In any case, many of the new pagination plug-ins functionally put their feature set as a part of Active Record, and pagination is, indeed, better suited in Active Record. However, no pagination is expected to be included directly in Active Record.

A World of Resources

Interestingly enough, a big part of the future of Active Record may not be Active Record at all but another component of Ruby on Rails called Active Resource. Active Resource exposes a Rails application, and therefore Active Record models, to the outside world via RESTful interfaces.

■**Note** In case you're not familiar with web service terminology, Representation State Transfer (REST) is a wide-sweeping term used to define an approach to distributed computing. There are currently a few camps of thought, which are often in heated debate, on what a system must support to truly be considered a REST system (or RESTful), but most people agree that, at the very least, a REST system involves at least two services exchanging data in some agreed-upon format. For example, the World Wide Web itself is considered to be a REST-based system. There are many great books on REST and web services available, including a short PDF written by one of this book's authors, Kevin Marshall, called "Web Services with Ruby on Rails;" it's available at `http://www.oreilly.com/catalog/websor/`.

During his keynote address at RailsConf 2006, DHH revealed that Ruby on Rails would include full support for REST and would encourage RESTful application development. Since that time, REST support has been growing rapidly, and the number of developers implementing RESTful applications has grown dramatically.

With Rails 2.0, REST will become the default application structure, unless otherwise specified. This means that, by default, an application will have a remote API built in, and the application will be exposed to remote access. The client-side library for this API access is Active Resource. A developer programming with Active Resource can program with local code, operating on remote resources in a syntax that is nearly identical to that of Active Record.

Like Active Record, Active Resource is also completely functional outside of the Ruby on Rails framework. Additionally, because Active Resource is merely a client-side implementation of the server-side API, RESTful clients can be implemented in pretty much any language. Alternate client libraries have already been created for JavaScript and Adobe Flex. Therefore, Active Resource and REST open up a new avenue for the integration of disparate or legacy systems with Rails or Active Record applications.

It should be noted though that, even within a RESTful system, it's likely that code will, at some point, need to access data stored within a database. So, while Active Resource (and web services as a whole) have been gaining a lot of traction as of late, they are not so much meant to replace libraries such as Active Record as to complement them (and maybe help to abstract the complexities of data stores a bit more).

Active Record on Its Own

As we've attempted to communicate throughout this book, Active Record is entirely functional outside of the Ruby on Rails framework for which it was created. As such, other frameworks have also started to use Active Record as their database ORM layer. Two such examples are Camping and Merb:

- Camping, a microframework, describes itself as a "little white blood cell in the vein of Rails" and was written and is maintained by "_why the lucky stiff". For more information about Camping, visit `http://code.whytheluckystiff.net/camping`.

- Merb, which is Mongrel plus Erb, is a small, fast web development framework written by Ezra Zygmuntowicz that is meant to complement Rails. For more information about Merb, visit `http://rubyforge.org/projects/merb`.

The needs and stresses that these and other frameworks put on Active Record continue to bring enhancements to Active Record. Merb, for instance, has provided insight and solutions to concurrency in Active Record. The benefits to Active Record from being used in new situations outside of Rails such as these are great. We also believe that these uses help to prove that Active Record is already a rich, dynamic, and robust ORM library that continues to get better!

Adding Your Own Two Cents

As we mentioned at the start of this section, the future of Active Record is really up to those of us (including you now) who use it day in and day out. If there's a feature you think is worth adding, or a problem you've hit that Active Record doesn't already address as you would like it to, you can try to get your solution added to the library source. If contributing to the development of Active Record sounds interesting to you, there are several resources for you to get started with:

`http://groups.google.com/group/rubyonrails-core` is the discussion forum for the core development of Active Record and the rest of the Ruby on Rails framework.

`http://rubyforge.org/projects/active record` is the location to download the latest Active Record release, as well as past releases (or you can install via the gem system outlined in Chapter 1).

`http://dev.rubyonrails.org` is the main web site for Active Record and Ruby on Rails development. Hosted within Trac, this site includes documentation for how to check out the latest version using SVN, as well as the bug and issue database.

As you can probably guess by now, we're big fans of Active Record, and we hope that we've helped to make you a big fan as well. Still, we wouldn't feel as if we were being complete, or totally honest, if we didn't acknowledge that Active Record doesn't do everything. It's not perfect for every situation, and there are alternatives. So before we can wrap up our coverage, we feel compelled to mention at least a few alternatives to Active Record you should know about.

Alternatives to Active Record

If there's one thing you can count on in the programming world, it's that any successful code implementation will be copied. Alternatives will emerge. Everyone wants to add their two cents and mold it to their specific needs. Sometimes these alternatives even turn out to be a better fit for specific tasks.

Active Record is no exception. In fact, there are a number of Ruby database-access library alternatives that you can choose from. Of course, we think Active Record is the cream of this crop (for the many reasons that we've outlined throughout this book), but perhaps one or two of these will be a better fit for your specific needs, and it's at least good to know you have options. So let's take a quick look at some of the more popular alternatives to Active Record and some of the pros and cons of each.

First, we feel compelled to point out the single biggest con, in our opinion, to each of the libraries mentioned below and, by contrast, the single biggest pro to the Active Record library—the built-in integration with the Ruby on Rails framework. If you're only planning on working with Rails applications, there is no need to bother with any of the libraries in the following sections at this time.

Also, it's important to note that the pros and cons we mention here are just our opinions when comparing each library to Active Record for our own applications. It is not our intention to demean or take anything away from each library. Again, each of these libraries could be a perfect choice for your application needs.

DBI

DBI stands for Database Interface and is actually at the core or behind the scenes of many of the other libraries mentioned in the following sections (it's also one of the backbones of Active Record). This description comes directly from its documentation, "The DBI package is a vendor-independent interface for accessing databases. It's similar, but not identical to, Perl's DBI module."

The official DBI site is http://ruby-dbi.rubyforge.org and installation files can be obtained at http://rubyforge.org/projects/ruby-dbi.

The Pros of DBI

The biggest advantage to the Ruby DBI package, as the documentation outlines, is that for the most part it's database independent. You only need to learn a couple of classes (DatabaseHandle and StatementHandle), and the majority of database-specific details are abstracted from your point of view.

In fact, viewing the source code reveals that many of the Active Record adaptors actually rely on DBI classes and logic.

The Cons of DBI

The first disadvantage to the DBI package is that, you are required to install the specific driver for each database that you intend to work with. This probably isn't a deal breaker, but it does mean at least a little extra work in switching from one database to another in the background.

The second biggest drawback to using DBI directly, as we see it, is that even though your database communication has been abstracted, your code really has not. It is not a true ORM library. Your database interaction is often embedded throughout various points of your code. You also have to do a lot of the legwork yourself, oftentimes resorting to pure SQL statements.

A DBI Example

The following example quickly shows some of the basic CRUD operations using DBI. For more information, examples, and options for implementing DBI, you should check the library's official web site.

```
require "dbi"

begin

  # connect to DB
  dbiexamp = DBI.connect("DBI:Mysql:test:localhost","root","rootpass")
  # add a record
  added = dbiexamp.do("insert into account(account_name) values('Kevin')")
  puts "added #{added} records" # => added 1 records

  # update the record
  dbiexamp.do("update account set account_name = 'Kevin Marshall' where " +
              "account_name = 'Kevin'")

  records = dbiexamp.execute("select * from account")
  records.fetch do |row|
    puts "found account for #{row["account_name"]}"
  end

  # delete a record
  dbiexamp.do("delete account where account_name = 'Kevin Marshall'")
rescue DBI::DatabaseError => error
  puts "Error: #{error}"
ensure
  dbiexamp.disconnect if dbiexamp
end
```

As you can see, all the basic CRUD operations are supported and easy enough to achieve. They just require a little more typing than their Active Record alternatives; there are no built-in helpers to abstract the SQL language, and you need to handle the opening and closing of your connections directly. Of course, many old-school developers coming from languages like Perl or Java are used to doing this type of work.

Og

Og is short for ObjectGraph and is probably the most full-featured Ruby ORM library alternative to Active Record available today. It was designed for handling the model section of the Nitro framework (a Ruby framework alternative to Ruby on Rails).

Og takes a slightly different approach to the ORM design pattern than Active Record. With Active Record, you define your database schema first and then Active Record creates the Ruby objects from that information. With Og, you define the Ruby objects, and Og takes care of creating the database schema for you.

You can learn more about Og (and the Nitro framework) and access its official documentation from its official web site, `http://www.nitroproject.org`.

The Pros of Og

Obviously, the biggest pro to Og is its integration with the Nitro framework. If you are looking for an alternative to the Ruby on Rails framework but don't want to give up working with Ruby or an ORM, Nitro is where you should look.

Another big advantage to Og is its reliance on Ruby objects to glean the database structure rather than the other way around (as Active Record does). If your background is that of a programmer more than of a database person, this probably feels more natural to you.

The use of the Og library is very similar to that of Active Record, which means the basic use and concepts from a coder's point of view are almost the same.

The Cons of Og

Honestly, from a top-level view, there aren't a lot of cons to the Og library, since it's so similar to that of Active Record (outside of the obvious fact that it's not integrated with the Ruby on Rails framework). If you are coming from a traditional database-driven application environment or are used to working with languages like Perl, the object approach might be a little confusing, but once you get over that hurdle, Og really is pretty simple and straightforward.

Also, to our knowledge, to date, documentation and publications covering Og are limited, and the Nitro framework has not gained quite the traction that the Ruby on Rails framework has.

An Og Example

The following example quickly shows some of the basic CRUD operations using Og. For more information, examples, and options for implementing Og, should check the library's official web site.

```
require 'og'

class Account
  property :account_name, String
end

# establish connection and create any tables that are not yet there.
Og.setup( { :destroy => false,
            :store => :mysql,
            :user => "root",
            :password => "rootpass",
            :name => "exampledb" })

test = Account.new
test.account_name = "Kevin"
test.save! # => saves the record into the account table
```

```
accs = Account.first
puts accs.account_name # => "Kevin"

test.account_name = "Kevin Marshall"
test.save!

puts test.account_username # => Kevin Marshall
test.delete! # => delete the record
```

ActiveRelation

ActiveRelation is a new ORM library that has been getting some attention recently. It was designed to build on Active Record concepts while adding support for some features that were intentionally left out of the Active Record library (like support for multicolumn primary keys, auto-detection of foreign keys, and eloquent handling of multiple-table joins).

Additional information and installation details can be found at http://rubyforge.org/projects/active-relation.

The Pros of ActiveRelation

Additional features such as support of multicolumn primary keys and auto-detection of foreign keys, while keeping the core functionality and beauty of Active Record, makes ActiveRelation very promising. Its support for handling more complex joins in a user-friendly way also intrigues us. If this library can really deliver on just these benefits (we have not extensively tested it), this is a library worth keeping your eyes on in the near future.

The Cons of ActiveRelation

The glaring problem with this library at the time of this writing was the lack of documentation, official support, or even word-of-mouth buzz. While we find the list of issues it's attempting to tackle inspiring, the fact that ActiveRelation has not seen more adoption probably shows the lack of need for many of these problems to actually be solved in most Ruby on Rails applications (these are issues that are generally found only in legacy systems, and most Rails applications are not currently legacy conversions).

Because of its lack of widespread use, only a couple of database adapters have been updated with support. If you wanted to start using this library with something like SQL Server, you would first need to update the adapter and library yourself.

The syntax for ActiveRelation, aside from configuration, if nearly identical to that of Active Record, so it should be relatively familiar to anyone reading this book.

Database-Specific Libraries

Though the concepts are generally the same, every database program is unique. They all have their own ways of allowing and handling connections. They all support a variety or version of SQL and different database features (like sequences, triggers, and stored procedures). So as you might expect, each database also has its own unique Ruby library that you can use for data access.

Check with your database vendor or the database community for details on existing Ruby libraries and Ruby support. Searching RubyForge.org is also a good place to find database-specific Ruby libraries and information.

The Pros of Database-Specific Libraries

Since these libraries are tightly coupled with a specific database implementation, they often provide the most complete support of the given database's feature set. If you know your application will only ever be connecting to a specific type and version of a database application, this approach will give you the most direct control from within your Ruby code.

The Cons of Database-Specific Libraries

Today's development world is full of rapid changes and updates. Using a database-specific library not only locks you into that database store, it generally locks you into a specific version of that database. For example, there are different Ruby libraries for working with different versions of Oracle (oracle for older version of Oracle, oci8 for Oracle 8*i*, and ruby9i for Oracle 9*i*).

This basically means that every time you update your database version, or switch to a completely new database store, you will, at a minimum, need to update your database-specific library (and rewrite large sections of your application code, at a maximum). Using database-specific libraries also has a lot of the same cons that we mentioned with using the DBI library, the most important of which is the coupling of your code and SQL statements.

Active Resource

For a few years now, web services have been a hot topic. It's been only recently, though, that many sites and services have started to actually implement web services as a core part of their applications and feature sets. The Ruby on Rails framework is no exception. DHH has been hard at work for the past year fleshing out the details of the Active Resource library, which is, in many ways, simply a web services take on the Active Record library.

While it's not directly intended to replace Active Record, in some situations, you may be able to use it as an alternative to Active Record. For more information on Active Resource, you should check out the official Ruby on Rails web site at http://www.rubyonrails.org.

The Pros of Active Resource

Implementation of true RESTful services is what has everyone talking about Active Resource right now, but on a more general level, it's the idea of a distributed data store, accessible through web service standards, that makes Active Resource an interesting potential alternative to Active Record.

The web service approach also allows you to remove the knowledge and support of a database from your core duties and focus on nothing more than your application code and the interaction with the web service.

The Cons of Active Resource

Eventually, data has to be stored—whether in a database, flat text files, or RAM, it's got to end up somewhere. So even behind a web service wall, there is likely a database that requires knowledge and support. Also, relying on web services means trusting that the service will continue to be available to your application at all times and will continue to support the features you have implemented. Basically, it means relinquishing control of and trusting your data to a third party, and that's something that most real-world programs have a tough time doing.

Even More Alternatives

We've already mentioned a handful of alternatives to Active Record, and as you are probably starting to notice, there is no shortage of them! In fact, there are so many that mentioning them all is outside of the scope of this book. So instead, we'll just mention some quick points on a handful more of the next best options we could find:

Kansas: Kansas is an older ORM library that sits on top of DBI. Essentially, it's designed to add ORM functionality to the DBI library without large amounts of overhead. You can learn more about Kansas at `http://enigo.com/projects/kansas`.

Criteria: Criteria is a little-known library designed to abstract the querying of various data sets. The idea is that regardless of what your data store is (a database, a flat file, or an array of Ruby objects for example) you can perform the same query without having to alter your code. You can learn more about Criteria at `http://mephle.org/Criteria`.

Lafcadio: Lafcadio is another ORM designed specifically for use with the MySQL database. You can learn more about Lafcadio at `http://lafcadio.rubyforge.org`.

LDAP and flat files: LDAP stands for Lightweight Directory Access Protocol, and while there are other directory services available, LDAP is the most commonly used one today. Basically, LDAP allows you to search directories like SQL allows you to search databases. As you can imagine, there are a lot of design issues that go into building a LDAP application, all of which are out of scope for this book. However, it should be noted that there are many times when using LDAP may be a smarter choice than Active Record for your application (if you are building a contacts application to run on your local computer for example). For more information about the Ruby LDAP library, you should visit `http://ruby-ldap.sourceforge.net`.

Common Active Record Questions and Answers

If you take a quick browse through the computer section at just about any book store, you'll probably notice a plethora of cookbooks or recipe books. There's a good reason for that: the real world of programming is all about problem solving and answering questions. A lot of times, you know exactly what you want to do, and you just want a quick answer on how to get it done without having to read an entire book or learn all the ins and outs.

So with that in mind, we've compiled this last section to provide quick answers to common problems. We've seen most of these questions mentioned on various forums and blogs or had them ourselves when we were starting out with Active Record.

How Do I Use Multiple Databases with Active Record?

It is possible to use Active Record seamlessly across multiple databases. This can be useful in many scenarios, from performing database maintenance and migrations to application integrations where separate models are stored in separate databases.

When working with multiple databases (and really when working with a single database as well), it can be handy to store your connection parameters in a YAML configuration file. For this example, the file will be called database.yml, but you can name it whatever you want. The file should look something like this:

```yaml
database1:
  adapter: mysql
  host: localhost
  username: myuser
  password: mypass
  database: db1

database2:
  adapter: mysql
  host: remote.host
  username: youruser
  password: yourpass
  database: db2
```

With the preceding configuration file in hand, we can now use it to individually configure our Active Record models to talk to the separate databases. We will first create a separate Active Record class that our real Active Record classes will extend, which will make our code cleaner and easier to maintain:

```ruby
require "rubygems"
require "activerecord"

@config = YAML.load_file(File.join(File.dirname(__FILE__), 'database.yml'))

class LocalDatabase < ActiveRecord::Base
  establish_connection @config['database1']
end

class RemoteDatabase < ActiveRecord::Base
  establish_connection @config['database2']
end
```

The Active Record classes LocalDatabase and RemoteDatabase can now be used to indicate which database each particular Active Record class uses. In this example, you have a remote database where your customers are stored, and a local database stores the users who belong to those customers. In addition, the local database also hosts a table containing the e-mail addresses of the users.

```ruby
class Customer < RemoteDatabase
  has_many :users
end

class User < LocalDatabase
  belongs_to :customer
```

```
  has_on :email
end

class Email < LocalDatabase
  belongs_to :user
end
```

You can now use the Customer, User, and Email Active Record classes normally, within the limitations of your database server.

■Caution In the first example, our databases are stored on different database servers. The ability to correctly interact with multiple servers varies among the different database servers. For instance, MySQL can make table joins across different databases only if they run on the same server. However, Oracle can make table joins across different servers.

In the first example of working with multiple databases, the Active Record models are using different models on each database. However, if you wanted to perform a migration of similar or identical models between two databases, it would be useful to put each of your classes inside of a module. For example, assume you have User and Email databases on both servers and you wish to copy a user from one database to the other:

```
Module LocalDb
  class User < LocalDatabase
    belongs_to :customer
    has_on :email
  end

  class Email < LocalDatabase
    belongs_to :user
  end
end

Module RemoteDb
  class User < RemoteDatabase
    belongs_to :customer
    has_on :email
  end

  class Email < RemoteDatabase
    belongs_to :user
  end
end
```

You can then reference the remote User model with RemoteDb::User and the local User model with LocalDb::User.

```
user = RemoteDb::User.find_by_name('Chad Pytel', :include => [:email], :limit => 1)
new_user = LocalDb::User.new user.attributes
new_user.email = LocalDb::Email.new user.email.attributes
new_user.save
```

How Do I Handle Internationalization and Localization?

Active Record does not include default support for internationalization or localization. The default validation error messages, for example, are all in English, regardless of your or your users' system language. Therefore, there are several things to consider to ensure that your Active Record program can handle internationalization.

First, if you have an international requirement, you will very likely want to make sure that your database is storing all characters with the UTF-8 character set. The mechanism for doing this may vary depending on your specific database. On most database servers, the character set can be specified at the database server, database, and table levels.

For example, to ensure that a MySQL database table for your Account model has default character set of UTF-8, you would use the following create_table statement:

```
create_table(:accounts, :options => 'DEFAULT CHARSET=utf8') do |t|
  t.column :first_name, :string
  t.column :last_name, :string
  t.column :email, :string
end
```

Additionally, there are problems with the String class in Ruby 1.8, as it does not support Unicode characters, except in regular expressions. These problems are present in any String method that expects each character of a string to be a single byte, such as String#count, String#slice, and so on. Fortunately, Active Support includes a module called Multibyte, which adds a chars accessor to the String class, on which you can safely perform these operations on multibyte (Unicode) strings. Therefore, instead of calling "hello".slice, you can safely call "hello".chars.slice. For more information about ActiveSupport::Multibyte, read the API documents for the chars method at

http://api.rubyonrails.org/classes/ActiveSupport/CoreExtensions/String/
Unicode.html#M000417

■**Note** The authors of Ruby have said that Ruby will get full Unicode support in Ruby 1.9 and 2.0, so hopefully, internationalization will be less of a problem.

Finally, it is likely necessary to provide translations for the messages displayed to users in your programs. There are several plug-ins available to assist with internationalization and localization. One of the simplest is the Localization plug-in, written by Thomas Fuchs. For more information about this plug-in, visit http://mir.aculo.us/2005/10/30/localization-plugin.

How Do I Use Composite Primary Keys?

Because Active Record is opinionated software, it includes no support for using composite primary keys. Even if, like the Active Record developers, you believe that composite primary keys are generally unnecessary, many legacy database schemas may use composite primary keys. Fortunately, there is an Active Record extension that adds composite primary key support. You can download and find documentation on this plug-in at http://compositekeys.rubyforge.org.

How Do I Use GUID/UUID Primary Keys?

Active Record not only uses sequential, integer primary keys by default, but contains no built-in support for any other type of primary key. Fortunately, it is relatively straightforward to override the default primary key behavior of Active Record to use nonsequential, noninteger primary keys.

There are actually two different methods of overriding Active Record to support Universally Unique Identifier (UUID) primary keys: including the UUID functionality in a module and using an abstract Base class. For completeness, let's run through both ways of implementing this functionality.

Regardless of which method you use to implement this functionality, you will need to generate a UUID to be used as the primary key. You can do this with the UUIDTools library, which is available via the Ruby Gems system. Install this gem with

```
gem install uuidtools
```

You can now use the UUIDTools library in Active Record by including the following lines:

```
require 'rubygems'
require 'uuidtools'
```

■**Note** UUIDTools is written by Bob Aman. Documentation can be found online at http://sporkmonger.com/projects/uuidtools.

To use a module to implement this functionality, define the module that provides a before_create method:

```
module UUIDKeys
  def before_create
    self.id = UUID.timestamp_create().to_s
  end
end
```

Next, in your ActiveRecord class, include the module:

```
class User < ActiveRecord::Base
  include UUIDKeys
  # your additional model code
end
```

The `before_create` method is a callback supported by Active Record that is called before the object is actually persisted to the database. As you can see, we are explicitly setting the ID of the object. Then, because our object already has a value in the `id` attribute, Active Record will not attempt to generate a new one.

The second way to implement this functionality is by using an abstract `Base` class. This abstract class will provide the same functionality as the previous module, by providing a `before_create` method:

```
class UUIDKeyClass < ActiveRecord::Base
  self.abstract_class = true

  def before_create
    self.id = UUID.timestamp_create().to_s
  end
end
```

Next, rather than having your Active Record class extend `ActiveRecord::Base`, your class will extend the class `UUIDKeyClass`:

```
class User < UUIDKeyClass
  # your additional model code
end
```

Can I Use Active Record in a Multithreaded Program?

Active Record can work inside of a multithreaded program. However, with all the Active Record adapters except those for PostgreSQL and Oracle, deadlocks can occur, because their underlying APIs do not use nonblocking I/O.

How Do I Ensure Proper Handling of Decimal Numbers?

Historically, Active Record, like many libraries, has had issues with ensuring that decimal values, such as currency, are handled correctly. However, as of Active Record 1.15, the `BigDecimal` class is supported for columns of type `:decimal`. Ruby's `BigDecimal` class provides arbitrary-precision floating-point arithmetic.

What Database Locking Mechanisms Does Active Record Support?

While Active Record supports its own optimistic and pessimistic record-level locking, there is no built-in support for table level locking. Fortunately, it is relatively straightforward to add this functionality. First, create the table locking module:

```
module TableLocking
  def lock_table(options = {})
    sql = "LOCK TABLES #{table_name}"
    sql += ' WRITE' if options[:write]
    sql += ' READ' if options[:read]
    execute sql
  end
```

```
  def unlock_table
    execute "UNLOCK TABLES"
  end
end
```

Next, in your Active Record class, include the module:

```
class User < ActiveRecord::Base
  include TableLocking
  # your additional model code
end
```

With the module included in your class, you can now lock and unlock the table at will for read access, write access, or both, as in the following example:

```
User.lock_table(:read => true, :write => true)
User.delete(1)
User.unlock_table
```

Does Active Record Support Prepared Statements?

Because of the dynamic nature of Active Record, it does not support prepared statements, and while this feature may be added in the future, it is currently not possible.

How Do I Select a Random Record from the Database?

This is a common problem, with a number of mediocre solutions. The most obvious solution follows:

```
random_record = Model.find(:all)[rand(Model.count)]
```

Because every single record is instantiated, this method is the incorrect and extremely inefficient method, unless the number of records is incredibly small.

You may be tempted to use the following solution:

```
random_record = Model.find(rand(Model.count)+1)
```

Because you cannot guarantee that all IDs are present in the database (there may be gaps caused by deleting records, for example), this is an incorrect solution. The best solution, which doesn't rely on database-specific functionality, is to select an ID less than a random number and limited to one result.

```
random_record = Model.find(:first, :conditions => ["id < ?", Model.maximum('id')])
```

There is one deficiency in the preceding code—if large sections of the database are deleted, there will be large gaps in the record IDs, so some records are less likely to be selected than others. If a more perfectly random selection method is important to you, you can solve this problem by creating a separate index column in your model that can be reindexed every once in a while, to remove gaps.

How Do I Model *X* with Active Record?

While each application may have its own data model needs, there are common patterns that will emerge once you start to use Active Record for your application. Also, if you are familiar with other ORM libraries, it may be helpful to see how data models with which you may be familiar are built using Active Record. Some common data models and explanations of how they would be coded follow in Listings 8-1 to 8-7.

Listing 8-1. *Customers and employees*

```
class Company < ActiveRecord::Base
  has_many :employees
end

class Employee < ActiveRecord::Base
  belongs_to :company
end
```

Listing 8-2. *E-commerce*

```
class Category < ActiveRecord::Base
  has_many :products
end

class Product < ActiveRecord::Base
  belongs_to :category
end

class Order < ActiveRecord::Base
  has_many :line_items
end

class LineItem < ActiveRecord::Base
  belongs_to :product
  belongs_to :order
end
```

Listing 8-3. *Role-Based Access Control*

```
class User < ActiveRecord::Base
  has_and_belongs_to_many :roles
end

class Roles < ActiveRecord::Base
  has_and_belongs_to_many :users
  has_and_belongs_to_many :permissions
end
```

```
class Permission < ActiveRecord::Base
  has_and_belongs_to_many :roles
end
```

Listing 8-4. *Surveys / Questionnaires / Quizzes*

```
class Survey < ActiveRecord::Base
  has_many :questions
  has_many :responses
end

class Question < ActiveRecord::Base
  belongs_to :survey
  has_many :choices
end

class Choice < ActiveRecord::Base
  belongs_to :question
end

class Response < ActiveRecord::Base
  belongs_to :survey
  has_many :response_choices
end

class ResponseChoice < ActiveRecord::Base
  belongs_to :response
  belongs_to :question
  belongs_to :choice
end
```

Listing 8-5. *Hierarchical Content Management*

```
class Page < ActiveRecord::Base
  acts_as_tree
  acts_as_list :scope => :parent
end
```

Listing 8-6. *Blogs*

```
class Post < ActiveRecord::Base
  has_many :comments, :dependent => true, :order => "created_at ASC"
end

class Comment < ActiveRecord::Base
  belongs_to :post
end
```

Listing 8-7. *Social Networking (Friends)*

```
class Users < ActiveRecord::Base
  has_many :friends, :through => :relationships
  has_many :relationships
end

class Relationship < ActiveRecord::Base
  belongs_to :user
  belongs_to :friend, :class => User
end
```

What Support Does Active Record Have for Database Foreign Keys?

The short answer is that Active Record does not include any support for database foreign keys. As opinionated software, Active Record takes the view that foreign key management should be managed at the ORM level, without any specific support for SQL foreign keys.

That said, you could always just use the execute method in your migrations to include raw SQL to create and modify your foreign key constraints.

In addition, several enterprising developers have made Active Record plug-ins that add various levels of foreign key support to Active Record. Plug-ins providing foreign key support essentially come in two flavors:

- Augmenting your existing relationship ID columns with foreign keys

- Actually establishing relationships based on foreign keys for you

If you are interested in using foreign keys with Active Record in either of these ways, there are a few resources you should check out. RedHill Consulting, has made several plug-ins related to foreign key support; you can find more about them at http://www.redhillonrails.org. Additionally, for magic support for foreign keys (and much more) explore Dr. Nic's Magic Models plug-in at http://magicmodels.rubyforge.org.

How Do I Properly Use find_by_sql?

The find_by_sql method simply accepts raw SQL, so you can essentially do any type of select statement for which you can generate the SQL code.

■**Note** We cover the find_by_sql method in detail in Chapter 7 as a part of our discussion on working with legacy database systems.

Honestly, if you find yourself using find_by_sql often for anything outside of legacy systems, you should probably take a step back and reevaluate what you are trying to accomplish. Using the normal find method and its various options, you should be able to accomplish many very complex database tasks. By relying on straight SQL to perform queries, you are circumventing some of the benefits of using Active Record, such as database abstraction. In addition, by not relying on straight SQL to perform your tasks, your code will be less brittle as your models change and much easier to maintain (for yourself and other Active Record developers).

How Do I Ensure that All My Records Are Valid?

Perhaps you are importing a large data set from another database to initially set up your application or adding new validations to an existing model, and you need to identify existing records that don't pass the new validations. Either way, it can be very handy to be able to ensure that all of your existing records are valid. The following script is a simple rake task that will validate all of your models; it is written specifically to be used within a Ruby on Rails application (another version modified to work with any model and YAML database configuration file will follow):

```
# file: validate_models.rake
# task: rake db:validate_models
namespace :db do
  desc "Run model validations on all model records in database"
  task :validate_models => :environment do
    puts "-- records - model --"
    Dir.glob(RAILS_ROOT + '/app/models/**/*.rb').each { |file| require file }
    Object.subclasses_of(ActiveRecord::Base).select { |c|
        c.base_class == c}.sort_by(&:name).each do |klass|
      total = klass.count
      printf "%10d - %s\n", total, klass.name
      chunk_size = 1000
      (total / chunk_size + 1).times do |i|
        chunk = klass.find(:all, :offset => (i * chunk_size), :limit => chunk_size)
        chunk.reject(&:valid?).each do |record|
          puts "#{record.class}: id=#{record.id}"
          p record.errors.full_messages
          puts
        end rescue nil
      end
    end
  end
end
```

■**Note** Special thanks go to Josh Susser (http://blog.hasmanythrough.com) for the preceding code.

The following script is a modification of the previous program that works with any Active Record models, even outside of a Ruby on Rails program. It will work on a Ruby on Rails program as well, given the correct arguments. It assumes that you have a YAML file to hold the database connection parameters, with the following format:

```
database:
  adapter: mysql
  host: localhost
  username: myuser
  password: mypass
  database: db1
```

The first argument is the path to the YAML configuration file; the second is the configuration root, in this case, database; and the remaining arguments are the paths to one or more Active Record models you'd like to validate:

```
require "rubygems"
require_gem "activerecord"

config_file = ARGV.shift
environment = ARGV.shift

@config = YAML.load_file(config_file)
ARGV.each { |file| puts file; require file }

Object.subclasses_of(ActiveRecord::Base).select { |c|
  c.base_class == c}.sort_by(&:name).each do |klass|
  klass.establish_connection @config[environment]
  total = klass.count
  printf "%10d - %s\n", total, klass.name
  chunk_size = 1000
  (total / chunk_size + 1).times do |i|
    chunk = klass.find(:all, :offset => (i * chunk_size), :limit => chunk_size)
    chunk.reject(&:valid?).each do |record|
      puts "#{record.class}: id=#{record.id}"
      p record.errors.full_messages
      puts
    end
  end rescue nil
end
```

Can I Use the Same Name for a Database Column and an Active Record Model?

No, you cannot have a column in your database with the same name as an Active Record model or database table, as it will cause errors. If the column is a reference (foreign key) to another model, Active Record conventions dictate it should be the name of the table followed by _id, but naming it anything other than the actual name of the table will avoid conflicts. For more information about Active Record naming conventions, see Chapter 3.

Does Active Record Support enum Column Types?

No, Active Record currently has no support for this database-specific feature. However, there is a way to create a read-only accessor to get at this data in your model, for use with a legacy database.

Given a table with the following enum column

```
`number` enum('ONE','TWO','THREE') NOT NULL default 'ONE'
```

use the following model with a custom accessor using the attributes_before_type_cast method to get the column value:

```
class Klass < ActiveRecord::Base
  def number
    attr = attributes_before_type_cast
    "#{attr['number']}"
  end
end
```

Does Active Record Support Adding Security to Individual Models or Columns?

Active Record does not include any support for security by default. Fortunately, there are ways to implement model-level security and plug-ins available that do it for you. One such plug-in is the ModelSecurity plug-in written by Bruce Perens, which is available at http://perens.com/FreeSoftware/ModelSecurity.

What Is the Difference Between has_one and belongs_to?

The difference between the two association types is in where the foreign key resides. In short, belongs_to is used when the related model's primary key is stored in the model's class, and has_one is used when the related model's primary key is stored in the other model's table. For more information about has_one, belongs_to, and the rest of the associations possible with Active Record, see Chapter 4.

How Can You Paginate Active Record Results?

Paging through result sets is a very common database-related task. At the time of this writing, Active Record has some limited support for pagination through the Action Controller library. However, it's buggy, to say the least, and therefore, in the near future, pagination is expected to be removed from this library and made available only as a plug-in to Active Record.

So our first recommendation would be to search for an Active Record pagination plug-in. Failing that, you can always deal with pagination via a fancy use of SQL LIMIT clauses. In SQL Server, for example, the following query allows you to get a subset of records you may want (records 10–20 here):

```
SELECT * FROM (SELECT TOP 10 * FROM (select top 20 * from comments order by id desc)
 as tmp1 ORDER BY id asc) AS tmp2 ORDER BY id desc
```

Most every flavor of SQL supports some form of the TOP or LIMIT clause and can therefore use a version of the preceding SQL statement. Refer to your specific SQL documentation for more details. You may also want to take a peek into your database adaptor source code to see if and how pagination is currently supported.

Where Can I Get More Active Record Help?

Throughout this book, we've tried to be as thorough as possible and cover everything about Active Record we could think of. Still, we've been around the block enough times to know that it's impossible to cover everything for everyone. If you've still got questions, a great place to start is by asking for help from the Ruby community itself by getting active on forums at sites like www.ruby-forum.com. You could also follow various blogs, like DHH's at http://www.loudthinking.com.

The Ruby on Rails official site at http://www.rubyonrails.org also has a number of helpful tips and tricks that are worth reading through.

Of course, if after reading this book and following those resources, you still have questions please feel free to e-mail us directly at info@falicon.com (Kevin Marshall), cpytel@thoughtbot.com (Chad Pytel), or jyurek@thoughtbot.com (Jon Yurek) with your comments and questions. We'll do our best to help you out, and we'll keep detailed notes, so we can improve later versions of this book!

■ ■ ■

Active Record Methods in Detail

ActiveRecord::Base

Public Class Methods

==(object_to_compare)

This method returns `true` if the `object_to_compare` is the same as the receiving object or is of the same Active Record class and has the same ID.

[](attribute_name)

This method returns the value of the specified attribute after it has been typecast and is an alias for the protected `read_attribute` method of an Active Record class. While a common method of accessing the attributes of an Active Record class is via a method call, like `account.first_name`, Active Record overrides the [ ] operator to make each of the attributes available as a hash parameter on the Active Record class. For example, you can also use the form `account[:first_name]`.

[]==(attribute_name, new_value)

This method is an alias for the protected `write_attribute` method of an Active Record class, and it allows you to set attribute values using a hash-like syntax, for example:

```
account[:last_name] = "Pytel"
```

abstract_class?()

`abstract_class?` returns `true` if the specified Active Record class is a base Active Record class and `false` if it is not.

attr_accessible(*attributes)

This method takes an array of attributes and makes them the only available attributes for mass assignment operations, such as with `new(attributes)` and `attributes=(attributes)`. All other attributes of the Active Record class become unavailable for mass assignment operations. The `attr_protected(*attributes)` method is the reverse of this operation.

attr_protected(*attributes)

This method takes an array of attributes and makes them unavailable for mass assignment operations, such as new(attributes) and attributes=(attributes). All other attributes of the Active Record class remain unchanged. The attr_accessible(*attributes) method is the reverse of this method.

base_class()

base_class returns the base Active Record class from which the specified Active Record class descends.

benchmark(title, log_level = Logger::DEBUG, use_silence = true) {|| . . .}

This method logs and benchmarks the statements that are specified in its block:

```
Account.benchmark("Creating and Finding Account") do
    account = Account.new(:username = > "cpytel")
    account.save
    accout.find_by_username("cpytel")
end
```

The benchmark is only performed if the current logging level matches the specified log_level. This allows you to specify benchmarking calls in production software without worrying about a performance hit from the benchmark.

Logging multiple statements of the benchmark is enabled by default but can be turned off by passing false to use_silence.

clear_active_connections!()

The method clears the cache that maps classes to database connections.

column_names()

column_names returns an array of strings that are the column names for the database table associated with this Active Record class.

columns()

With columns, you can return an array of column objects for the database table associated with this Active Record class.

columns_hash()

This method returns a hash of column objects for the database table associated with this Active Record class.

connected?()

The `connected?` method returns `true` if a database connection that is usable by this class has been opened.

connection()

To return the connection currently associated with the class, use the `connection` method. This method can also be used to obtain the connection in order to work directly with the database, for example:

```
Account.connection.select_values("SELECT id FROM accounts WHERE created_at < " +
Time.now - 1.day)
```

connection=(connection_specification)

This method manually sets the database connection for an Active Record class.

content_columns()

This method returns an array of `column` objects that Active Record considers the actual content, or data, of the Active Record class. Therefore, this array does not include the primary ID column, any columns ending in `_id` or `_count`, and any columns used for single table inheritance.

count_by_sql(sql_query_string)

The method returns the result of an SQL query that should only include `COUNT(*)` in the `SELECT` part of the SQL query:

```
Account.count_by_sql("SELECT COUNT(*) FROM accounts")
```

create(attributes = nil)

The `create` method instantiates and immediately saves the Active Record class with the values specified in the attributes hash, if validations permit. The newly created Active Record object is returned regardless of whether the save succeeded.

decrement_counter(counter_name, id)

This method works just like the `increment_counter(counter_name, id)` method, but it decrements the counter instead.

delete(id)

This method deletes the database record with the given `id` but does not instantiate the object first. Therefore, the `destroy` method and any other callbacks are not triggered. If an array of IDs is provided, all of the records matching the IDs are deleted.

delete_all(conditions = nil)

This method deletes all of the database records that match the given `conditions` but does not instantiate the objects first. Therefore, the `destroy` method and any other callbacks are not triggered. The format of `conditions` is the same as those given to the `find` method. If no conditions are specified, all of the database records for this class will be removed.

destroy(id)

`destroy` removes the database record associated with the given primary key by first instantiating the object and then calling the `destroy` method on the object. Therefore, when using this method, the `destroy` callbacks are triggered. If an array of IDs is provided, all of the records matching the IDs are destroyed.

destroy_all(conditions = nil)

Use this method to destroy all the database records that match the given `conditions` by first instantiating each object and then calling the `destroy` method. Therefore, when using this method, the `destroy` callbacks are triggered. The format of `conditions` is the same as those given to the `find` method. If no conditions are specified, all of the database records for this class will be destroyed.

establish_connection(connection_specification = nil)

This method is used to establish a connection to a database. It accepts a hash of connection parameters, where the `:adapter` key must be specified with the name of a valid database adapter:

```
ActiveRecord::Base.establish_connection(
  :adapter => "mysql",
  :host => "localhost",
  :username => "project",
  :database => "project_development")
```

exists?(id)

`exists?` returns `true` if the specified `id` matches the primary key of a record in the database.

find(*args)

The `find` method can retrieve a record by its `id`, the first record matching a query, or all records matching a query. When retrieving records by `id`, the `find` method can take a single `id`, a list of `ids`, or an array of `ids`, as shown in the following examples:

```
Account.find(1)
Account.find(1, 2, 3)
Account.find([1, 2, 3])
```

Return only the first matching record like this:

```
Account.find(:first)
```

Return all matching records like this:

`Account.find(:all)`

All of these approaches to returning records take an optional hash as the final parameter. The valid options in this hash follow:

:conditions: The :conditions options supplied to the find method will be converted into the WHERE clause of the SQL statement. You can pass a string or a hash of column names and values, or you can specify a more complex string of SQL along with values to interpolate inside an Array.

:order: The :order parameter defines the sorting order that would normally appear in the ORDER clause of the resulting SQL statement. When you specify the :order option, you are literally specifying a snippet of the SQL statement that will be sent to your database server.

:group: The :group parameter defines the GROUP BY portion of the resulting SQL statement, and like the :order parameter, the string supplied will directly translate to the GROUP BY portion of the SQL statement.

:limit: The :limit parameter takes an integer and directly corresponds to the LIMIT portion of the resulting SQL statement.

:offset: The :offset parameter takes an integer and directly corresponds to the OFFSET portion of the resulting SQL statement.

:include: The :include option is used to augment the FROM portion of the resulting SQL statement. The :include parameter will take a nested hash of symbols that correspond to the names of relationships you've defined for your model and add use them as joining conditions.

:joins: While the :joins parameter is similar in function to the :include option, it works on a lower level in the resulting SQL statement. The value given to the :joins option is a string that will get added to the FROM clause of the SQL statement. You can use this to join on tables to which you don't have a defined Active Record relationship.

:from: Whereas the :joins option will let you specify extra tables to join to in the FROM clause, the :from option allows you to specify the entire contents of the FROM clause of the SQL statement.

:select: You can use the :select option to specify extra columns in the SELECT clause of the resulting SQL statement. Any extra columns will be added as additional attributes on the returned objects, called piggyback attributes. However, because Active Record doesn't know how to save these extra attributes, the objects it returns will automatically be marked as read only.

:readonly: Specifying true for this parameter will mark the records returned from this find call as read only and prevent changes to the objects from being saved. Likewise, specifying false for this parameter will ensure that the records returned will not be marked as read only, regardless of whether they should (such as when the :select parameter is used).

:lock: You can use the :lock option to have the database lock the selected rows. The value given for the :lock option is either the Boolean true or an SQL fragment like LOCK IN SHARE MODE. If you pass in true, Active Record will use the default locking syntax for your connection.

For a complete description of the find method, see Chapter 2.

find_by_sql(sql_query)

This method works like find(:all) but takes a complete SQL query. For each of the results returned by the query, an Active Record object is instantiated.

increment_counter(counter_name, id)

This method increments the specified counter by one. A counter, in this context, is any integer Active Record attribute. Changes are made to the database record immediately, without instantiating the Active Record object. This method is most commonly used, along with the decrement_counter method, to maintain a cache of an aggregate value, such as the number of posts in a forum.

inheritance_column()

This method defines the name of the database column used with single table inheritance, in which the name of the subclass will be stored. Unlike many Active Record configuration methods, this does not take an argument. Rather, you override the method in the Active Record subclass itself. The following example changes the column used for the Account class from the default of "type" to "object_type":

```
class Account < ActiveRecord::Base
  def inheritance_column
    "object_type"
  end
end
```

new(attributes=nil) { |self if block_given?| . . . }

The new method is used to instantiate a new instance of an Active Record object. It takes parameters as a hash or can be used in block form. A hash example follows:

```
account = Account.new(:first_name => "Chad", :last_name => "Pytel")
```

Here's an example of an initialization of an Active Record object via a block:

```
Account.new do |account|
    account.first_name = "Chad"
    account.last_name = "Pytel"
end
```

Finally, you can specify no parameters and set the attributes at a later time.

```
account = Account.new
account.first_name = "Chad"
account.last_name = "Pytel"
```

primary_key()

This method defines the name of the database column that holds the primary key for the Active Record class. This method is overridden in the Active Record class. The following example overrides the primary key column for the Account class from the default of "id" to "account_key":

```
class Account < ActiveRecord::Base
  def primary_key
    "account_key"
  end
end
```

remove_connection(klass=self)

This method removes the connection for the specified class, which includes closing the active and defined connections. This method will default to the current class if no class is specified. It also returns the specification for the connection that was just removed. This specification can be used as an argument for establish_connection, to reestablish the connection.

reset_column_information()

Reset all of the cached information about the database columns for the specified Active Record class with this method. The columns will be reloaded on the next request.

serialize(attribute_name, class_name = Object)

It is possible to serialize an object to an Active Record attribute. The data in this object is stored in YAML format, which makes it possible to store arrays, hashes, and other objects for which Active Record does not include default mappings.

```
class Account < ActiveRecord::Base
  serialize :preferences
end

account = Account.find(1)
account.preferences = { "receive_email_alerts" => "weekly", "default_sort" =>
"price" }
```

The class_name parameter to this method takes a specific class name. When the serialized object is retrieved from the database, if it is not a descendent in the class hierarchy, a SerializationTypeMismatch exception will be raised.

serialized_attributes()

serialized_attributes returns a hash of all the Active Record attributes for this class that have been specified as serialized (using the serialize method). The keys of the hash are the attribute names; the values are the class restrictions.

set_inheritance_column(value = nil, &block)

This method defines the name of the database column used with single table inheritance in which the name of the subclass will be stored. Unlike many Active Record configuration methods, this does not take an argument. Rather, you override the method in the Active Record subclass itself. The following example changes the column used for the Account class from the default of "type" to "object_type":

```
class Account < ActiveRecord::Base
  def set_inheritance_column
    "object_type"
  end
end
```

set_locking_column(value = nil, &block)

Active Record supports optimistic locking if the database column lock_version is present. For more information about the optimistic locking features of Active Record, see Chapter 2. You can override the name of the expected database column from lock_version to something different with this method, for example:

```
class Account < ActiveRecord::Base
  set_locking_column "locking_column"
end
```

set_primary_key(value = nil, &block)

Set the name of the database column that holds the primary key as follows:

```
class Account < ActiveRecord::Base
  set_primary_key "accountid"
end
```

set_sequence_name(value = nil, &block)

Set the name of the sequence to use for the generation of primary keys with this method; use it with Oracle or other databases that use sequences for primary key generation.

If the sequence name is not specifically set when using an Oracle or Firebird database, the common sequence name of #{table_name}_seq will be used.

When using a PostgreSQL database, if the sequence name is not explicitly set, Active Record will discover the sequence for your primary key for you:

```
class Account < ActiveRecord::Base
  set_sequence_name "accountseq"
end
```

set_table_name(value = nil, &block)

Set the name of the database table to use for this Active Record class as follows:

```
class Account < ActiveRecord::Base
  set_table_name "account_table"
end
```

silence() { || . . . }

Silence the logger for the given block with this method.

table_exists?()

This method returns true if the database table associated with this Active Record class exists; it returns false if it does not.

table_name()

table_name returns the name of the database table based on the name of the class in the inheritance hierarchy directly descending from Active Record. So, if called on the class CustomerAccount with a class hierarchy of CustomerAccount < Account < ActiveRecord, the Account class is still used to generate the table name.

The rules for table name generation are provided by the Inflector class in Active Support. In addition, the table names are always lowercase, and any settings specified for table_name_prefix and table_name_suffix are applied to the generated table name.

update(id, attributes)

This method finds the record in the database with the specified primary key, sets the values in the specified attribute hash, and instantly saves the object back to the database. This method does instantiate an object for each record. Therefore, this method does ensure that validations are applied. If the validations fail, the unsaved class is returned. If the object is successfully saved, the newly saved object is returned.

```
Account.update(1, { :first_name => "Test", :last_name => "Account" })
```

You can also pass in arrays as the arguments of this method to update several objects at once, for example:

```
accounts = {  1 => { :first_name => "Test", :last_name => "Account" },
              2 => { :first_name => "Test", :last_name => "Account 2" }}
Account.update(accounts.keys, accounts.values)
```

update_all(update_sql, conditions)

This method applies the specified updates all of the matching rows in the database; it takes in SQL for the SET part of the UPDATE statement as the first argument, and the conditions to find the matching records are the second argument. The format of the conditions argument is the same as the Active Record find method. This method performs its operation directly on the database records, without instantiating a copy of each object. Therefore, any validations and callbacks are not performed.

```
Account.update_all("first_name = 'Test', last_name = 'Account'", ["account = ?", 1])
```

with_exclusive_scope(method_scoping = {}, &block)

This method works like `with_scope` but ignores any nested properties.

with_scope(method_scoping = {}, action = :merge) { || . . . }

Scope parameters to method calls within the specified block with this method, which takes a hash of method names and parameter hashes. Valid method names are `:find` and `:create`. Valid parameters for the options hash to the `find` method are `:conditions`, `:joins`, `:include`, `:offset`, `:limit`, and `:readonly`. The parameters to the `create` method are an attribute hash.

```
Account.with_scope(:find => { :conditions => "site_id = 1" },
                   :create => { :site_id => 1} do
  # => SELECT * FROM accounts WHERE last_name = 'Pytel' AND site_id => 1
  Account.find_by_last_name("Pytel")
  a = account.create(:last_name => "Pytel")
  a.site_id # => 1
end
```

It is also possible to nest multiple calls to `with_scope`. In nested calls to `with_scope`, all previous parameters are overwritten, except for the `:conditions` parameter to the `find` method, whose hash is merged:

```
Account.with_scope(:find => { :conditions => "site_id = 1" },
                   :create => { :site_id => 1} do
  Account.with_scope(:find => { :conditions => "creator_id = 1", :limit => 1 } do
    # => SELECT * FROM accounts WHERE last_name = 'Pytel'
    #    AND side_id = 1 AND creator_id = 1 LIMIT 1
    Account.find_all_by_last_name("Pytel")
  end
end
```

If you wish to overwrite all previous scoping, including `:conditions` to find, then you should use the `with_exclusive_scope` method.

Protected Class Methods

class_of_active_record_descendant(klass)

This method returns the class that is directly descended from Active Record in the class hierarchy:

```
class Account < ActiveRecord::Base
end
class CustomerAccount < Account
  class_of_active_record_descendant(self) # => Account
end
```

compute_type(type_name)

`compute_type` returns the class type of the record using the current module as a prefix. For example, descendents of `MyApp::Business::Account` would appear as `MyApp::Business::AccountSubclass`.

sanitize_sql(sql_to_sanitize)

This method accepts either an `Array` or a `String`. If the argument is a `String`, the string will be returned unchanged. If the argument is an Array, this method expects the first element of the array to be an SQL statement. This SQL statement will be sanitized and the remaining elements of the array will be interpolated into the SQL statement. These additional elements will also be sanitized. The following code

```
sanitize_sql(["last_name = '%s', first_name = '%s'", "Mc'Donald", "Old"])
```

would return `"last_name = 'Mc\'Donald', first_name = 'Old'"`.

Public Instance Methods

==(object_to_compare)

This method returns `true` if the `object_to_compare` is the same as the receiving object or is of the same Active Record class and has the same `id`.

[](attribute_name)

This method returns the value of the specified attribute after it has been typecast and is an alias for the protected `read_attribute` method of an Active Record class. While a common method of accessing the attributes of an Active Record class is via a method call, like `account.first_name`, Active Record overrides the [ ] operator to make each of the attributes available as a hash parameter on the on Active Record class. For example, you can also use the form `account[:first_name]`.

[]==(attribute_name, new_value)

This method is an alias for the protected `write_attribute` method of an Active Record class and allows setting of attribute values using a hash-like syntax, for example:

```
account[:last_name] = "Pytel"
```

attribute_names()

This method returns an alphabetically sorted array of the names of all the attributes available on this Active Record class.

attribute_present?(attribute)

`attribute_present?` returns `true` if the specified attribute has a value that was either set by you or loaded from the database. To return `true`, the value should be neither `nil` nor return `false` to `empty?`.

attributes(options = nil)

This method returns a hash of all of this object's attributes, with the attribute names as keys and clones of the attribute objects as their values:

```
Account.find(1).attributes # => { "last_name" => "Pytel", "first_name" => "Chad"}
```

The only options are :except and :only, and each should be an array of the attribute names. :except specifies that all attributes should be included in the return hash *except* for those in the specified array. :only specifies that *only* the attributes whose names match those in the specified array should be included in the returned hash:

```
Account.find(1).attributes({:only => ["last_name"]})
# => { "last_name" => "Pytel" }
Account.find(1).attributes({:except => ["last_name"])
# => { "first_name" => "Chad" }
```

attributes=(new_attributes)

This method accepts a hash with keys matching the attribute names of this object and sets all of the object's attributes at once using this hash. You can protect sensitive attributes from this form of mass assignment by using the attr_protected and attr_accessible methods:

```
Account.find(1).attributes = { :last_name => "Pytel", :first_name => "Chad" }
```

attributes_before_type_cast()

Return a hash of attributes and their cloned values before typecasting and deserialization with this method.

clone()

This method returns a clone of the Active Record object where all the attributes are cloned copies; the id remains unset, and the clone is treated as a new record. Be advised that this is a shallow clone in that it only applies to the object's attributes and not to its associations.

Active Record takes the opinion that a deep clone, one in which the entire object and all related objects are replicated, is application specific, and its implementation should be left up to you.

column_for_attribute(attribute_name)

Return the Column object for the specified attribute with this method.

connection()

connection returns the database connection that is currently being used by the Active Record object. You can then use this connection to perform miscellaneous database work unrelated to the Active Record object itself.

decrement(attribute)

Decrease the specified attribute by one with this method. If the attribute is nil, the attribute will be initialized to zero before being decremented (resulting in a value of -1). This method does not cause the Active Record object to be saved.

decrement!(attribute)

This method also decreases the specified `attribute` by one. If the attribute is `nil`, the attribute will be initialized to zero before being decremented (resulting in a value of -1). This method does save the changed attribute to the database. However, when the attribute is saved, the object validations are not run, allowing the attribute to be saved even if the full object is not valid.

destroy()

`destroy` deletes the database record for this Active Record object and freezes the attributes of the object.

eql?(object_to_compare)

`eql?` returns `true` if the specified object is equal to the current Active Record object or `false` if it is not. This method simply calls the equals operator (`==`).

freeze()

This method freezes the attributes of the Active Record object so that they cannot be changed. Also, it allows you to access the associations of an object, even after the object has been destroyed.

frozen?()

`frozen?` returns `true` if the attributes of this object have been frozen; otherwise, it returns `false`.

has_attribute?(attribute)

This method returns `true` if the specified attribute is in the attribute hash of this object.

hash()

`hash` delegates to `id()` in order to allow standard operations on Active Record objects of the same type and id, for example:

```
[Acccount.find(1), Account.find(3)] & [Account.find(1), Account.find(4)]
# => [ Account.find(1) ]
```

id()

The `id()` method makes it so that an Active Record object's primary key attribute is always available as `ar_object.id`, even if its name has been overridden. This method is also aliased to `to_param()`.

id=(value)

This method sets the primary key of this Active Record object. The method is always available, even if you have overridden the name of the primary key attribute to something besides `id`.

increment(attribute)

Increase the specified attribute by one with this method. If the attribute is `nil`, the attribute will be initialized to zero before being incremented (resulting in a value of 1). This method does not cause the Active Record object to be saved.

increment!(attribute)

You can increase the specified `attribute` by one with this method as well. If the attribute is `nil`, the attribute will be initialized to zero before being incremented (resulting in a value of 1). This method does save the changed attribute to the database. However, when the attribute is saved, the object validations are not run, allowing the attribute to be saved even if the full object is not valid.

new_record?()

`new_record?` returns `true` if this Active Record object has not been saved yet. In other words, if there is not yet a row in the database for this object, this method will return `true`.

readonly?()

This method returns `true` if the attributes of this object have been marked as read only, which will happen when piggyback attributes have been added to the object. For more information on piggyback attributes, see `find()`.

reload()

`reload` causes the attributes of this object to be reloaded from the database.

respond_to?(method, include_priv=false)

This method returns `true` if the specified method name appears on the Active Record object. An `Account` object with a `last_name` attribute would return `true` to `account.respond_to?` (`"last_name"`), `account.respond_to?("last_name=")`, and `account.respond_to?("last_name?")`.

save()

Save the current Active Record object with this method. If the object has not yet been saved, a new record is created in the database. If the object already has a corresponding database record, that record is updated with the current values of this object's attributes. If the object has been marked as read only, this method will raise a `ReadOnlyRecord` exception. If the save was successful, this method will return `true`; otherwise, it will return `false`.

By default, Active Record mixes in the `Validation` module, which overrides the default implementation of this method with the `ActiveRecord::Validations.save_with_validation` method. This method takes in a Boolean value that indicates whether validations should be run, the default of which is to run validations. Therefore, the default behavior of this method is to trigger validations before the object is saved. If you wish to save the Active Record object without validations, you can call the method as follows:

```
account.save(false)
```

save!()

This method also saves the current Active Record object. If this object has not yet been saved, a new record is created in the database. If the object already has a corresponding database record, that record is updated with the current values of this objects attributes. If the save was successful, this method will return `true`; otherwise, it will raise a `RecordNotSaved` exception.

By default, Active Record mixes in the `Validation` module, which overrides the default implementation of this method with the `ActiveRecord::Validations.save_with_validation!` method. Therefore, the default behavior of this method is to trigger validations before the object is saved.

to_param()

This method is an alias for `id()`.

to_xml(options = {})

This method returns an XML representation of the Active Record object. While this method does take a hash of configuration options, for more complex XML generation, using Active Support's `Builder` class is generally recommended.

The XML generated by default will include all attributes for the object, and a `type` attribute for attributes that are not of type `String`. In addition, associations are not expanded by default. An example of the XML for an object of our `Account` class would be

```
<?xml version="1.0" encoding="UTF-8"?>
<account>
  <id type="integer">1</id>
  <last-name>Pytel</last-name>
  <first-name>Chad</first-name>
  <site-id>1</site-id>
</account>
```

Valid options for the options hash are `:skip_instruct`, `:root`, `:except`, `:only`, and `:include`. The `:skip_instruct` option, if set to true, will cause the XML processing instruction line to be excluded from the resulting XML:

```
account.to_xml(:skip_instruct => true)
# => <account>
  <id type="integer">1</id>
  <last-name>Pytel</last-name>
  <first-name>Chad</first-name>
  <site-id>1</site-id>
  <created-at type="datetime">2006-11-10T10:22:56-05:00</created-at>
</account>
```

The default name for the root element is the class name of the Active Record object we are formatting. The `:root` option should be a string and allows you to override the name of the root element:

```
account.to_xml(:root => "myaccount")
# => <myaccount>
```

```
<id type="integer">1</id>
<last-name>Pytel</last-name>
<first-name>Chad</first-name>
<site-id>1</site-id>
<created-at type="datetime">2006-11-10T10:22:56-05:00</created-at>
</myaccount>
```

You can use the :only and :except options to explicitly include or exclude attributes from the resulting XML:

```
account.to_xml(:only => [ :last_name ])
# => <account>
  <last-name>Pytel</last-name>
</account>
account.to_xml(:except => [ :last_name ])
# => <account>
  <id type="integer">1</id>
  <first-name>Chad</first-name>
  <site-id>1</site-id>
  <created-at type="datetime">2006-11-10T10:22:56-05:00</created-at>
</account>
```

As previously mentioned, associations are not expanded in the XML by default. To cause certain associations to also be included in the XML, use the :include option:

```
account.to_xml(:include => [ :site ])
# => <?xml version="1.0" encoding="UTF-8"?>
<account>
  <id type="integer">1</id>
  <last-name>Pytel</last-name>
  <first-name>Chad</first-name>
  <site>
    <id type="integer">1</id>
    <name>Account Site</name>
  </site>
  <site-id>1</site-id>
  <created-at type="datetime">2006-11-10T10:22:56-05:00</created-at>
</account>
```

toggle(attribute)

The method sets the specified attribute to true if the current value is false and sets it to false if the current value is true. This method does not cause the Active Record object to be saved.

toggle!(attribute)

This method also sets the specified attribute to true if the current value is false and sets it to false if the current value is true. This method does save the changed attribute to the database. However, when the attribute is saved, the object validations are not run, allowing the attribute to be saved even if the full object is not valid.

update_attribute(name, value)

This method updates the specified attribute with the specified value and saves the record. By default, Active Record mixes in the `Validation` module, which overrides the default implementation of this method with the `ActiveRecord::Validations.update_attributes` method. Therefore, the default behavior of this method is to skip validations, allowing the attribute to be saved even if the full object is not valid.

update_attributes(attributes)

This method takes in a hash with attribute names as the keys and the corresponding attribute values as the values. The corresponding attributes on the object are updated, and the record is saved. This method does cause validations to be run. Therefore, if the object is invalid, the save will fail, and `false` will be returned.

ActiveRecord::Calculations::ClassMethods

Public Instance Methods

average(column_name, options = {})

Calculate the average of the data in the specified column with this attribute. Valid options are the same as those for the `calculate` method.

```
Account.average('age')
```

calculate(operation, column_name, options = {})

This method calculates aggregate values of columns on the database table backing the Active Record class. Valid operations are `count(:count)`, `sum(:sum)`, `average(:avg)`, `minimum(:min)`, and `maximum(:max)`. When the aggregate value is a single value, the type of the returned value is `Fixnum` for count, `Float` for average, and the actual of the column we are aggregating for all other operations.

```
Account.calculate(:count, :all) # The same as Account.count
Account.average(:age) # SELECT AVG(age) FROM accounts...
# Select the minimum age for everyone with a last name other than 'Pytel'
Account.minimum(:age, :conditions => ['last_name != ?', 'Pytel'])
# Select the minimum age for any family without any minors
Account.minimum(:age, :having => 'min(age) > 17', :group => :last_name)
```

The `:group` option takes either the name of a column or the name of a `belongs_to` association, and it causes the `calculate` method to return an ordered hash of the values, where the keys are the grouped object:

```
values = Account.average(:age, :group => :last_name)
values["Pytel"] # => 42
this_site = Site.find(1)
values = Account.average(:age, :group_by => :site)
values[this_site] # => 42
```

The options valid to the `calculate` method are the same options valid to `find`, including `:conditions`, `:joins`, `:order`, `:group`, `:select`, `:having`, and `:distinct`.

count(*args)

This method returns a `Fixnum` equal to the number of rows returned by the resulting database query. If no arguments are passed in, this method will return the total number of rows in the database table.

```
Account.count # => SELECT COUNT(*) FROM accounts
```

This method also will take one or two strings as arguments, representing, respectively, conditions for the WHERE part of the SQL query and a string to be added to the FROM part of the query.

```
Account.count("site_id != 1") # SELECT COUNT(*) FROM accounts WHERE side_id != 1
Account.count("name != 'My Site'", "LEFT JOIN sites on accounts.site_id = sites.id")
# SELECT COUNT(*) FROM accounts LEFT JOIN sites on accounts.site_id = sites.id
#    WHERE name != 'My Site'
```

Finally, this method also accepts arguments similar to the arguments to `find`, including an `options` hash containing options for `:conditions`, `:joins`, `:order`, `:group`, `:select`, `:having`, and `:distinct`.

```
Account.count(:conditions => "site_id != 1"
# SELECT COUNT(*) FROM accounts WHERE side_id != 1

Account.count(:conditions => "name != 'My Site'", :include => :site)
# SELECT COUNT(*) FROM accounts LEFT JOIN sites WHERE name != 'My Site'

Account.count('id', :conditions => "site_id != 1"
# SELECT COUNT(id) FROM accounts where site_id != 1

Account.count(:all, :conditions => "site_id != 1"
# SELECT COUNT(*) FROM accounts where site_id != 1
```

maximum(column_name, options = {})

This method returns the maximum value present in the specified column. Valid options are the same as those for the `calculate` method, which in turn derives its `options` from the `find` method.

```
Account.maximum('age')
```

minimum(column_name, options = {})

Return the minimum value present in the specified column with this method. Valid options are the same as those for the `calculate` method, which in turn derives its `options` from the `find` method.

```
Account.average('age')
```

sum(column_name, options = {})

Calculate the sum of the specified column with this method, for which valid options are again the same as those for the `calculate` method, which in turn derives its `options` from the `find` method.

```
Account.sum('age')
```

ActiveRecord::Callbacks

Public Instance Methods

after_create()

This method is called after `Base.save()` only on objects that have not been saved yet. Override this method in your Active Record model to specify functionality. For more information on callbacks, see Chapter 4.

after_destroy()

This method is called after `Base.destroy()`. Therefore, the corresponding database record has already been deleted, and the attributes have already been frozen. Override this method in your Active Record model to specify functionality. For more information on callbacks, see Chapter 4.

after_save()

This method is also called after `Base.save()`, and it's called regardless of whether the object was being created or updated. Override this method in your Active Record model to specify functionality. For more information on callbacks, see Chapter 4.

after_update()

This method is also called after `Base.save()` only when the object has already been saved and already has a corresponding record in the database. Override this method in your Active Record model to specify functionality. For more information on callbacks, see Chapter 4.

after_validation()

`after_validation` is called after the `Validations.validate()` method. `Validations.validate()` is included in calls to `Base.save()`. Override this method in your Active Record model to specify functionality. For more information on callbacks, see Chapter 4.

after_validation_on_create()

After the `Validations.validate()` method is called, you can call this method only on objects that have not been saved yet. `Validations.validate()` is included in calls to `Base.save()`. Override this method in your Active Record model to specify functionality. For more information on callbacks, see Chapter 4.

after_validation_on_update()

This method is also called after the `Validations.validate()` method is called; this one is called only when the object has already been saved and already has a corresponding record in the database. `Validations.validate()` is included in calls to `Base.save()`. Override this method in your Active Record model to specify functionality. For more information on callbacks, see Chapter 4.

before_create()

Call `before_create` before `Base.save()` only on objects that have not yet been saved. Override this method in your Active Record model to specify functionality. For more information on callbacks, see Chapter 4.

before_destroy()

This method is called before `Base.destroy()`. Therefore, the corresponding database record has not yet been deleted, and the attributes have not yet been frozen. Override this method in your Active Record model to specify functionality. For more information on callbacks, see Chapter 4.

before_save()

`before_save` is called before `Base.save()`, regardless of whether the object was being created or updated. Override this method in your Active Record model to specify functionality. For more information on callbacks, see Chapter 4.

before_update()

`before_update` is called before `Base.save()` as well but only when the object has already been saved and already has a corresponding record in the database. Override this method in your Active Record model to specify functionality. For more information on callbacks, see Chapter 4.

before_validation()

Call `before_validation` before the `Validations.validate()` method is called; `Validations.validate()` is included in calls to `Base.save()`. Override this method in your Active Record model to specify functionality. For more information on callbacks, see Chapter 4.

before_validation_on_create()

This method is called before the `Validations.validate()` method but only on objects that have not yet been saved. `Validations.validate()` is included in calls to `Base.save()`. Override this method in your Active Record model to specify functionality. For more information on callbacks, see Chapter 4.

before_validation_on_update()

This method, also called before the `Validations.validate()` method, is called only when the object has already been saved and already has a corresponding record in the database.

Validations.validate() is included in calls to Base.save(). Override this method in your Active Record model to specify functionality. For more information on callbacks, see Chapter 4.

ActiveRecord::ConnectionAdapters::AbstractAdapter

Public Instance Methods

active?()

active? returns true if the connection is active and ready to perform database queries.

adapter_name()

adapter_name returns the human readable name of the connection adapter.

disconnect!()

disconnect! closes the database connection associated with this adapter.

prefect_primary_key?(table_name = nil)

This method returns true if the primary key for a new record must be retrieved before the insert statement is executed. If this is true, then next_sequence_value is called before each insert to get the new record's primary key value. This is currently only true for the Firebird database adapter.

raw_connection()

Return the underlying database connection with this method, which can be used to call proprietary database methods.

reconnect!()

Close the current connection and open a new connection to the database with reconnect!.

requires_reloaded?()

This method returns true if it is safe to reload the database connection between requests. It is used in development mode and is currently unsafe for the Ruby/MySQL adapter and unnecessary for any database adapter except SQLite.

supports_count_distinct?()

This method returns true if this connection adapter supports using DISTINCT with COUNT. This is currently true for all adapters except SQLite.

supports_migrations?()

Return true with this method if this connection adapter supports Active Record migrations.

verify!(timeout)

This method calls and returns the value of active? only if it has not been called for timeout seconds.

Protected Instance Methods

format_log_entry(message, dump = nil)

This method adds color to the log message if ActiveRecord::Base.colorize_logging = true and returns the given log message with formatting applied.

log(sql_statement, name) { || . . .}

This method writes the given SQL statement to the log. If given a block, the method will benchmark the statements contained within it while also logging them.

log_info(sql, name, runtime)

Log the given SQL statement and its runtime with this method, which is called by log(sql_statement, name) { || . . . } and calls format_log_entry(message, dump = nil).

ActiveRecord::ConnectionAdapters::Column

Public Class Methods

binary_to_string(value)

This method is used to convert BLOBs to Strings.

new(name, default, sql_type = nil, null = true)

Create a new column in the database table with this method: name is the name of the new column; default is the typecasted default value for the new column; sql_type specifies the type, including the length of the new column; and null specifies whether this column allows NULL as a value.

string_to_binary(value)

Convert Strings to BLOBs with this method.

string_to_date(value)

This method converts the given value, which is a String, to a Date.

string_to_dummy_time(value)

string_to_dummy_time converts the given value, which is a String containing only time information, with dump information.

string_to_time(value)

This one converts the given value, which is a String containing date and time information, to a Time value.

value_to_boolean(value)

Convert the given value to a boolean with this method. It returns true for true, "true", "t", and "1" and returns false for all other values.

value_to_decimal(value)

With this method, you can convert the given value to a BigDecimal.

Public Instance Methods

human_name()

Return the human readable version of the column name as follows:

```
Column.new("first_name", nil, "varchar(255)").human_name #=> "First name"
```

klass()

klass returns the Ruby class that corresponds to the abstract data type of the column. For example, if the SQL column is of type :integer, the class returned from this method is Fixnum. Table A-1 lists the abstract data types for columns and the corresponding classes that this method will return.

Table A-1: *Abstract Data Types and Corresponding Classes*

Type	Class
:integer	Fixnum
:float	Float
:decimal	BigDecimal
:datetime	Time
:date	Date
:timestamp	Time
:time	Time
:text	String
:string	String
:binary	String
:boolean	Object

number?()

number? returns true if the data type of this Column is a float, integer, or decimal.

text?()

text? returns `true` if the data type of this `Column` is `string` or `text`.

type_cast(value)

type_cast casts the given column `value` to an appropriate instance. Valid column types are `string`, `text`, `integer`, `float`, `decimal`, `datetime`, `timestamp`, `time`, `date`, `binary`, and `boolean`.

type_cast_code(var_name)

This method returns the Ruby code that would be used to convert a variable with the given name to the type of this `Column`.

ActiveRecord::ConnectionAdapters:: DatabaseStatement

Public Instance Methods

add_limit!(sql, options)

This method is an alias for `add_limit_offset!(sql, options)`.

add_limit_offset!(sql, options)

Modify the given SQL by adding `LIMIT` and `OFFSET` statements to it, as in the following example:

```
add_limit_offset!("SELECT * FROM accounts", {:limit => 10, :offset => 30})
```

The preceding code would return the following SQL query:

```
SELECT * FROM accounts LIMIT 10 OFFSET 30
```

add_lock!(sql, options)

Modify the given SQL by adding a locking statement with `add_lock!`. The statement `"FOR UPDATE"` will be added if the `:lock` option is `true`; otherwise, the given locking statement will be added.

```
add_lock("SELECT * FROM accounts", :lock => true)
#=> "SELECT * FROM accounts FOR UPDATE"
add_lock("SELECT * FROM accounts", :lock => " FOR UPDATE")
#=> "SELECT * FROM accounts FOR UPDATE"
```

begin_db_transaction()

This method begins the transaction and turns off automatic committing. See `transaction(start_db_transaction = true) { ||| . . . }`.

commit_db_transaction()

This method commits the transaction and turns on automatic committing. See
`transaction(start_db_transaction = true) { ||| . . . }`.

default_sequence_name(table, column)

Return the default sequence name for the current adapter with this method.

delete(sql, name = nil)

This `delete` method executes the given SQL statement in the context of the current connection and returns the number of rows deleted.

execute(sql, name = nil)

Execute the given SQL statement in the context of the current connection with this method, which raises a `NotEmplementedError` by default and must be implemented by the specific database connection adapters.

insert(sql, name = nil, pk = nil, id_value = nil, sequence_name = nil)

This method executes the given SQL `INSERT` statement in the context of the current connection and returns the automatically generated ID that the new record was given. The method raises a `NotEmplementedError` by default and must be implemented by the specific database connection adapters.

reset_sequence!(table, column, sequence = nil)

Reset the given sequence to the maximum value of the given table's column with this method; it does nothing by default and must be implemented by the specific database connection adapters.

rollback_db_transaction()

You must roll back the database transaction with this method if the transactional block raises an exception or returns `false`. See `transaction(start_db_transaction = true) { ||| . . . }`.

select_all(sql, name = nil)

`select_all` returns an array of database record hashes with the column names as keys and the column values as values.

select_one(sql, name = nil)

`select_one` returns a record hash of the first record to be returned by the given SQL statement with the column names as keys and the column values as values.

select_value(sql, name = nil)

Return the value from the first column of the first record that matches the given SQL statement with `select_value`.

select_values(sql, name = nil)

Return an array of values of the first column of the records that match the given SQL with `select_values`.

transaction(start_db_transaction = true) { || . . . }

This method wraps the given block in a database transaction and returns the value of the block.

update(sql, name = nil)

Execute the given `UPDATE` SQL statement and return the number of rows that were affected.

Protected Instance Methods

select(sql, name = nil)

Execute the given `SELECT` SQL statement and return an array of record hashes with the column names as keys and the column values as values with this method. It raises a `NotEmplementedError` by default and must be implemented by the specific database connection adapters.

ActiveRecord::ConnectionAdapters::Quoting

Public Instance Methods

quote(value, column = nil)

This method quotes the given value to help prevent SQL injection attacks. If a column is given, this method will use the column type to determine how this value should be quoted; otherwise, it will use the value's type to determine the quoting method.

quote_column_name(name)

This method returns a quoted form of the given column name. The method of quoting is highly database specific, and therefore, this method is typically overridden by the connection adapter.

quote_string(value)

Quote the given `String` with this method, which escapes any single quotation mark (') and backslash (\) characters.

quoted_date(value)

Format the given date value as a String with this method.

quoted_false()

This quoted method returns the String 'f'.

quoted_true()

This method returns the String 't'.

ActiveRecord::ConnectionAdapters:: SchemaStatements

Public Instance Methods

add_column(table_name, column_name, type, options = {})

This method adds a new column to the given table with the given name and type. See TableDefinition#column for details on what options you can use.

add_index(table_name, column_name, options = {})

add_index adds a new database index to the given table for the given column. column_name can be a single Symbol or an Array of Symbols. The index will be named after the table and the column name (or the first column name if given an array), unless you give this method the :name option.

The following example creates a simple index on only the email column of our accounts table:

```
add_index(:accounts, :email)
```

Here's the SQL statement generated for the preceding example:

```
CREATE INDEX accounts_email_index ON accounts(name)
```

You can also create a multicolumn index by passing in an Array of symbols for the column name attribute:

```
add_index(:accounts, [:first_name, :last_name])
```

The SQL statement generated for that example would be

```
CREATE INDEX accounts_first_name_last_name_index ON accounts(first_name, last_name)
```

To override the name given to the index, you use the :name option:

```
add_index(:accounts, [:first_name, :last_name], :name => "name_index")
```

The SQL generated for the :name example would be CREATE INDEX name_index ON accounts(first_name, last_name).

Lastly, if you wish the create a `UNIQUE` index, use the `:unique` option:

```
add_index(:accounts, [:first_name, :last_name], :unique => true)
```

The SQL generated for this example would be `CREATE UNIQUE INDEX accounts_first_name_last_name_index ON accounts(first_name, last_name)`.

add_order_by_for_association_limiting!(sql, options)

With this method, you can modify the given SQL statement by adding the clause specified in `options[:order]` to it. The PostgreSQL connection adapter overrides this method because of its stricter standards compliance.

```
sql = "SELECT last_name FROM accounts"
add_order_by_for_association_limiting!(sql, :order => "last_name")
sql #=> "SELECT last_name FROM accounts ORDER BY last_name"
```

change_column(table_name, column_name, type, options = {})

The `change_column` method changes the specified column definition to match those specified in `options`. See `TableDefinition#column` for details on what options you can use.

This method raises a `NotEmplementedError` by default and must be implemented by the specific database connection adapters.

change_column_default(table_name, column_name, default)

You can use this method to change the default value for the specified column. Unfortunately, you cannot use it to set the default value of a column to `NULL`. To do that, you must use `DatabaseStatements#execute` to run the appropriate SQL statement manually.

This method raises a `NotEmplementedError` by default and must be implemented by the specific database connection adapters.

columns(table_name, name = nil)

`columns` returns an `Array` of `Column` objects for the given table.

create_table(name, options = {}) { || . . . }a

This method creates a new table with the given name, and by default, automatically adds a column for the primary key to the table.

You can use the method either in regular or block form. The regular form does not add any columns besides the one for the primary key to the table, and you would then use `add_column` to add additional columns to the table.

For example, we could use the regular form of this method to create our `accounts` table:

```
create_table(:accounts)
add_column(:accounts, :first_name, :string)
add_column(:accounts, :last_name, :string)
add_column(:accounts, email, :string)
```

However, if, instead, you wish to use the block form of this method to create the same table, the code would be

```
create_table(:accounts) do |t|
  t.column :first_name, :string
  t.column :last_name, :string
  t.column :email, :string
end
```

The valid options for the options hash are :id, :primary_key, :options, :temporary, and :force.

The :id option, which defaults to true, specifies whether the primary key column should be added to the table automatically.

The :primary_key option, which defaults to :id, specifies the name of the primary key column in the table.

The :options option specifies any additional options that you wish to append to the table definition. For instance, if you are using a MySQL database and wish to use an InnoDB table and to set the default character set of the table to be UTF-8, you would specify :options => 'ENGINE=InnoDB DEFAULT CHARSET=utf8'.

The :temporary option defaults to false; if set to true, it indicates that this table should be a temporary table.

The :force option defaults to false; if set to true, it indicates that the table should be dropped before attempting to create it.

distinct(columns, order_by)

distinct executes a SELECT DISTINCT SQL statement, with the given ORDER BY clause for the given set of columns. The PostgreSQL and Oracle database connection adapters override this method to account for their custom DISTINCT syntax. The following example executes a SELECT DISTINCT statement on the id column for the accounts table, ordered by the created_at column:

```
distinct("accounts.id", "accounts.created_at DESC")
```

drop_table(name, options = {})

This method drops the specified table from the database. The following example drops the accounts table from your database:

```
drop_table(:accounts)
```

The options hash is available for database-specific options.

initialize_schema_information()

Initialize the schema information in the database by creating the schema information table, named schema_info by default, and inserting the current schema version into the table. You should not need to call this method under standard operation, as the migration process handles this automatically. However, calling this method is nondestructive; if the schema information table already exists, this method completes silently.

native_database_types()

This method returns a Hash where the keys are the abstract data types and the values are the native database types. See TableDefinition#column for details regarding the recognized abstract data types.

remove_column(table_name, column_name)

Remove the specified column from the specified table with this method.

remove_index(table_name, options = {})

Remove the specified index from the specified table with this method. The index to remove is specified in the options hash, whose syntax is taken from the add_index method. For example, to remove the index on the email column you would call

```
remove_index(:accounts, :email)
```

Remove a multicolumn index by passing in an Array of symbols for the :column option:

```
remove_index(:accounts, :column => [:first_name, :last_name])
```

If the name of the index does not conform to the standard index naming conventions, you can specify that it should be removed with the :name option:

```
remove_index(:accounts, :name => "name_index")
```

rename_column(table_name, column_name, options = {})

Rename the specified column on the specified database table with this method, which raises a NotEmplementedError by default and must be implemented by the specific database connection adapters.

rename_table(name, new_name)

With this method, you can rename the specified table to the name of new_name. It raises a NotEmplementedError by default and must be implemented by the specific database connection adapters.

structure_dump()

structure_dump returns a string that contains the CREATE TABLE statements needed to re-create the entire structure of the database.

table_alias_for(table_name)

Return the alias for the table name, truncated to comply with the maximum table name length of the specific database connection adapter, using this method.

table_alias_length()

This method will return the maximum possible length of a table alias for this database connection adapter.

Protected Instance Methods

options_include_default?(options)

This internal method checks the supplied options to see if they contain a `:default` key.

ActiveRecord::ConnectionAdapters:: TableDefinition

Public Class Methods

new(base)

Instantiate a new table definition with the specified base class as the base with this method.

Public Instance Methods

[](name)

Use this method to return a `ColumnDefinition` for the column with the specified name.

column(name, type, options = {})

This `column` method instantiates a new column with the specified name for the table, returning the `TableDefinition` instance on which the `column` method was called. Valid values for the type parameter are `:primary_key`, `:string`, `:text`, `:integer`, `:float`, `:decimal`, `:datetime`, `:timestamp`, `:time`, `:date`, `:binary`, and `:boolean`.

The available options are `:limit`, `:default`, `:null`, `:precision`, and `:scale`. None of the options have a default value.

The `:limit` option specifies the maximum length for values in the column. This option is only valid for columns of type `:string`, `:text`, `:binary`, and `:integer`.

The `:default` option specifies the default value of this database column. Specifying `:default => nil` will result in a default of `NULL`.

The `:null` option, either `true` or `false`, specifies whether `NULL` values should be allowed in this database column.

The `:precision` option specifies the precision of the database column. This option is only valid for columns of type `:decimal`.

The `:scale` option specifies the scale of the database column values. This option is only valid for columns of type `:decimal`.

The SQL standard declares that the default scale for a decimal column should be zero and that scale should be less than or equal to the precision. However, the standard makes no requirements for precision. In addition, you should note the following points regarding columns of type `:decimal` for various database implementations.

- *MySQL*: The valid values for decimal precision in MySQL are 1 to 63, and the valid values for decimal scale are 0 to 30. The default scale is 10, and the default precision is 0.

- *PostgreSQL*: The valid values for decimal precision in PostgreSQL are 1 to infinity, and the valid values for decimal scale are 0 to infinity. PostgreSQL does not have a default precision or scale.

- *SQLite2*: Any precision or scale can be used, as this database stores everything as strings. SQLite2 does not have a default precision or scale.

- *SQLite3*: The valid values for decimal precision in SQLite3 are 1 to 16, and there is no limit on the values for decimal scale. SQLite3 does not have a default precision or scale.

- *Oracle*: The valid values for decimal precision in Oracle are 1 to 38, and the valid values for decimal scale are -84 to 127. The default scale is 38, and the default precision is 0.

- *DB2*: The valid values for decimal precision in DB2 are 1 to 63, and the valid values for decimal scale are 0 to 62. The default precision is 38, and the default scale is 0.

- *Firebird*: The valid values for decimal precision in Firebird are 1 to 18, and the valid values for decimal scale are 0 to 18. The default scale is 9, and the default precision is 0.

- *FrontBase*: The valid values for decimal precision in FrontBase are 1 to 38, and the valid values for decimal scale are 0 to 38. The default scale is 38, and the default precision is 0.

- *SQL Server*: The valid values for decimal precision in SQL Server are 1 to 38, and the valid values for decimal scale are 0 to 38. The default scale is 38, and the default precision is 0.

- *Sybase*: The valid values for decimal precision in Sybase are 1 to 38, and the valid values for decimal scale are 0 to 38. The default scale is 38, and the default precision is 0.

- *OpenBase*: The valid values for decimal precision in OpenBase are unspecified.

primary_key(name)

This method adds a new primary key definition to the table; it can be called multiple times.

to_sql()

Returns a String that is the column definitions for the columns in this table concatenated together. This string and be prepended and appended to generate the final table-creation SQL statement.

ActiveRecord::Errors

Public Instance Methods

[](attribute)

This method is an alias for on().

add(attribute, msg = @@default_error_messages[:invalid])

This method adds an error message to the specified attribute. The error message will be returned when you call on(attribute) and will ensure that object.errors[:attribute].empty? returns false. If no message is supplied, the default error message of "invalid" is used.

add_on_blank(attributes, msg = @@default_error_messages[:blank])

This method takes an array of attributes. The specified error message will be added to each of the blank attributes in the array. If no message is supplied, the default error message of "blank" is used.

add_on_boundary_breaking(attributes, range, too_long_message = @@default_error_messages[:too_long], too_short_message = @@default_error_messages[:too_short])

This method takes an array of attributes. For each of the specified attributes, if the length of the attribute is longer than the given range, the too_long_message error message will be used. If the attribute is shorter than the given range, the too_short_message will be used. If either error message is not supplied, the default error messages will be used. This method is also aliased as add_on_boundary_breaking().

add_on_boundary_breaking(attributes, range, too_long_message = @@default_error_messages[:too_long], too_short_message = @@default_error_messages[:too_short])

This method is an alias for add_on_boundary_breaking().

add_on_empty(attributes, msg = @@default_error_messages[:empty])

This method takes an array of attributes. For each empty attribute in an object, the specified error message will be added. If no error message is supplied, the default error message for "empty" will be used.

add_to_base(msg)

Use this method to add the specified error message to the actual Active Record object instance instead of to any particular attribute. These messages do not get prepended with any attribute name when iterating the errors with each_full(), so the error messages should be a complete sentence.

clear()

clear removes all of the errors that have been added to this object.

count()

This method is an alias for size().

each() { lattribute, msgl . . . }

each yields each attribute and error message.

each_full() { lmsgl . . . }

each_full yields each error message for all of the attributes on the object.

empty?()

This method returns true if there are no errors on the object.

full_messages()

This method returns the full error messages (as returned by each_full) in an Array.

invalid?(attribute)

This method returns true if the specified attribute has had any errors added for it.

length()

This method is an alias for size().

on(attribute)

This method returns the error, or errors, that have been added for the specified attribute. If no errors have been added, nil will be returned. If only one error has been added, a String will be returned. If more than one error has been added, an Array of the errors will be returned. This method is also aliased as [ ].

on_base()

on_base returns the error, or errors, that have been added directly on the Active Record class (as opposed to onto a specific attribute). If no errors have been added, nil will be returned. If only one error has been added, a String will be returned. If more than one error has been added, an Array of the errors will be returned.

size()

size returns the number of errors that have been added to the specified Active Record object, which includes all of the individual errors on each attribute, as well as errors added directly to object itself. This method is also aliased as length() and count().

ActiveRecord::Migration

Public Class Methods

announce(message)

By default, migrations log what they are doing and the amount of time it takes to run them to the console. You can add your own messages to the console with this method.

method_missing(method, *arguments, &block)

This class method overrides `method_missing()` as a mechanism for performing actions on the many different types of databases that Active Record migrations will run. There should be no need for you to call this method during standard operation.

migrate(direction)

This method executes a migration in the specified direction. Valid directions are `:up` and `:down`.

say(message, subitem = false)

By default, migrations log what they are doing and the amount of time it takes to run them to the console. You can add your own messages to the console with this method. This method formats its messages beginning with `--` (or `->` for subitems), which is different than `announce()`. If `subitem` is `true`, the message will have additional formatting to indent the message on the console.

say_with_time(message) { || . . . }

By default, migrations log what they are doing and the amount of time it takes the console to run them. You can add your own messages to the console with this method. This method formats its messages beginning with `--`, which is different than `announce()`, and will also call benchmark for each of the statements contained within the given block.

suppress_messages() { || . . . }

By default, migrations log what they are doing and the amount of time it takes the console to run them. This method will suppress this logging for all statements contained within the given block.

write(text="")

This is the method used by `announce()`, `say()`, and `say_with_time()` to output text to the console. The given text will only be written to the console if `ActiveRecord::Migration.verbose` is `true`.

ActiveRecord::Observer

Public Class Methods

new()

This new method instantiates this observer class, starting the observation of the declared classes and their subclasses.

observe(*models)

Attach the observer to the specified Active Record model classes with this method.

observed_class()

This method returns the class observed by this observer. The class observed by default is determined by the class name of the observer class. For example, the AccountObserver class will observe the Account class, and the EmailObserver class will observe the Email class.

Protected Instance Methods

add_observer!(klass)

This method adds the observer class as an observer to the class specified with klass.

observed_classes()

This one returns the classes that are currently observed by this observer.

observed_subclasses()

And this method returns the subclasses that are currently observed by this observer.

ActiveRecord::Observing::ClassMethods

Public Instance Methods

instantiate_observers()

Instantiate all of the global Active Record observers using this method.

observers()

Returns the current Active Record observers with observers.

observers=(*observers)

Set the Active Record observers and activate them with this method. However, the assigned observers are not instantiated by this method, rather instantiate_observers() is called during Active Record startup and before each request when running in development mode.

Protected Instance Methods

inherited(subclass)

This method notifies all of the observers of this class that the class has been subclassed. The notification sent is `:observed_class_inherited`.

ActiveRecord::Reflection::ClassMethods

Public Instance Methods

create_reflection(macro, name, options, active_record)

Creates a new reflection, that is, either an `AssociationReflection` or an `AggregateReflection` depending on the macro specified. An `AssociationReflection` will be created when macro is `:has_many`, `:belongs_to`, `:has_one`, or `:has_and_belongs_to_many`. An `AggregateReflection` will be created when the macro specified is `:composed_of`.

reflect_on_aggregation(aggregation)

Return the `AggregateReflection` object for the named reflection specified by aggregation with this method.

reflect_on_all_aggregations()

This method returns an `Array` of all the `AggregateReflection` objects for the aggregations in the class.

reflect_on_all_associations(macro = nil)

With this method, you can return an `Array` of all the `AssociationReflection` objects for the associations in this class. If you only want the associations of a specific type, specify its symbol in a macro. The valid types are `:has_many`, `:belongs_to`, `:has_one`, or `:has_and_belongs_to_many`.

reflect_on_association(association)

Return the `AssociationReflection` object for the named reflection specified by association with this method.

reflections()

Use this method to return a `Hash` containing all of the `AssociationReflection` and `AggregateReflection` objects for the class.

ActiveRecord::Reflection::MacroReflection

Public Class Methods

new(macro, name, options, active_record)

This new method creates a new reflection class with the given macro, name, and options.

class_name()

Return the class name of this reflection class with this item.

klass()

klass returns the class for the reflection.

macro()

macro returns the name of the macro that this reflection represents. For example, this method would return :has_many for the association has_many :accounts.

name()

Returns the name that was specified for the aggregate or association reflection. For example, this method returns :accounts for the association has_many :accounts.

options()

Return the hash of options that were used for the association or aggregation with the options method. For example, this method would return { :conditions => "active = 1" } for the association has_many :accounts, :conditions => "active = 1".

ActiveRecord::Schema

Public Class Methods

define(info = {}, &block)

This method allows you to define a database schema in a portable Domain Specific Language (DSL) within the given block. All methods available to the current connection adapter are available within the block, allowing you to call create_table, add_index, and so forth.

The optional info hash allows you to pass in additional metadata for the schema, such as the schema's version number.

ActiveRecord::Schema is very similar to the migrations class and, as such, is only available when using a database connection adapter that supports migrations.

ActiveRecord::Transactions::ClassMethods

Public Instance Methods

transaction(*objects, &block)

This method executes all of the statements in the given block within an atomic action. An atomic action is a group of operations that all must succeed in order for the action to be completed. If one of the statements in the block fails (throws an exception), none of the statements will take effect.

For example, when a user creates a new account in our computer system, their old account is deleted; if we do not want to delete the previous account unless the creation of the new account succeeds, we might wrap these two actions in a transaction, to ensure that they are atomic:

```
old_account = Account.find(1)
Account.transaction do
  new_account = Account.create(:last_name => old_account.last_name,
                               :first_name => old_account.first_name)
  old_account.destroy()
end
```

In the preceding example, if either of the statements raises an exception, ROLLBACK will be called on the database. Rollbacks return the database to the state it was in before the transaction began. You should be aware that, by default, Active Record objects *will not* have their instance data returned to the state it was in before the transaction began. In order to return the instance data its pretransaction state, you must explicitly pass the objects as arguments to the transaction method, for example:

```
account = Account.find(1)
account2 = Account.find(2)
Account.transaction(account, account2) do
  account.site_id = account2.site_id
  account2.destroy()
end
```

Both ActiveRecord::Base.save() and ActiveRecord::Base.destroy() are already wrapped in a transaction to ensure that the entire save or destroy action, including callbacks and validations, will be atomic. Therefore, you can take advantage of this fact in your callbacks and validations and raise exceptions to cause the entire save or destroy action to be rolled back.

The exceptions thrown by a statement in a transaction continue to propagate. Therefore, it is likely that you will want to specifically handle the transactions as well.

Another important point regarding transactions is that they are only valid on a single database connection. Therefore, if you have multiple database connections that are class specific, the transaction will not protect the individual statements of each record. A workaround for this problem is to nest the transactions. For example, if we are using a different database to store our Site objects than our Account objects, we would need to nest a transaction that involved both objects:

```
account = Account.find(1)
Site.transaction do
  Account.transaction do
    new_site = Site.create(:name => "New Site")
    account.site_id = new_site.id
  end
end
```

Please note that this is a generally poor solution, but fully distributed transactions are outside of the scope of Active Record.

ActiveRecord::Validations

Public Instance Methods

errors()

This method returns the Errors object associated with the Active Record object. Each Active Record object has an Errors object automatically assigned to it.

save_with_validation(perform_validation = true)

This method causes the Active Record object to be saved, but it first runs all of the validations of the object. This method returns false if there are validation errors. This method overrides the default ActiveRecord::Base.save() method when the Validations module is mixed in, which is the default behavior of Active Record.

save_with_validation!()

This method causes the Active Record object to be saved, but it first runs all of the validations of the object. If the save fails, the RecordInvalid exception is raised. This method overrides the default ActiveRecord::Base.save!() method when the Validations module is mixed in, which is the default behavior of Active Record.

update_attribute_with_validation_skipping(name, value)

This method updates the specified attribute with the specified value and saves the record. However, when the attribute is saved, the object validations are not run, allowing the attribute to be saved even if the full object is not valid. This method overrides the default ActiveRecord::Base.update_attributes method when the Validations module is mixed in, which is the default behavior of Active Record.

valid?()

valid? runs validate and validate_on_create or validate_on_update. It returns true if no errors were detected and false if there were validation errors.

Protected Instance Methods

validate()

This method is run for all saves (both `create` and `update`). Override this method in your class to provide validations, and use `errors.add(attribute, msg)` to register validation errors. `ActiveRecord::Validations::ClassMethods` contains several higher level validation helper methods.

validate_on_create()

This method is run on a `save` action for an Active Record object when the object has not yet been saved to the database. Override this method in your class to provide validations, and use `errors.add(attribute, msg)` to register validation errors. `ActiveRecord::Validations::ClassMethods` contains several higher level validation helper methods.

validate_on_update()

This method is run for all saves where the Active Record object already has been saved and has a corresponding record in the database table. Override this method in your class to provide validations, and use `errors.add(attribute, msg)` to register validation errors. `ActiveRecord::Validations::ClassMethods` contains several higher level validation helper methods.

ActiveRecord::Validations::ClassMethods

Public Instance Methods

condition_block?(condition)

This method returns `true` if the supplied block responds to `call` and has an arity of 1 or -1.

create!(attribute = nil)

The `create!` method instantiates the Active Record class with the values specified in the attributes hash and immediately saves it, if validations permit, just like `ActiveRecord::Base.create`. However, this method calls `save!` so that an exception is raised if the record is not able to be saved.

evaluate_condition(condition, record)

Use this method to determine, based on the given condition, whether or not to validate the given record. This method is used by the `validate_each` method.

validate(*methods, &block)

The `validate` method is overridden in an Active Record class and is called each time a record of that class is created or saved. In the example `Account` class that follows, each time the `Account` class is saved or created, the `first_name` and `last_name` attributes will be checked to make sure they are not empty:

```
class Account < ActiveRecord::Base
  protected
    def validate
      errors.add_on_empty %w( first_name last_name )
    end
end
```

Additionally, it is possible to supply validation method names with the nonblock form of this method:

```
class Account < ActiveRecord::Base
  protected
    validate :check_names

    def check_names
      errors.add_on_empty %w( first_name last_name )
    end
end
```

For more information regarding validations, see Chapter 4.

validate_on_create(*methods, &block)

The validate_on_create method is overridden in an Active Record class and is called only before a record of that class is created. In the example Account class that follows, each time the Account class is saved or created, the first_name and last_name attributes will be checked to make sure they are not empty:

```
class Account < ActiveRecord::Base
  protected
    def validate_on_create
      errors.add_on_empty %w( first_name last_name )
    end
end
```

Additionally, it is possible to supply validation method names with the nonblock form of this method:

```
class Account < ActiveRecord::Base
  protected
    validate_on_create :check_names

    def check_names
      errors.add_on_empty %w( first_name last_name )
    end
end
```

For more information regarding validations, see Chapter 4.

validate_on_update(*methods, &block)

The `validate_on_update` method is overridden in an Active Record class and is called only before an existing record of that class is saved. In the example `Account` class that follows, each time an existing `Account` record is saved, the `first_name` and `last_name` attributes will be checked to make sure they are not empty:

```
class Account < ActiveRecord::Base
  protected
    def validate_on_update
      errors.add_on_empty %w( first_name last_name )
    end
end
```

Additionally, it is possible to supply validation method names with the nonblock form of this method:

```
class Account < ActiveRecord::Base
  protected
    validate_on_update :check_names

    def check_names
      errors.add_on_empty %w( first_name last_name )
    end
end
```

For more information regarding validations, see Chapter 4.

validates_acceptance_of(*attribute_names)

This method is used to validate that an attribute value when you do not want to store the attribute as an actual column in the database. This would typically be used for an acceptance of terms check box on a web page.

```
class Account < ActiveRecord::Base
  validates_acceptance_of :terms_of_service
end
```

The preceding class definition adds a virtual `terms_of_service` attribute to the `Account` class. The `terms_of_service` attribute is *not* represented by a column in the database.

In addition to the virtual attributes to create, this method takes the configuration options of `:message`, `:on`, `:accept`, or `:if`.

The `:message` option provides a custom error message. The default error message is `"must be accepted"`:

```
validates_acceptance_of :terms_of_service, :message => "must be verified"
```

The `:on` option specifies for what methods this validation should be active. Valid options are `:save`, `:create`, and `:update`. The default value is `:save`.

```
validates_acceptance_of :terms_of_service, :on => :create
```

The :accept option specifies exactly what value should be considered as an indication of acceptance. The default is the string "1", which makes it easy to use with an HTML check box.

```
validates_acceptance_of :terms_of_service, :accept => true
```

The :if option specifies a method, proc, or string that is called in order to determine whether the validation should occur at all.

```
validates_acceptance_of :terms_of_service, :if => :check_acceptance
validates_acceptance_of :terms_of_service, :if => "check_acceptance"
validates_acceptance_of :terms_of_service, :if => Proc.new {|a| a.create_step == 2 }
```

For more information regarding validations, see Chapter 4.

validates_associated(*attribute_names)

This method validates whether the associated object or objects specified also successfully validate. This method will work for any type of association. But, be careful of infinitely recursive validations on bidirectional associations.

```
class Account < ActiveRecord::Base
  validates_associated :site
end
```

Also, you should note that this validation will not fail if the association has not yet been set (if it is nil or empty). If you wish to validate that the attribute is both present and valid, you need to also use validates_presence_of.

In addition to the association attributes to validate, this method takes the configuration options of :on and :if.

The :on option specifies for what methods this validation should be active. Valid options are :save, :create, and :update. The default value is :save.

```
validates_associated :site, :on => :create
```

The :if option specifies a method, proc, or string that is called in order to determine whether the validation should occur at all:

```
validates_associated :site, :if => :check_site
validates_associated :site, :if => "check_site"
validates_associated :site, :if => Proc.new {|a| a.create_step == 2 }
```

For more information regarding validations, see Chapter 4.

validates_confirmation_of(*attribute_names)

This method is used to validate that a virtual attribute matches the value of a real attribute, such as dual e-mail or password entry boxes on a web form.

```
validates_confirmation_of :email_address
```

In the preceding example, email_address is an actual database-backed attribute. A new virtual attribute that is not represented by a column in the database is created named email_address_confirmation.

In addition to the attributes to validate the confirmation, this method takes the configuration options of :message, :on, and :if.

The :message option provides a custom error message. The default error message is "doesn't match confirmation".

```
validates_confirmation_of :email_address, :message => "does not match"
```

The :on option specifies for what methods this validation should be active. Valid options are :save, :create, and :update. The default value is :save.

```
validates_confirmation_of :email_address, :on => :create
```

The :if option specifies a method, proc, or string that is called in order to determine whether the validation should occur at all:

```
validates_confirmation_of :email_address, :if => :check_email
validates_confirmation_of :email_address, :if => "check_email"
validates_confirmation_of :email_address, :if => Proc.new {|a| a.create_step == 2 }
```

For more information regarding validations, see Chapter 4.

validates_each(*attribute_names) { |record, attribute, value| . . . }

This method validates each of the specified attributes against the specified block:

```
class Account < ActiveRecord::Base
  validates_each(:first_name, :last_name) do |record, attribute, value|
    record.errors.add(attribute, "is Chad") if value == "Chad"
  end
end
```

In addition to the attributes to validate, this method takes the configuration options of :on, :allow_nil, and :if.

The :on option specifies for what methods this validation should be active. Valid options are :save, :create, and :update. The default value is :save.

```
class Account < ActiveRecord::Base
  validates_each(:first_name, :last_name, :on => :create) do |record, attr, value|
    record.errors.add(attr, "is Chad") if value == "Chad"
  end
end
```

The :allow_nil option, if true, specifies that that the validation should be skipped if the attribute is nil:

```
class Account < ActiveRecord::Base
  validates_each(:first_name, :last_name, :allow_nil => true) do |record, attr, value|
    record.errors.add(attr, "is Chad") if value == "Chad"
  end
end
```

The :if option specifies a method, proc, or string that is called in order to determine whether the validation should occur at all:

```
class Account < ActiveRecord::Base
  validates_each(:first_name,
                 :last_name,
                 :if => :check_each) do |record, attr, value|
    record.errors.add(attr, "is Chad") if value == "Chad"
  end
end

class Account < ActiveRecord::Base
  validates_each(:first_name,
                 :last_name,
                 :if => "check_each") do |record, attr, value|
    record.errors.add(attr, "is Chad") if value == "Chad"
  end
end

class Account < ActiveRecord::Base
  validates_each(:first_name,
                 :last_name,
                 :if => Proc.new {|a| a.create_step == 2 }) do |record, attr, value|
    record.errors.add(attr, "is Chad") if value == "Chad"
  end
end
```

For more information regarding validations, see Chapter 4.

validates_exclusion_of(*attribute_names)

This method adds errors to the specified attributes if the attributes values appear in the specified enumerable object:

```
class Account < ActiveRecord::Base
  validates_exclusion_of(:first_name, :in => %w(Chad Jon Kevin))
end
```

In addition to the attributes to validate, this method takes the configuration options of :in, :message, :allow_nil, and :if.

The :in option specifies an enumerable object against which the attribute values should be checked:

```
validates_exclusion_of(:first_name, :in => %w(Chad Jon Kevin))
```

The :message option provides a custom error message. The default error message is "is reserved".

```
validates_exclusion_of(:first_name, :in => %w(Chad Jon Kevin), :message => "cannot
be one of the authors' names")
```

The :allow_nil option, if true, specifies that that the validation should be skipped if the attribute is nil:

```
validates_exclusion_of(:first_name, :in => %w(Chad Jon Kevin), :allow_nil => true)
```

The :if option specifies a method, proc, or string that is called in order to determine whether the validation should occur at all:

```
validates_exclusion_of(:first_name, :in => %w(Chad Jon Kevin), :if => :check_name)
validates_exclusion_of(:first_name, :in => %w(Chad Jon Kevin), :if => "check_name")
validates_exclusion_of(:first_name,
                       :in => %w(Chad Jon Kevin),
                       :if => Proc.new {|a| a.create_step == 2 })
```

For more information regarding validations, see Chapter 4.

validates_format_of(*attribute_names)

This validation method matches each attribute against a specified regular expression, adding errors to the attributes if they do not match the given regular expression:

```
class Account < ActiveRecord::Base
  validates_format_of(:first_name, :with => /^chad$/i)
end
```

In addition to the attributes to validate, this method takes the configuration options of :with, :message, :on, and :if.

The :with option specifies the regular expression against which the attribute values should be checked:

```
validates_format_of(:first_name, :with => /^chad$/i)
```

The :message option provides a custom error message. The default error message is "is invalid".

```
validates_format_of(:first_name, :with => /^chad$/i, :message => "is not correct")
```

The :on option specifies for what methods this validation should be active. Valid options are :save, :create, and :update. The default value is :save.

```
validates_format_of(:first_name, :with => /^chad$/i, :on => :create)
```

The :if option specifies a method, proc, or string that is called in order to determine whether the validation should occur at all:

```
validates_format_of(:first_name, :with => /^chad$/i, :if => :check_name)
validates_format_of(:first_name, :with => /^chad$/i, :if => "check_name")
validates_format_of(:first_name,
                    :with => /^chad$/i,
                    :if => Proc.new {|a| a.create_step == 2 })
```

For more information regarding validations, see Chapter 4.

validates_inclusion_of(*attribute_names)

This method adds errors to the specified attributes if the attribute's values do not appear in the specified enumerable object:

```
class Account < ActiveRecord::Base
  validates_inclusion_of(:first_name, :in => %w(Chad Jon Kevin))
end
```

In addition to the attributes to validate, this method takes the configuration options of :in, :message, :allow_nil, and :if.

The :in option specifies an enumerable object against which the attribute values should be checked:

```
validates_inclusion_of(:first_name, :in => %w(Chad Jon Kevin))
```

The :message option provides a custom error message. The default error message is "is not included in the list".

```
validates_inclusion_of(:first_name,
                       :in => %w(Chad Jon Kevin),
                       :message => "must be one of the authors' names")
```

The :allow_nil option, if true, specifies that that the validation should be skipped if the attribute is nil:

```
validates_inclusion_of(:first_name, :in => %w(Chad Jon Kevin), :allow_nil => true)
```

The :if option specifies a method, proc, or string that is called in order to determine whether the validation should occur at all:

```
validates_inclusion_of(:first_name, :in => %w(Chad Jon Kevin), :if => :check_name)
validates_inclusion_of(:first_name, :in => %w(Chad Jon Kevin), :if => "check_name")
validates_inclusion_of(:first_name,
                       :in => %w(Chad Jon Kevin),
                       :if => Proc.new {|a| a.create_step == 2 })
```

For more information regarding validations, see Chapter 4.

validates_length_of(*attribute_names)

This method adds errors to the specified attributes if the attribute's values do not match the specified restrictions on length:

```
class Account < ActiveRecord::Base
  validates_length_of :first_name, :maximum => 30
end
```

The validates_length_of method takes only one length-check operation. Valid operations are :minimum, :maximum, :is, :within, and :in.

The :minimum operation checks whether the attribute is longer than the specified minimum length. Either :message or :too_short can be used to customize the error message when this check is used. The default is "is too short (minimum is %d characters)".

```
validates_length_of(:first_name, :minimum => 5, :message => "is too short")
```

The :maximum operation checks whether the attribute is shorter than the specified maximum length. Either :message or :too_long can be used to customize the error message when this check is used. The default is "is too long (maximum is %d characters)".

```
validates_length_of(:first_name, :maximum => 35, :message => "is just too long")
```

The :is operation checks whether the length of the attribute exactly matches the specified length. Either :message or :wrong_length can be used to customize the error message when this check is used. The default is "is the wrong length (should be %d characters)".

```
validates_length_of(:first_name,
                    :is => 35,
                    :message => "must be exactly 35 characters long")
```

The :within operation checks whether the length of the attribute falls within the specified range. The options :too_long and :too_short should be used to customize the error messages when this check is used. The defaults are "is too long (maximum of %d characters)" and "is too short (minimum of %d characters)", respectively.

```
validates_length_of(:first_name,
                    :within => 5...35,
                    :too_short => "is too short",
                    :too_long => "is too long")
```

The other valid configuration options for this method are :on, :allow_nil, and :if.

The :on option specifies for what methods this validation should be active. Valid options are :save, :create, and :update. The default value is :save.

```
validates_length_of(:first_name, :maximum => 35, :on => :create)
```

The :allow_nil option, if true, specifies that that the validation should be skipped if the attribute is nil:

```
validates_length_of(:first_name, :maximum => 35, :allow_nil => true)
```

The :if option specifies a method, proc, or string that is called in order to determine whether the validation should occur at all:

```
validates_length_of(:first_name, :maximum => 35, :if => :check_name)
validates_length_of(:first_name, :maximum => 35, :if => "check_name")
validates_length_of(:first_name,
                    :maximum => 35,
                    :if => Proc.new {|a| a.create_step == 2 })
```

For more information regarding validations, see Chapter 4.

validates_numericality_of(*attribute_names)

This method adds errors to the specified attributes if the value of the attribute is not numeric. By default, this is done by attempting to convert it to a float with Kernel.Float, but this can be overridden with the :only_integer options.

```
class Account < ActiveRecord::Base
  validates_numericality_of :value
end
```

In addition to the attributes to validate, this method takes the configuration options of
:only_integer, :on, :message, :allow_nil, and :if.

The :only_integer option specifies that we are only looking for integers, not floats. The
default is :only_integer => false. When this option is used, the attribute value is matched
against the regular expression /^[+\-]?\d+$/ instead of using Kernel.Float.

The :on option specifies for what methods this validation should be active. Valid options
are :save, :create, and :update. The default value is :save.

```
validates_numericality_of(:value, :on => :create)
```

The :message option provides a custom error message. The default error message is "is
not a number".

```
validates_numericality_of(:value, :message => "must be a number")
```

The :allow_nil option, if true, specifies that the validation should be skipped if the
attribute is nil:

```
validates_numericality_of(:value, :allow_nil => true)
```

The :if option specifies a method, proc, or string that is called in order to determine
whether the validation should occur at all:

```
validates_numericality_of(:value, :if => :check_value)
validates_numericality_of(:value, :if => "check_value")
validates_numericality_of(:value, :if => Proc.new {|a| a.create_step == 2 })
```

For more information regarding validations, see Chapter 4.

validates_presence_of(*attribute_names)

This validation method adds errors to the specified attributes whose values are blank:

```
class Account < ActiveRecord::Base
  validates_presence_of :first_name
end
```

For association attributes, it is important to validate the presence of the foreign key, not
the object itself:

```
validates_presence_of :site # Incorrect
validates_presence_of :site_id # Correct
```

In addition to the attributes to validate, this method takes the configuration options of
:on, :message, and :if.

The :on option specifies for what methods this validation should be active. Valid options are :save, :create, and :update. The default value is :save.

```
validates_presence_of(:first_name, :on => :create)
```

The :message option provides a custom error message. The default error message is "can't be blank".

```
validates_presence_of(:first_name, :message => "must be provided")
```

The :if option specifies a method, proc, or string that is called in order to determine whether the validation should occur at all:

```
validates_presence_of(:first_name, :if => :check_first_name)
validates_presence_of(:first_name, :if => "check_first_name")
validates_presence_of(:first_name, :if => Proc.new {|a| a.create_step == 2 })
```

For more information regarding validations, see Chapter 4.

validates_size_of(*attribute_names)

This method is an alias for validates_length_of. For more information regarding validations, see Chapter 4.

validates_uniqueness_of(*attribute_names)

Use this method to add errors to the specified attributes if the attribute value is not unique in the database table. This can be useful, for example, for ensuring that each account has a unique username.

```
class Account < ActiveRecord::Base
  validates_uniqueness_of :username
end
```

In addition to the attributes to validate, this method takes the configuration options of :scope, :on, :message, and :if.

The :scope option indicates one or more database columns that should be used to limit the scope of the uniqueness check. For instance, if you wanted usernames to be unique only on a site-by-site basis, you could use this line:

```
validates_uniqueness_of :username, :scope => :site_id
```

The :on option specifies for what methods this validation should be active. Valid options are :save, :create, and :update. The default value is :save.

```
validates_uniqueness_of(:username, :on => :create)
```

The :message option provides a custom error message. The default error message is "has already been taken".

```
validates_uniqueness_of(:username, :message => "must be unique")
```

The :if option specifies a method, proc, or string that is called in order to determine whether the validation should occur at all:

```
validates_uniqueness_of(:username, :if => :check_username)
validates_uniqueness_of(:username, :if => "check_username")
validates_uniqueness_of(:username, :if => Proc.new {|a| a.create_step == 2 })
```

For more information regarding validations, see Chapter 4.

Index

Symbols

* (asterisk), 30
[]==(attribute_name, new_value), 215, 225
[](attribute), 246
[](attribute_name), 215, 225
[](name), 245
~:as attribute, 78–79
==(object_to_compare), 215, 225

A

abstract_adapter.rb file, 191
abstract_class?( ), 215
:accept option, 85
Account class, 3, 19, 22, 40, 146, 182
Account model, 165, 176, 204
account objects, 3, 65
Account record, 92
Account table, 60, 167
Account_fullname attribute, 63
account_id primary key, 165, 171
account_id table, 167
account_id type, 128
Account_initialized attribute, 64
Account_lastsaved attribute, 65
account_name value, 83, 129
account_number primary key, 21
account_password field, 107
Account_updated attribute, 65
account_updated field, 64, 66
Account_Username attribute, 6
Account_Username field, 6, 107
account_username table, 43
Account.find method, 157
AccountObserver class, 91
Accounts class, 21
accounts table, 167
accounts.yml file, 140, 184
account.yml file, 141
Action Controller library, 194
ActionView::Helpers::DateHelper#date_selec
    t helper method, 152
active?( ), 235
Active Record Schema, 46
Active Server Pages (ASP), 44
active_record/deprecated_finders library,
    189
active_record.rb file, 188

Active Record, 1
    advantages of, 7
    alternatives to, 196–201
        ActiveRelation, 199
        Active Resource, 200–201
        Database Interface (DBI), 196
        database-specific libraries, 199–200
        ObjectGraph (Og), 197–199
    associations, 69–80
    callbacks, 59–69
    create, read, update, and delete (CRUD)
        database transactions, 4
    debugging, 153–160
        benchmarking, 159–160
        logging, 153–158
    development of, 2
    error methods, 144–153
    establishing connections to databases,
        10–16
        DB2, 11
        Firebird, 11–12
        FrontBase, 12
        learning more, 16–17
        MySQL, 12–13
        OpenBase, 13–14
        Oracle, 14
        PostgreSQL, 14–15
        SQL Server, 15–16
        SQLite, 15
        Sybase, 16
    extending, 109–123
        adding class methods, 120–123
        column_names array, 116–117
        metaprogramming, 110–112
        method_missing method, 112–115
        retrieving association names, 117–119
    frequently asked questions, 201–214
    future of, 192–195
        Active Resource, 194
        enterprise-level functionality, 192–193
        feedback, 195
        minor changes, 193
        plug-ins, 193–194
        use as database ORM layer, 195
    getting help, 214
    installing, 8–10
        additional libraries, 9–10
        gems, 8–10

localization, 204
model, view, controller (MVC) framework, 4
object relational mapping (ORM) concept, 2–3
objects, 5–6
overview, 1–2
Ruby code, 5
source code, 187–191
    abstract_adapter.rb file, 191
    active_record.rb file, 188
    base.rb file, 189–191
    connection_specification.rb file, 191
    finding, 188
unit testing, 125–144
    assertion methods, 129–139
    fixtures, 139–144
    reasons for, 126–127
    writing tests, 127–129
validations, 80–88
writing programs, 18–24
    assumptions, 19–20
    coding conventions, 19–20
    overriding assumptions, 20–21
    relationships among objects, 22–24
    retrieving objects from databases, 21–22
ActiveRecord::Base class, 109, 145, 164–165, 167, 169, 175
ActiveRecord::Base#reflect_on_all_associations method, 117
ActiveRecord::Base#save argument, 122
ActiveRecord::Base.connection.select_all statement, 176
ActiveRecord::Base.create call, 64
ActiveRecord::Base.delete statement, 68
ActiveRecord::Base.delete_all statement, 68
ActiveRecord::Base.destroy statement, 68
ActiveRecord::Base.destroy_all statement, 68
ActiveRecord::Base.establish_connection method, 10, 47
ActiveRecord::Base.find class, 110, 112
ActiveRecord::Base.find operation, 63
ActiveRecord::Base.observers method, 91
ActiveRecord::Base.save method, 6, 64–65, 67
ActiveRecord::Base.update statement, 65
ActiveRecordError class, 144, 145
ActiveRecord::Error object, 80, 82
ActiveRecord::RecordNotFound error, 132
ActiveRecord::Schema class, 46
ActiveRecord::Schema format, 169
ActiveRecord::SchemaDumper class, 46, 50
ActiveRecord::StaleObjectError exception, 41
ActiveRecord::Validations.validate statement, 66
ActiveRecord::Validations.validate_on_create statement, 67
ActiveRelation, 199
Active Resource, 194, 200–201
acts_as features, 92

acts_as_* method, 92
acts_as_list method, 93–97
    adding, 94–95
    decrement_position method, 97
    defining integer columns used for sorting lists, 94
    first? method, 97
    higher_item method, 97
    increment_position method, 96–97
    insert_at(value), 95
    insert_at(value) method, 95
    last? method, 97
    lower_item method, 97
    move_higher method, 96
    move_lower method, 95
    move_to_bottom method, 96
    move_to_top method, 96
    remove_from_list method, 96
    setting up associations, 93
acts_as_nested-set method, 93, 101–105
    add_child method, 104
    all_children method, 105
    before_destroy method, 105
    child? method, 104
    children_count method, 104
    defining, 101–103
        left_column parameter, 102
        parent_column parameter, 102
        right_column parameter, 102
        scope parameter, 102–103
    defining foreign keys, 101
    direct_children method, 105
    full_set method, 105
    root? method, 104
    unknown? method, 104
acts_as_tree method, 93, 97–101, 123
    ancestors method, 100
    defining, 98–99
    root method, 100
    siblings method, 100–101
adapter parameter, 11–16
adapter_name( ), 235
AdapterNotFound error, 148
AdapterNotSpecified error, 147
adapters, 10–16
    DB2, 11
    Firebird, 11–12
    FrontBase, 12
    MySQL, 12–13
    OpenBase, 13–14
    Oracle, 14
    PostgreSQL, 14–15
    SQL Server, 15–16
    SQLite, 15
    Sybase, 16
add_child method, 104
add_column method, 52–54

add_column(table_name, column_name, type, options = {}), 241
add_index method, 54
add_index(table_name, column_name, options = {}), 241–242
add_limit_offset!(sql, options), 238
add_limit!(sql, options), 238
add_lock!(sql, options), 238
add_observer!(klass), 250
add_on_blank(attributes, msg = @@default_error_messages[:blank]), 247
add_on_empty(attributes, msg = @@default_error_messages[:empty]), 247
add_order_by_for_association_limiting!(sql, options), 242
add_to_base(msg), 247
add(attribute, msg = @@default_error_messages[:invalid]), 247
ADO directory, 10
ADO.rb file, 10
after_create( ), 233
after_create method, 65
after_destroy( ), 233
after_destroy method, 68–69
after_find method, 63
after_initialize method, 64
after_save( ), 233
after_save method, 64–65
after_update( ), 233
after_update method, 66
after_validation( ), 233
after_validation method, 66–67
after_validation_on_create( ), 233
after_validation_on_create method, 67
after_validation_on_update( ), 234
after_validation_on_update method, 68
aggregations, 105–109
    composed_of method, 106–107
        class_name parameter, 107
        mapping parameter, 107
        names of value objects, 106
    defining value objects, 107–108
    using, 108–109
aid_seq sequence, 173
alias_method call, 111
:all control, 27
all_children method, 105
allow_concurrency attribute, 168–169
allow_concurrency parameter, PostgreSQL, 15
:allow_nil option, 84, 86
ALTER TABLE statements, 50
ancestors method, 99, 100
announce(message), 249

ar_hello_world.rb file, 110
Array form, 28
:as option, 78
ASP (Active Server Pages), 44
assert method, 129–130
assert_equal method, 131
assert_in_delta method, 132
assert_instance_of method, 133
assert_kind_of method, 134
assert_match method, 135
assert_nil method, 130
assert_no_match method, 135
assert_not_nil method, 131
assert_not_same method, 136
assert_nothing_raised method, 133
assert_operator method, 136–137
assert_raise method, 132–133
assert_raised method, 133
assert_respond_to method, 134
assert_same method, 135–136
assert_send method, 138
assert_throws method, 137–138
assertion methods, 129–139
    assert, 129–130
    assert_equal, 131
    assert_in_delta, 132
    assert_instance_of, 133
    assert_kind_of, 134
    assert_match, 135
    assert_nil, 130
    assert_no_match, 135
    assert_not_nil, 131
    assert_not_same, 136
    assert_nothing_raised, 133
    assert_operator, 136–137
    assert_raise, 132–133
    assert_respond_to, 134
    assert_same, 135–136
    assert_send, 138
    assert_throws, 137–138
    flunk, 138–139
:association_foriegn_key attribute, 79
AssociationReflection object, 117
associations, 59, 69–80
    example of, 69–70
    modifiers, 76–79
        :as, 78–79
        :association_foriegn_key, 79
        :class_name, 77
        :dependent, 79
        finder options, 77
        :foreign_key, 77
        :join_table, 79
        :polymorphic, 78–79
        :through, 78
    overview, 69
    setting up, 93

types of, 70–76
    belongs_to, 70–71
    has_and_belongs_to_many, 74–75
    has_many, 71–72
    has_many:through, 75–76
    has_one, 72–73
AssociationTypeMismatch error, 146–147
assumptions, 19–20
asterisk (*), 30
attr_accessible(*attributes), 215
attr_accessor class method, 120
attr_protected(*attributes), 216
attribute_names( ), 225
attribute_present?(attribute), 225
AttributeAssignmentError error, 152
attributes, 6
attributes method, 152
attributes_before_type_cast( ), 226
attributes_before_type_cast method, 213
attributes=(new_attributes), 226
attributes(options = nil), 225–226
Audit class, 122
auditing_columns method, 122
audits class method, 122
audits method, 121
autocommit parameter, 16, 180
average(column_name, options = {}), 231
:awesome symbol, 137

B
balance field, 106
Base class, 144, 154, 189
base_class( ), 216
base64 library, 189
Base.establish_connection method, 191
base.rb file, 189–191
before_create( ), 234
before_create method, 65, 205
before_destroy( ), 234
before_destroy callback, 79
before_destroy method, 68, 105
before_save( ), 234
before_save method, 64
before_update( ), 234
before_update method, 65–66
before_validation( ), 234
before_validation method, 66
before_validation_on_create( ), 234
before_validation_on_create method, 67
before_validation_on_update( ), 234–235
before_validation_on_update method, 67–68
BEGIN statement, 38
begin_db_transaction( ), 238
belongs_to association, 70, 71, 213
belongs_to method, 22, 78, 93
belongs_to relationship, 70–71
benchmark method, 159

benchmarking, 159–160, 190
benchmark(title, log_level = Logger::DEBUG,
    use_silence = true) {|| . . .}, 216
between clause, 101
BigDecimal class, 206
:binary type, 181
binary_to_string(value), 236
BLOB data type, 16
boolean attribute, 20
Boolean data types, 44
Boolean type, 181
Builder class, 182
building programs, 18–24
    assumptions, 19–20
    coding conventions, 19–20
    objects
        relationships among, 22–24
        retrieving from databases, 21–22
by_other_artist method, 108

C
calculate(operation, column_name, options
    = {}), 231–232
callbacks, 59–69
    callback macros, 61–63
    implementing, 60
    overview, 59–60
    types of, 63–69
        after_create, 65
        after_destroy, 68–69
        after_find, 63
        after_initialize, 64
        after_save, 64–65
        after_update, 66
        after_validation, 66–67
        after_validation_on_create, 67
        after_validation_on_update, 68
        before_create, 65
        before_destroy, 68
        before_save, 64
        before_update, 65–66
        before_validation, 66
        before_validation_on_create, 67
        before_validation_on_update, 67–68
cattr_accessor method, 63, 190
change_column method, 54
change_column_default(table_name,
    column_name, default), 242
change_column(table_name, column_name,
    type, options = {}), 242
char type, 181
chars accessor, 204
charset parameter, 12
child? method, 104
:children option, 36
children_count column, 99
children_count method, 104

class methods, 120, 123
class_name( ), 252
:class_name attribute, 77
class_name option, 77
class_name parameter, 107
class_of_active_record_descendant(klass), 224
ClassMethods module, 121
clear( ), 247
clear_active_connections!( ), 216
CLOB data type, 16
clone( ), 226
colorize_logging attribute, 167
column method, 52
Column objects, 114
column parameter, 94
column_for_attribute(attribute_name), 226
column_names( ), 216
column_names array, 116–117
column(name, type, options = {}), 245–246
columns( ), 216
columns
    adding security to, 213
    changing, 53–54
    enum, 213
    foreign key, defining, 98
    indexing, 54–55
    integer, defining, 94
    naming, 212
    removing, 53–54
columns_hash( ), 216
columns(table_name, name = nil), 242
comma separated value (CSV) format, 142–143, 185–186
comment association, 77
Comment model class, 103
Comments association, 158
comments table, 174
COMMIT statement, 38, 40
commit_db_transaction( ), 239
composed_of method, 106–107
composite primary keys, 205
compute_type(type_name), 224
condition_block?(condition), 255
:conditions argument, 115
:conditions array, 114
:conditions option, 28–29, 36
config directory, 10
configuration options, 164–173
    allow_concurrency attribute, 168–169
    colorize_logging attribute, 167
    default_timezone attribute, 167–168
    generate_read_methods attribute, 169
    pluralize_table_names attribute, 166–167
    primay_key_prefix_type attribute, 164–165
    schema_format attribute, 169–170
    set_Inheritance_column attribute, 171–172

set_primary_key attribute, 171
set_sequence_name attribute, 172–173
set_table_name attribute, 170–171
table_name_prefix attribute, 165–166
table_name_suffix attribute, 166
ConfigurationError error, 152
configuring connections to databases, 10–16
    DB2, 11
    Firebird, 11–12
    FrontBase, 12
    MySQL, 12–13
    OpenBase, 13–14
    Oracle, 14
    PostgreSQL, 14–15
    SQL Server, 15–16
    SQLite, 15
    Sybase, 16
connected?( ), 217
connection( ), 217, 226
connection_specification.rb file, 191
connection=(connection_specification), 217
ConnectionAdaptors module, 191
connection.delete method, 177, 190
connection.execute method, 179, 180
ConnectionFailed error, 148
connection.insert statement, 177
ConnectionNotEstablished error, 148
connection.select_all method, 177, 179, 190
connection.update method, 177, 190
content_columns( ), 217
content_columns method, 185
convenience methods, 83–88
    validates_acceptance_of, 85
    validates_associated, 87–88
    validates_confirmation_of, 84–85
    validates_each, 83–84
    validates_exclusion_of, 87
    validates_format_of, 87
    validates_inclusion_of, 87
    validates_length_of, 86
    validates_numericality_of, 88
    validates_presence_of, 85–86
    validates_uniqueness_of, 86
count( ), 247
count(*args), 232
count_by_sql(sql_query_string), 217
counter_cache attribute, 99
counter_cache method, 98
cows table, 51
cows_farmer_id_index index, 55
create method, 6, 26, 190
create, read, update, delete (CRUD), 1, 4, 25, 51, 148, 175, 177, 190
create_attributes method, 183
create_fixtures method, 140
create_from_xml method, 183

create_reflection(macro, name, options, active_record), 251
create_table method, 51–52, 204
create_table(name, options = {}) { || . . . }a, 242–243
create!(attribute = nil), 255
create(attributes = nil), 217
created_at field, 44
created_on field, 44
CRUD (create, read, update, delete), 1, 4, 25, 51, 148, 175, 177, 190
CSV (comma separated value) format, 142–143, 185–186
.csv extension, 142

D

data models, 208, 210
data types, 181
data validations. *See* validations
database administrator's (DBA), 80
database configuration root, 212
database foreign keys, 210
Database Interface (DBI), 196–197
database locking mechanisms, 206–207
database management system (DBMS), 166
database parameter, 11–16
databases, 17, 43–57
    Active-Record friendly tables, 43–44
    DB2, 11
    Firebird, 11–12
    FrontBase, 12
    learning more about specific, 16–17
    migrations, 46–57
        anatomy of, 50
        Domain Specific Language (DSL), 46–47
        example of, 50–57
        executing, 48–50
        using, 47–48
    MySQL, 12–13
    OpenBase, 13–14
    Oracle, 14
    PostgreSQL, 14–15
    retrieving objects from, 21–22
    saving attributes as records in, 6
    selecting random records from, 207
    SQL Server, 15–16
    SQLite, 15
    Sybase, 16
    traditional management of, 44–46
    using multiple with Active Record, 201–203
database-specific libraries, 199–200
database.yml file, 10, 49
date object, 152
DB2, 9, 11
DBA (database administrator's), 80
DbB2 database, 17
db:bootstrap option, 56

DBD directory, 10
DBI (Database Interface), 196–197
db/migrate/002_add_farmer_id_column file, 53
db/migrations folder, 48
DBMS (database management system), 166
debugging, 153–160
    benchmarking, 159–160
    logging, 153–158
decimal numbers, 206
decrement_counter(counter_name, id), 217
decrement_position method, 97
decrement(attribute), 226
decrement!(attribute), 227
def call, 111
def to_s method, 117
default_sequence_name(table, column), 239
default_timezone attribute, 167–168
define_column_methods method, 116
define_method call, 111
define_method method, 113, 122
define(info = {}, &block), 252
defining
    acts_as_nested-set method, 101–103
        left_column parameter, 102
        parent_column parameter, 102
        right_column parameter, 102
        scope parameter, 102–103
    acts_as_tree method, 98–99
    foreign key columns, 98
    foreign keys, 101
    integer columns used for sorting lists, 94
    value objects, 107–108
delete method, 35, 190
:delete_all attribute, 79
delete_all method, 35
delete_all(conditions = nil), 218
delete(id), 217
delete(sql, name = nil), 239
deleting records, 35–37
:dependent => :delete_all option, 37
:dependent => :destroy option, 36–37
:dependent attribute, 79
:dependent option, 36
deposit method, 39
destroy( ), 227
:destroy attribute, 79
destroy method, 35, 38, 191
destroy_all method, 35
destroy_all(conditions = nil), 218
destroy_author method, 60
destroy_readers method, 60
destroy(id), 218
development decisions, 162–164
    efficiency, 163–164
    process, 163
    responsibility, 163
    scope, 162–163

development of Active Record, 2
DHH (Hansson, David Heinemeier), 2
direct table, 174
direct_children method, 105
directs table, 168
disconnect!( ), 235
distinct(columns, order_by), 243
Domain Specific Language (DSL), 46–47
down method, 50, 54
downcase method, 175
drop_table method, 53
drop_table(name, options = {}), 243
DSL (Domain Specific Language), 46–47
dsn parameter, SQL Server, 15
dynamic finders, 33–34

E
each( ) { |attribute, msg| . . . }, 248
each_full( ) { |msg| . . . }, 248
Email database, 203
embedded Ruby (ERb), 141
empty?( ), 248
encoding parameter, PostgreSQL, 15
enterprise-level functionality, 192–193
enum columns, 213
eql?(object_to_compare), 227
ERb (embedded Ruby), 141
error methods, 144–153
    ActiveRecordError, 145
    AdapterNotFound, 148
    AdapterNotSpecified, 147
    AssociationTypeMismatch, 146–147
    AttributeAssignmentError, 152
    ConfigurationError, 152
    ConnectionFailed, 148
    ConnectionNotEstablished, 148
    MultiparameterAssignmentErrors, 153
    PreparedStatementInvalid, 150–151
    ReadOnlyRecord, 152
    RecordNotFound, 149
    RecordNotSaved, 149
    SerializationTypeMismatch, 147
    StaleObjectError, 151–152
    StatementInvalid, 149–150
    SubclassNotFound, 145–146
errors( ), 254
establish_connection method, 10
establish_connection(connection_specificati
    on = nil), 218
establishing connections to databases, 16
eval methods, 61
evaluate_condition(condition, record), 255
Evans, Clark, 184
Event logging, 190
:except option, 182
Exception class, 189
execute method, 32, 37, 56, 210

execute(sql, name = nil), 239
exists?(id), 218
exporting
    comma separated value (CSV) format, 185
    XML format, 182–183
    YAML format, 184
extend method, 120
extending Active Record, 109–123
    adding class methods, 120–123
    column_names array, 116–117
    metaprogramming, 110–112
    method_missing method, 112–115
    retrieving relationship names, 117–119

F
farmer_id column, 53
feedback table, 170
find method, 21, 27, 33, 36, 42, 63, 152, 157,
        175, 210
find operations, 149
find(*args), 218–220
find_all_by method, 33
find_by method, 23, 33
find_by_sql method, 32, 37, 43, 149, 158, 176,
        210–211
find_by_sql(sql_query), 220
find_by_username method, 22
find_or_create_by method, 33
find_or_create_by_* dynamic finder, 23
find_with_rquery method, 111
find_without_rquery method, 111, 113–114
Finder methods, 190
finder options, 77
finders
    dynamic, 33–34
    nondynamic, 37–38
finding source code, 188
Firebird, 11–12
Firebird adapter, 9
Firebird database, 17
:first control, 27
first? method, 97
fixnum type, 181
fixtures, 139–144
    benefits of, 139–141
    formats, 142–144
        comma separated value (CSV), 142–143
        single file, 143–144
        YAML, 142
    transaction support with, 141–142
Fixtures.create_fixtures method, 140
flat files, 201
float type, 181
floating point values, 132
flunk method, 138–139
FOR UPDATE statement, 42
:force => true option, 52

foreign key columns, 98
foreign keys, 101
:foreign_key attribute, 77, 99
foreign_key method, 98
foreign_key name, 77
foreign_key value, 101
format_log_entry(message, dump = nil), 236
freeze( ), 227
FROM clause, 29, 32
:from option, 32
from_xml method, 183
FrontBase, 9, 12, 17
frozen?( ), 227
full_messages( ), 248
full_set method, 105
fullname attribute, 63
functions, custom, 179–181

G
gems, installing, 8–10
generate command, 50
generate_read_methods attribute, 169
generate_read_methods method, 169
:group option, 31–32, 33
GUID primary keys, 205–206

H
Hansson, David Heinemeier (DHH), 2
has_and_belongs_to_many relationship,
74–75, 79
has_attribute?(attribute), 227
has_many association, 70, 72, 76, 78
has_many class method, 120
has_many relationship, 71–72, 74, 158
has_many :through association type, 70
has_many:through relationship, 75–76
has_one association, 70, 71–72, 78, 213
has_one relationship, 72–73
has_parent? method, 98
hash( ), 227
hello_world method, 110
higher_item method, 97
host parameter, 12–16
human_name( ), 237

I
id( ), 227
:id => false option, 52
id attribute, 21, 206
id primary key, 43
id=(value), 227
:if operates, 85
:if option, 86
implementing
    callbacks, 60
    validations, 81–83

importing
    comma separated value (CSV) format,
        185–186
    XML format, 183–184
    YAML format, 184
:in option, 86–87
include method, 120
:include option, 31, 118, 183
:include parameter, 29, 31
increment_counter(counter_name, id), 220
increment_position method, 96–97
increment(attribute), 228
increment!(attribute), 228
indexing columns, 54–55
Inflector class, 165–166, 190
inheritance_column( ), 220
inherited(subclass), 251
initialize method, 108
initialize_schema_information( ), 243
init.rb file, 109
Inner joins, 71
INSERT statement, 25, 38
insert_at(value) method, 95
insert(sql, name = nil, pk = nil, id_value = nil,
        sequence_name = nil), 239
installing
    additional libraries, 9–10
    gems, 8–10
InstanceMethods module, 121–122
instantiate_observers( ), 250
insult method, 132
integer columns, 94
integer type, 99
internationalization, 204
invalid?(attribute), 248

J
Java, 44
:join_table attribute, 79
:joins option, 31, 32

K
key: value format, 142
keys
    composite primary, 205
    database foreign, 210
    GUID primary, 205–206
    Universally Unique Identifier (UUID)
        primary, 205–206
klass( ), 237, 252

L
Lafcadio, 201
last? method, 97
LDAP (Lightweight Directory Access
        Protocol), 201

Left joins, 71
left_column parameter, 101, 102
legacy schema, configuration options, 164–173
  allow_concurrency attribute, 168–169
  colorize_logging attribute, 167
  default_timezone attribute, 167–168
length( ), 248
lib directory, 188
libraries, installing additional, 9–10
Lightweight Directory Access Protocol (LDAP), 201
LIMIT clause, 32, 213
:limit option, 32–33
LineItem model, 56
listdetails[0] record, 96
listdetails[1] record, 96
LocalDatabase class, 202
localization, 204
lock! method, 42
:lock option, 33, 42
lock_version column, 41
lock_version field, 152
locking, 40–42
log_info(sql, name, runtime), 236
Log4r class, 190
Logger class, 154, 158
Logger::DEBUG method, 158
logging, 153, 158
log(sql_statement, name) { || . . .}, 236
lower_item method, 97

M
macro( ), 252
macros, 61–63
mapping option, 107
mapping parameter, 107, 108
maximum(column_name, options = {}), 232
member table, 175
members table, 170, 174, 176
Merb, 195
:message => "" method, 85
:message option, 86
metaprogramming, 110–112
method_missing error, 177
method_missing function, 22
method_missing method, 112–115, 169, 190
method_missing(method, *arguments, &block), 249
methods, assertion. See assertion methods
methods, error. See error methods
migrate(direction), 249
migrate.rb file, 49
migrations, 46–57, 193
  anatomy of, 50
  Domain Specific Language (DSL), 46–47

example of, 50–57
  columns, 53–55
  managing data, 55–57
  tables, 51–53
executing, 48–50
  outside of Ruby on Rails, 49–50
  within Ruby on Rails, 48–49
using, 47–48
min_messages parameter, PostgreSQL, 14
minimum(column_name, options = {}), 232
mode parameter, SQL Server, 15
model, view, controller (MVC) framework, 1
models
  adding security to, 213
  naming, 212
modifiers, association, 76–79
  :as, 78–79
  :association_foriegn_key, 79
  :class_name, 77
  :dependent, 79
  finder options, 77
  :foreign_key, 77
  :join_table, 79
  :polymorphic, 78–79
  :through, 78
move_higher method, 96, 97
move_lower method, 95, 97
move_to_bottom method, 96
move_to_top method, 96
MultiparameterAssignmentErrors error, 153
multiple databases, using with Active Record, 201–203
multithreaded programs, using Active Record in, 206
MVC (model, view, controller) framework, 1
mylog.txt file, 155
MySQL, 9, 12–13, 17

N
name( ), 252
:name option, 55
naming columns and models, 212
native_database_types( ), 244
new( ), 250
new method, 6
new_attributes method, 183
new_record?( ), 228
new(attributes=nil) { |self if block_given?| . . . }, 220
new(base), 245
new(macro, name, options, active_record), 252
new(name, default, sql_type = nil, null = true), 236
nil field, 44
nil value, 20, 128

nondynamic finders, 37–38
N-tier applications, 162
:nullify attribute, 79
number?( ), 237

O

object relational mapping (ORM), 2–3, 18,
    192
object_id values, 135
Object.blank? method, 85
ObjectGraph (Og), 197–199
objects
    attributes of, 6
    creating, 6
    relationships among, 22–24
    retrieving from databases, 21–22
observe method, 92
observe(*models), 250
observed_class( ), 250
observed_classes( ), 250
observed_subclasses( ), 250
observers, 91–92
observers( ), 250
observers=(*observers), 250
OFFSET clause, 32
:offset option, 32–33
Og (ObjectGraph), 197–199
omap type, 142
:on => :create method, 85
:on => :save method, 85
:on => :update method, 85
:on option, 84, 86
on_base( ), 248
on(attribute), 248
:only option, 182
OpenBase, 13–14
OpenBase adapter, 9
OpenBase database, 17
optimistic locking, 41
options( ), 252
:options option, 52
options_include_default?(options), 245
Oracle, 14
Oracle adapter, 10
Oracle database, 17
ORDER BY clause, 99
order method, 98
:order option, 31, 33
order parameter, 31, 99
Orders model, 55
ORM (object relational mapping), 2–3, 18,
    192
overriding assumptions, 20–21

P

paginating results, 213–214
parent_column parameter, 101, 102

password attribute, 107
password parameter, 11–16
Perl, 44
pessimistic locking, 42
PHP, 44
plug-ins, 193–194
pluralize_table_name attribute, 171
pluralize_table_names attribute, 166–167
pluralize_table_names parameter, 21
:polymorphic attribute, 78–79
port parameter, 12–16
position column, 95
position method, 94
PostgreSQL, 10, 14–15, 17
prefect_primary_key?(table_name = nil), 235
prepared statements, 207
PreparedStatementInvalid error, 150–151
price method, 56
primary_key( ), 221
:primary_key option, 52
primary_key_prefix_type class attribute, 175
primary_key_prefix_type method, 165
primary_key_prefix_type setting, 164
primary_key(name), 246
primay_key_prefix_type attribute, 164–165
private methods, 190
proc method, 84
proc statement, 137
procedures, stored, 179–181
project_development database, 19
protected methods, 190
public methods, 191

Q

quantity method, 56
quote_column_name(name), 240
quote_string(value), 240
quoted_date(value), 241
quoted_false( ), 241
quoted_true( ), 241
quote(value, column = nil), 240

R

railsroot/log directory, 153
raise clause, 144
rake db:migrate method, 51, 53–54
rake db:schema:dump task, 170
rake task, 48, 56, 211
raw_connection( ), 235
reading (R) task, 3
reading records
    :conditions options, 28–29
    dynamic finders, 33–34
    :from option, 32
    :group option, 31–32
    :include parameter, 29, 31
    :joins option, 32

:limit option, 32–33
:lock option, 33
:offset option, 32–33
:order parameter, 31
:readonly option, 33
:select option, 31
readonly?( ), 228
:readonly => false option, 33
:readonly => true option, 33
:readonly option, 33
ReadOnlyRecord error, 152
realtedID attribute, 102
reconnect!( ), 235
RecordNotFound error, 79, 149
RecordNotSaved error, 25, 149
records
    creating, 25–26
    deleting, 35–37
    reading, 27–34
        :conditions options, 28–29
        dynamic finders, 33–34
        :from option, 32
        :group option, 31–32
        :include parameter, 29–31
        :joins option, 32
        :limit option, 32–33
        :lock option, 33
        :offset option, 32–33
        :order parameter, 31
        :readonly option, 33
        :select option, 31
    selecting random from databases, 207
    updating, 34–35
    validation of, 211–212
RedHill Consulting, 210
reflect_on_aggregation(aggregation), 251
reflect_on_all_aggregations( ), 251
reflect_on_all_associations(macro = nil), 251
reflect_on_association(association), 251
reflections( ), 251
related_id method, 103
relationships
    general discussion, 22–24
    retrieving names of, 117–119
reload( ), 228
RemoteDatabase class, 202
remove_column method, 54
remove_column(table_name,
        column_name), 244
remove_connection(klass=self), 221
remove_from_list method, 96
remove_index(table_name, options = {}), 244
removing columns, 53–54
rename_column(table_name,
        column_name, options = {}), 244
rename_table(name, new_name), 244
Representation State Transfer (REST), 194

requires_reloaded?( ), 235
rescue clause, 144
reset_column_information( ), 221
reset_sequence!(table, column, sequence =
        nil), 239
respond_to?(method, include_priv=false),
        228
REST (Representation State Transfer), 194
RESTful interfaces, 194
results, paginating, 213–214
retrieving objects from databases, 21–22
revisions_for method, 123
right_column parameter, 101, 102
Role class definition, 22
ROLLBACK statement, 38, 40
rollback_db_transaction( ), 239
root method, 99, 100
root? method, 104
:root option, 182
RQuery::Conditions object, 112
Ruby Gem system, 8
ruby migrate.rb command, 49
Ruby on Rails
    executing migrations outside of, 49–50
    executing migrations within, 48–49

S

sanitize_sql(sql_to_sanitize), 225
save( ), 228
save!( ), 229
save method, 6, 25, 34, 38, 122
save! method, 149
save_with_validation!( ), 254
save_with_validation(perform_validation =
        true), 254
saving attributes as records in databases, 6
say_with_time(message) { || . . . }, 249
say(message, subitem = false), 249
schema, legacy. *See* legacy schema
schema parameter, DB2, 11
schema_format attribute, 169–170
schema_info database, 49
schema_info table, 49, 52
schema_search_path parameter, PostgreSQL,
        14
SchemaDumper method, 50
scope, 190
:scope option, 86
scope parameter, 94, 102–103
script/generate migration
        add_farmer_id_column file, 53
script/generate migration command, 49
script/generate migration create_users_table
        command, 48
security, adding to models/columns, 213
select * type, 177
SELECT clause, 30, 38

:select option, 31
SELECT statement, 27, 94, 210
select_all statement, 178, 181
select_all(sql, name = nil), 239
select_one(sql, name = nil), 239
select_value(sql, name = nil), 240
select_values(sql, name = nil), 240
selecting random records from databases,
    207
select(sql, name = nil), 240
self.down method, 52
self.included method, 121
self.up method, 53
send command, 138
sequences, custom, 179–181
SerializationTypeMismatch error, 147
serialize(attribute_name, class_name =
    Object), 221
serialized_attributes( ), 221
service parameter, Firebird, 12
set library, 189
set_Inheritance_column attribute, 171–172
set_inheritance_column(value = nil, &block),
    222
set_locking_column(value = nil, &block), 222
set_primary_key attribute, 171
set_primary_key method, 43, 164–165,
    174–175
set_primary_key(value = nil, &block), 222
set_sequence_name attribute, 172–173
set_sequence_name(value = nil, &block), 222
set_table_name attribute, 170–171
set_table_name method, 43, 174
set_table_name(value = nil, &block), 222–223
setup method, 141
Sexy Migrations, 193
siblings method, 99, 100–101
silence( ) { ‖ . . . }, 223
simplification, 173–181
    CRUD operations, 175–177
    custom functions, 179–181
    custom sequences, 179–181
    data types, 181
    improving performance, 177–178
    low-level operations, 177–178
    SQL statements, 175–177
    stored procedures, 179–181
single file format, 143–144
SingletonMethods module, 121, 123
size( ), 248
size method, 112
socket parameter, MySQL, 13
some_array.size method, 112
sorting lists, 94
source code
    abstract_adapter.rb file, 191
    active_record.rb file, 188

base.rb file, 189–191
connection_specification.rb file, 191
finding, 188
SQL, 25–42
    creating records, 25–26
    deleting records, 35–37
    locking, 40–42
    nondynamic finders, 37–38
    reading records, 27–34
        :conditions options, 28–29
        dynamic finders, 33–34
        :from option, 32
        :group option, 31–32
        :include parameter, 29, 31
        :joins option, 32
        :limit option, 32–33
        :lock option, 33
        :offset option, 32–33
        :order parameter, 31
        :readonly option, 33
        :select option, 31
    transactions, 38, 40
    updating records, 34–35
SQL Server, 15–16
SQL statements, 5, 175–177
SQL syntax, 45
:sql value, 169
SQLite, 15
SQLite adapter, 10
SQLite database, 17
SQLServer adapter, 10
sqlserver value, 148
sslca parameter, MySQL, 13
sslcapath parameter, MySQL, 13
sslcert parameter, MySQL, 13
sslcipher parameter, MySQL, 13
sslkey parameter, MySQL, 13
StaleObjectError error, 151–152
StandardError class, 144, 189
StatementInvalid error, 149–150
statements, prepared, 207
stored procedures, 179–181
String class, 112, 204
:string type, 181
string_to_binary(value), 236
string_to_date(value), 236
string_to_dummy_time(value), 236
string_to_time(value), 237
structure_dump( ), 244
SubclassNotFound error, 145–146
sum(column_name, options = {}),
    232–233
super command, 60
supports_count_distinct?( ), 235
supports_migrations?( ), 235
suppress_messages( ) { ‖ . . . }, 249
Sybase, 16, 17

T

table_alias_for(table_name), 244
table_alias_length( ), 245
table_exists?( ), 223
table_name( ), 223
:table_name option, 165
table_name_prefix attribute, 165–166
table_name_suffix attribute, 166
:table_name_with_underscore class
        attribute, 175
:table_name_with_underscore option, 165
tablename_allcolumnnames_index index, 55
tablename_id field, 44
tables
    Active-Record friendly, 43–44
    creating, 51–53
Talbott, Nathaniel, 127
teardown method, 141
temp object, 138
:temporary => true option, 52
TestCase.fixture_path method, 142–143
testing, unit. *See* unit testing
text?( ), 238
the find_by_sql method, 190
:through attribute, 78
Time object, 26
to_csv method, 185
to_find_conditions method, 114, 118
to_param( ), 229
to_s method, 117
to_sql( ), 246
to_xml method, 182–183
to_xml(options = {}), 229–230
to_yaml method, 184
toggle!(attribute), 230
toggle(attribute), 230
TOP clause, 214
transaction class-level method, 39
transaction support, with fixtures, 141–142
transaction(*objects, &block), 253–254
transactions, 38, 40
transaction(start_db_transaction = true) { || . .
        . }, 240
transform method, 184
type attribute, 182
type_cast_code(var_name), 238
type_cast(value), 238

U

:unique => true option, 55
unit testing, 125–144
    assertion methods, 129–139
        assert, 129–130
        assert_equal, 131
        assert_in_delta, 132
        assert_instance_of, 133
        assert_kind_of, 134

assert_match, 135
assert_nil, 130
assert_no_match, 135
assert_not_nil, 131
assert_not_same, 136
assert_nothing_raised, 133
assert_operator, 136–137
assert_raise, 132–133
assert_respond_to, 134
assert_same, 135–136
assert_send, 138
assert_throws, 137–138
flunk, 138–139
fixtures, 139–144
    benefits of, 139–141
    formats, 142–144
    transaction support with, 141–142
reasons for, 126–127
writing tests, 127, 129
Unit::Test library, 127
universal time (UTC), 167
Universally Unique Identifier (UUID)
        primary keys, 205–206
unknown? method, 104
up method, 50–51
upcase method, 134
update call, 5
update method, 190
UPDATE statement, 38, 68
update_all(update_sql, conditions), 223
update_attribute method, 34, 191
update_attribute_with_validation_skipping(
        name, value), 254
update_attribute(name, value), 231
update_attributes method, 34, 39
update_attributes! method, 149
update_attributes method, 183
update_attributes(attributes), 231
updated_at field, 44
updated_on field, 44
update(id, attributes), 223
update(sql, name = nil), 240
updating (U) task, 3
updating records, 34–35
use_silence parameter, 159
use_transactional_fixtures method, 141
User database, 203
User model, 203
Userinfo class, 107
username attribute, 107
username parameter, 11–16
UTC (universal time), 167
:utc class, 167
UUID (Universally Unique Identifier)
        primary keys, 205–206
UUIDKeyClass class, 206
UUIDTools library, 205

V

valid?( ), 254
validate( ), 255
validate method, 82
validate(*methods, &block), 255–256
validate_exclusion method, 87
validate_on_create( ), 255
validate_on_create method, 82
validate_on_create(*methods, &block), 256
validate_on_update( ), 255
validate_on_update method, 82
validate_on_update(*methods, &block), 257
validates_acceptance_of method, 85
validates_acceptance_of(*attribute_names),
    257–258
validates_associated method, 87–88
validates_associated(*attribute_names), 258
validates_confirmation_of method, 84–85
validates_confirmation_of(*attribute_names
    ), 258–259
validates_each method, 83–84
validates_each(*attribute_names) { |record,
    attribute, value| . . . }, 259–260
validates_exclusion_of method, 87
validates_exclusion_of(*attribute_names),
    260–261
validates_format_of method, 87
validates_format_of(*attribute_names), 261
validates_inclusion_of method, 87
validates_inclusion_of(*attribute_names),
    262
validates_length_of method, 86
validates_length_of(*attribute_names),
    262–263
validates_numericality_of method, 88
validates_numericality_of(*attribute_names)
    , 263–264
validates_presence_of class method, 120
validates_presence_of method, 85–86, 88
validates_presence_of(*attribute_names),
    264–265
validates_size_of(*attribute_names), 265
validates_uniqueness_of method, 86
validates_uniqueness_of(*attribute_names),
    265–266
validations, 80–88
    convenience methods, 83–88
        validates_acceptance_of, 85
        validates_associated, 87–88
        validates_confirmation_of, 84–85
        validates_each, 83–84

validates_exclusion_of, 87
validates_format_of, 87
validates_inclusion_of, 87
validates_length_of, 86
validates_numericality_of, 88
validates_presence_of, 85–86
validates_uniqueness_of, 86
    implementing, 81–83
    overview, 80
    of records, 211–212
    uses, 80–81
value objects
    defining, 107–108
    names of, 106
value_to_boolean(value), 237
value_to_decimal(value), 237
varchar type, 181
verify!(timeout), 236
version column, 52
VERSION parameter, 49

W

WHERE clause, 28, 36, 94, 103
Wikipedia, 46
:with option, 87
with_exclusive_scope(method_scoping = {},
    &block), 224
with_scope(method_scoping = {}, action =
    :merge) { || . . . }, 224
withdraw method, 39
:within option, 86
write(text=""), 249
writing programs, 18–24
    assumptions, 19–20
    coding conventions, 19–20
    objects
        relationships among, 22–24
        retrieving from databases,
            21–22

X

XML configuration file, 164
XML format
    exporting, 182–183
    importing, 183–184

Y

YAML format, 56, 142, 184
yaml library, 189
yamldata field, 147
.yml extension, 142

You Need the Companion eBook

Your purchase of this book entitles you to buy the companion PDF-version eBook for only $10. Take the weightless companion with you anywhere.

We believe this Apress title will prove so indispensable that you'll want to carry it with you everywhere, which is why we are offering the companion eBook (in PDF format) for $10 to customers who purchase this book now. Convenient and fully searchable, the PDF version of any content-rich, page-heavy Apress book makes a valuable addition to your programming library. You can easily find and copy code—or perform examples by quickly toggling between instructions and the application. Even simultaneously tackling a donut, diet soda, and complex code becomes simplified with hands-free eBooks!

Once you purchase your book, getting the $10 companion eBook is simple:

❶ Visit **www.apress.com/promo/tendollars/**.

❷ Complete a basic registration form to receive a randomly generated question about this title.

❸ Answer the question correctly in 60 seconds, and you will receive a promotional code to redeem for the $10.00 eBook.

2560 Ninth Street • Suite 219 • Berkeley, CA 94710

eBookshop

THE EXPERT'S VOICE™